THE THAMES

Landscapes of the Imagination

Landscapes

THE THAMES

A *Cultural History*

MICK SINCLAIR

Signal Books
Oxford

First published in 2007 by
Signal Books Limited
36 Minster Road
Oxford OX4 1LY
www.signalbooks.co.uk

A catalogue record for this book is available from the British Library

ISBN 1-904955-27-4 Paper

Cover Design: Baseline Arts
Production & Design: Devdan Sen
Cover Images: © Peter Adams Photography/Alamy; Mayfair Picture Library; Darren
Baker/istockphoto
Photographs and Images © Mick Sinclair pp.40, 50, 100, 125, 147, 165, 195, 205, 214,
222, 228, 230, 251; Catriona Davidson pp.2, 4, 20, 22, 25; Alamy pp.xxii, 75, 87, 89, 202;
Margaret Smeaton/istockphoto pp.i, 36; Ben Battersby/istockphoto p.x; Jon
Tarrant/istockphoto p.xii; Graeme Purdy/istockphoto pp.34, 70; Sean Nel/istockphoto p.80;
John Tate/istockphoto p.115; Dave Roberts/istockphoto p.190; Chris Schmidt/istockphoto
p.198

Printed in India

CONTENTS

Part Three
London's River   79

Preface

The Thames is much more than a mere river and writing a book about it, as I discovered when it was too late to turn back, is much more than describing a body of water. In fact, I was often writing not so much the story of a river but what seemed an entire history of England, from the trading habits of Roman settlers and the role of Thames bridges in the civil war to the effects of industrialization and the impact of the Blitz.

Not that examining history as far back as it has been recorded—and sometimes even further—revealed the whole tale. Its surface may at times be frozen but the Thames never stops flowing; its waters and their surrounds document the present (think Canary Wharf or the Millennium Dome) as thoroughly as they do the past while also offering pointers to the future.

As activists activate, speculators speculate and environmentalists tangle with developers, the river itself is suddenly a focus of debate. Should regeneration necessarily include preservation? How many anchors embedded in the pavement are needed to suggest "heritage" on London's riverside? Refreshingly less contentious are matters such as the upper river's conservation of historic locks, the lengthening Thames Path, and the post-industrial (partial) greening of the Thames estuary, allowing the broadest sections of the river to be enjoyed with fresh air rather than toxic fumes for company. On the subject of company, I have to mention Fred Thacker, without whom the Thames would seem a very different river and any serious account of it would be much the poorer. Thacker's three books of the early 1900s saved subsequent generations of Thames writers serious legwork in unearthing documents of the early river while his personal asides offer matchless insights.

Whether fiction or fact, several other books with the river at their heart deserve particular mention: Sydney R. Jones' *Thames Triumphant* (1943) casts the waterway as a fixed reference point in the turmoil of the Second World War; William Morris' *News From Nowhere* (1891) embraces a post-apocalypse England and takes us onto the Thames to view it; the real Thameside scenes of the late nineteenth century are described with revealing (if often unintentionally so) insights by the well-to-do gentlemen who authored *The Royal River* (1885). Jerome K.

Jerome's seemingly immortal *Three Men in a Boat* (1889) still brings easy laughs but at another level reflects an attitude to the river and its surrounds that, a hundred years on, might be seen (if only by me) as hardening into Iain Sinclair's *Downriver* (1991), an intense, abrasive and worrying book—for all the right reasons.

As should any account unhindered by mooring details and lock-keepers' telephone numbers, mine describes the Thames as a source of power, a provider of livelihood and an object of pleasure, and above all as a waterway imbued with a cultural and historical meaning acquired over many centuries of human interaction.

Seen in this light, the Thames reveals itself to be less a river than a mirror, a reflection of who we are.

Introduction

A SYMBOLIC RIVER

And we came to realize more than ever that the Thames is the true symbolic river of England, the river that has nurtured within its embrace many of the people and systems, ideas, aims, and ideals, which in no small measure through the centuries have built up the character and trends of the race, reflected on the pages of ancient and modern history by deeds accomplished, some failures, and many triumphs.

Sydney R. Jones, *Thames Triumphant*, 1943

The River Thames should be a simple thing: a body of water that rises from the ground some three hundred feet above sea-level in a Gloucestershire meadow and flows for 215 miles downhill in a generally easterly direction until reaching the North Sea. Yet as Sydney R. Jones noted, albeit in the emotionally-charged atmosphere of an England at war, this is a river with a significance far greater than its mere physical form would suggest.

The Thames has been a source of sustenance, a provider of raw materials, a means of transport for kings, queens and commoners, linked rural England to the centres of national power as well as the markets of Europe and beyond, been a site for palaces and prisons, and seen the plots, conspiracies and political intrigues—from Magna Carta to the Profumo Affair—that have shaped the course of English history.

For generations, the river provided a living, and a lifestyle, for many on its course, be they the osier gatherers, eel-catchers and isolated lock-keepers of the upper river or the shipwrights and ferrymen, and later the dockers, of London. For almost as long as people have lived along its banks, the Thames has inspired novels, poetry and song, and since Victorian times it has been a major provider of pleasure and sport, originating the Oxford-Cambridge Boat Race, hosting regattas by the score, and still lined by countless rowing clubs and boatyards.

Watched over by grazing cows in quiet meadows and crossed by medieval bridges that once linked manor houses and monasteries, some sections have barely changed since the days horses pulled barges and transported Cotswold wool to market. By stark contrast, many other parts of the Thames have been, or are being, transformed almost beyond recognition. In London, the river has entered the twenty-first century as one of the capital's most discussed aspects: new architecture a feature of its banks; regeneration the buzzword of the riverside; new pathways making its course through the metropolis publicly accessible.

East of London along the Thames estuary, toxicity and pollution have been reduced and enabled the river to again be seen as a desirable natural asset. The potential of the "Thames Gateway", a media-friendly term for the estuary and much around it, to become, despite political controversies and ecological concerns, the solution to south-east Britain's housing crisis, confirms the continuing rediscovery of the river—and a growing affirmation of its contribution to the well-being of the nation.

Early History
Its course determined by successive ice ages and its name and character by successive invaders, occupiers and inhabitants of Britain, the Thames (as it would become) may well have existed for millions of years but almost certainly, 600,000 to 475,000 years ago, flowed across southern England to become a tributary of the Rhine, Britain then connected by land to Europe. Later glaciation forced the Thames south by perhaps twenty miles and gave it sufficient force to slice through the Chiltern Hills and create what is now Goring Gap. Its velocity lessening as the ice receded, the river eventually acquired its present course.

Belief that the fertile Thames Valley, west of London, may have been a site of human habitation for 300,000 years is supported by discovery of simple stone tools along the river and evidence of boatbuilding: typically simple rafts made from logs held together with animal hides for moving heavy loads over slow-moving water, and simple dug-out canoes and coracles enabling travel across faster-moving stretches. Continuing occupation, following the Ice Age which ended 10,000 years ago, is revealed by later finds including those connected with the Celts who arrived from Gaul (having crossed the English Channel, which since around 65000BC had divided Britain from Europe) and introduced the Iron Age to Britain. Boatbuilding advances and greater use of the river for trade and communication ensued. Agriculture benefited significantly from the wheeled plough, brought to Britain by the Belgae (a Celtic-

Germanic group) from around 75BC. Such advances stimulated population growth. and larger settlements spread along the river.

Aided by the Dobunni people of the upper Thames Valley, who resisted the advance of the Celts and Belgae, lasting Roman occupation of Britain began under Claudius in 43AD. Initially, the Romans made Colchester the capital of their new territory but recognizing the importance of the Thames (named Tamesis by the Romans, possibly from a Celt word, *Tems*, or the Sanskrit *tamas*, each meaning "darkness" and presumably a reference to the colour of its waters) for commerce and communications, a small riverside settlement was developed into a trade and administrative centre called Londinium, today's London.

At strategic points, the Romans built pile-driven wharves, sturdier and able to handle a far greater weight of cargo than previous landing stages, as developing boatbuilding technology allowed larger loads to be carried. Ceramics and roof tiles, prerequisites for Roman villas, joined hay and grain among the staples of expanding river commerce. Romans introduced techniques for strengthening the river bank and gave the Thames its first fixed crossing: the earliest London Bridge, constructed around AD50, of squared beams of oak arranged for stability in an interlocking pattern, and built another crossing at Staines, known to the Romans simply as *Pontes* or Bridge. The Roman road system, which included the creation of post-houses and inns at major fording points, speeded the movement of produce to market and fuelled the rise of a Romano-British merchant class, in turn heightening the importance of riverside settlements.

As the Roman empire declined in the fourth century, Saxons steadily penetrated Britain, advancing along the Thames as far as Dorchester and creating settlements (recognized by the ending "ing" in their names, such as Reading and Sonning) on its banks. Doing much to forge the lasting character of the river, the Saxons began the process of diverting water to power corn mills with "weirs" (a word of Saxon origin, as was "eyot", meaning island and still in common usage on the Thames). River trade was stimulated by abbeys established at towns such as Abingdon and Chertsey following St. Augustine's arrival in Britain during 59, charged with converting the pagan population to Christianity.

By the time of Alfred (reigned 871-99), Britain faced attack from the Danes, though the conflict was largely resolved, after Alfred's death, by the Thames becoming a dividing line between the rule of Anglo-Saxons (the Saxons and other Germanic tribes, the Jutes and Angles, from whom the word England was derived) in the south and that of the Danes in the north. As a result of succession struggles in England following the death of Edward the Confessor (reigned 1042-66), the Normans under William I ("the Conqueror") invaded. Prevented from crossing the Thames at Southwark, the Normans marched along the south side of the river, crossing at Wallingford to advance again on London, this time successfully.

Once established, Normans not only introduced feudalism to Britain, but also the stone buildings that signalled a rise in Cotswold quarrying, the local stone well-suited to construction uses and moved along the Thames to build William's new defensive positions in and around London, notably that which became Windsor Castle. In protecting hunting rights on lands adjacent to the river, William effectively asserted royal control over the river itself.

Weirs, Locks and Other Hazards

Know ye all that we, for the health of our soul, our father's soul, and all our ancestors' souls, and also for the common weal of the City of London, and of all our realm have granted and steadfastly commanded that all weirs that are in the Thames be removed...

Second Charter of Richard I, 1197

Royal control may have formally existed over the entire Thames, but in practice the waterway was a free-for-all. Richard's barely-implemented declaration reflected long-running conflicts between those for whom the river was a means of transport and the riparian landowners who constructed weirs for their mills and usually owned the adjacent locks where tolls were levied on passing river traffic. Weirs typically altered navigation channels and created shallows, thereby hindering barges and regularly flooding riverside hamlets and farmland.

The earliest Thames weirs were simple manipulations of the river's flow, commonly using parallel timber beams and any available debris, such as chalk or stone, to change the river's course, depth and speed over a small section. As barges grew larger, there evolved a more sophisticated form of lock known as "rhymer-and-paddle", or "flash" lock. These began with a cill of wood and stone driven into the river bed across its width, with further beams at intervals above, the top one being at the highest water level. A vertical series of "paddles", wooden planks that slotted into grooves cut into the upstream side of the horizontal beams, were similarly set across the width of the river and kept firm against the frame by water pressure. The gaps between the paddles were filled by overlapping wooden "rymers". Often there were several layers of rymers to provide greater control over water levels.

When a barge wished to pass (subject to the whim of the lock-keeper and payment of a sometimes extortionate toll), the paddles and rymers were raised by the lock-keeper using poles attached to them; the resulting "flash" of water continued until levels on both sides of the lock were equal. Moving a barge upstream, against the flow, could be slow and arduous; larger barges (which by the eighteenth century were able to carry two hundred tons) sometimes required up to eighty men aided by a dozen horses. A bargeman moving in the other direction would often save time by simply allowing the water flow to carry his vessel through, sometimes at dangerous speed and with its success dependent on the bargeman's skill in assessing whether the speed was sufficient to clear the shallows. The "flash" meanwhile continued downriver to the next lock, raising water levels as it went, a process eventually regulated by a daily schedule of lock openings.

Already resentful of high tolls, bargemen were further irritated by mill locks, used to create a head of water to power one or more waterwheels. Many of the earliest and largest mills were run by monks to grind cereals; with the rise of industrialization mills produced paper, cloth and metal products. Mill locks typically diverted water as the river flowed through a narrow channel, such as at the downriver end of an island, or in some cases a bank would be dug to create a new channel. Both methods affected river navigation and could cause flooding.

The threat to mercantile trade from unnavigable river stretches led to the creation in 1605 of the Oxford-Burcot Commission, charged with ensuring clear passage between Oxford and Burcot (east of Lechlade) where cargo had to be transferred from river to road as shallows made the waterway impassable. Under the commission, the Thames acquired its first pound locks, early examples of modern locks with two sets of swing gates spanning the river a short interval apart. Such locks were built at Iffley, Sandford and the Swift Ditch near Abingdon, though no more followed until 1772 with the opening of Boulter's Lock at Maidenhead under the auspices of the Thames Navigation Commission.

Further hazards for bargeman were various devices used by Thames fisherman. At their simplest, these were "kidles" (sometimes called "stops" or "hedges") set close to the bank often at an angle across the current and composed of brushwood formed into V- or W-shaped structures, creating a channel at the end of which were placed nets in which migrating fish became trapped. Despite becoming increasingly sophisticated, such traps were unstable and liable to collapse in the heavy flows that followed rainfall, causing logs and debris to block the river's navigation channels. During the seasonal eel migration, sections of flash locks might be converted into eel bucks. From a wooden frame, several elongated baskets, sometimes ten feet in length, were lowered into the river, trapping eels inside. Eels were also caught with "grigwels", a baited basket laid on the river bed and left overnight. Another widespread Thames trade was osier farming, usually on islands since they were inaccessible to cattle. A cut of willow would be planted, harvested a year later and, after preparation, sold primarily for use in basketry and furniture.

Controlling the Thames

To raise revenue for the Crusades, Richard I (reigned 1189-99) sold rights over the river to the City of London Corporation, acknowledging the supremacy of mercantile interests in disputes over Thames navigation, even though the ability of the corporation to assert control over the river away from the capital was negligible. In 1215 Magna Carta included provisions prohibiting navigational obstructions on the river and in 1285 the authority of the City of London Corporation was recognized as extending only as far west as Staines. In 1350 Edward III re-affirmed royal control over the river but, as before, there was no practical method of such control being fully implemented and disputes between landowners and bargemen continued.

In *The Thames Highway: Vol.2*, Thacker notes that around 1535 "a ferocious crusade against weirs was waged all over the country, instigated apparently by the king himself: a piquant little parergon in the intervals of harrying the monasteries; to which, and to pricate Catholics, it is notable that many of the weirs belonged." Thacker illustrated the lack of maintenance of weirs, locks and the river bank by quoting sections of *Thames Isis*, John Taylor's 1632 book of linked verses detailing river obstructions. At Sutton Courtenay Taylor found:

> ...there are left
> Piles that almost our barges bottome cleft;
> These Sutton locks are great impediments.
> The waters fall with such violence.

And downriver at Datchet:

> A stop, a weare, a dangerous sunke tree
> Not far from Datchet ferry are all three.

In the eighteenth century, the Thames Navigation Commission was created to oversee improvements as industrialization made smooth river passage increasingly important. An unwieldy body composed of several hundred members that included members of parliament, Oxford University officials and assorted mayors, clergymen and riverside landowners, it might be surprising that the commission achieved anything at all. Yet it oversaw construction of towpaths, sometimes by compulsory purchase of riverside land, sought to ensure the maintenance of flash locks and to synchronize their opening, thereby reducing queuing and problems downriver due to the sudden release of water. Many flash locks were improved by use of chains and wooden axles on which the paddles could be turned, rather than raised, giving the lockkeeper greater control of water flow, though subsequently the commission replaced many such locks with the safer and more efficient pound locks: by 1809 there were 26 such locks in operation, allowing a load to travel from Lechlade (the western limit of navigation) to London in five days.

The rise of industry and the creation of canals highlighted the necessity of ensuring swift and problem-free movement on the Thames. Canals could make a well-maintained and easily-navigated Thames part of a nationwide conduit for the movement of goods, be it the passage from London of imported tea and sugar to the provinces, or the converse movement of food—huge amounts of cheese, flour, cereals, hay, timber and hides—to the fast-growing metropolis. A Thames hindered by delays, high tolls and localized disputes would lose its customers and those employed along its course would lose their livelihoods. Attempts to evade the tolls, often applied per ton of cargo, were common, and became particularly widespread at Lechlade, where young, inexperienced lock-keepers were no match for, as Thacker puts it, "truculent and hard swearing bargemen".

By the mid-nineteenth century, the failings of the increasingly outmoded Thames Commission were apparent as it faced substantial debts and the loss of many workers; it was replaced by the more streamlined Thames Conservancy, which by 1866 controlled the river from Cricklade to the estuary. Despite caveats allowing continued private ownership of certain channels and weirs, the Conservancy effectively oversaw the river's development under public control, with an Act of Parliament stating that "private interests should no longer interfere with the navigation of one of the most important highways of the kingdom." The Conservancy presided over bank stabilization, dredging to improve existing navigation channels and the creation of quicker, straighter channels (the numerous "cuts" that are a feature of today's river). Innovations included electric alarms to signal changing water levels at locks close to the mills and the requirement of lock-keepers to keep their grounds, as well as their locks, in good condition: prizes for lock gardens were first awarded in 1898.

In banning shooting for hunting purposes between Teddington and Cricklade in 1885 on grounds that the river had "come to be largely used as a place of public recreation and resort," the Conservancy recognized the changing role of the Thames. Railways had usurped the waterway's role as a primary transport route and, in 1897, it was ruled that passenger steamers would take precedence over barges at Richmond and Teddington locks, a reversal of previous rulings giving rights of way to cargo carriers. It was, as Thacker noted, something that "might make the old bargemasters turn in their grave," but it signalled a new era in the life of the Thames: as a river of leisure and relaxation.

Messing about on the Thames

The Thames had long been a source of pleasure for society's upper crust but during the late nineteenth century, following the transformations wrought by industrialization, it began providing recreation for the expanding middle class and the more affluent sections of the working class. Besides the rise of leisure travel on the river itself, people could travel on the new railways, which made daytrips and weekend jaunts to riverside towns feasible and affordable, and actively encouraged by rail companies. Thacker noted in *The Thames Highway Vol. 2* that, "having ruined the water traffic upon the Thames [railways] began to discern the possibility of exploiting the river's allurement for their own profit."

Lock-keepers responded by providing refreshments, as previously hard-working river towns sought to re-invent themselves as glamorous resorts. Maidenhead gained a collection of fashionable hotels such as Skindles (along with many cheaper, seedier alternatives) as punts, skiffs and other craft rented by holiday makers jammed Boulter's Lock. On the estuary, Gravesend enjoyed a few halcyon decades as a vacation destination for Londoners, while river features such as the islands of Eel Pie and Taggs became popular picnic and entertainment venues.

Steamboats were another aspect of Thames pleasure. In 1843 the first steam passenger service appeared, though after causing £300 of damage to the riverbank between Teddington and Hampton Court, its speed was limited to 2mph. The Oxford company, Salter's, began a twice-weekly scheduled steamer service between Oxford and Kingston in 1878, its popularity leading to a daily service by 1891. Passengers could board at any lock or stop, carry bicycles, and could buy tickets enabling travel in one direction by boat and in the other aboard the Great Western Railway. Boatyards switched production from commercial to pleasure craft, including such items as the houseboat and the camping skiff: essentially a simple boat equipped with canvas cover and camping paraphernalia, enabling the occupants to spend the night, as well as the day, on the river. The Thames Conservancy recognized the changes by introducing registration fees for pleasure craft. By 1889, 12,000 such vessels were recorded, a fifty per cent increase on the previous year. From the early 1880s river income from pleasure usage exceeded that from commercial use.

Published in 1912, James Englefield's *The Delightful Life of Pleasure on the Thames* described the river's changing face as it appeared to the fisherman:

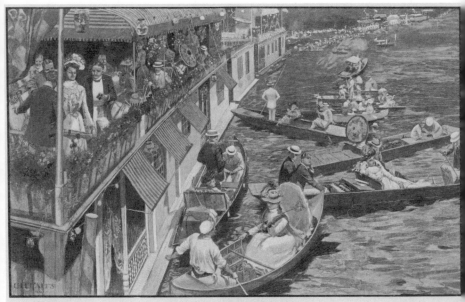

THE REGATTA AT HENLEY OPENED ON WEDNESDAY

…the continual and increasing disturbance of the river from the wash and hurry and turmoil caused by hundreds of steam launches and the endless procession of every description of floating craft, from the light canoe, dinghy or outrigger, to the lordly, much decorated, or hotel-like houseboat. Its banks will then be thronged by gaily dressed and joyous holiday makers, merry and loving couples towing boats along, horses also drawing skiffs and houseboats, and by an innumerable host of spectators, especially at the locks; by idlers, loafers and roughs.

Three Men—and Some Servants—in a Boat

With great commercial success, the changing mood of the river was also evoked by Jerome K. Jerome's *Three Men in a Boat*. Published in 1889 and based on personal experiences of Thames trips, the story uses humour and *faux* naivety to chronicle the adventures of three river novices—two of them, typically for the time, clerks—threatened not only by treacherous currents and dangerous weirs but grumpy lock-keepers and cheating boatyards. Yet while the presence of clerks in a small boat was part of the river's changing scene, the book reveals that even among such people there was nostalgia for times recently past:

> We had a good deal of trouble with steam launches that morning. It was just before the Henley week, and they were going up in large numbers; some by themselves, some towing houseboats. I do hate steam launches: I suppose every rowing man does. I never see a steam launch but I feel I should like to lure it to a lonely part of the river, and there, in the silence and the solitude, strangle it.

Steamboats became the dominant mode of travel on the Thames but houseboats were the most elegant, enabling the rich to tackle the river complete with serving staff, bedrooms, a living and dining area with well-equipped kitchen, railing-enclosed decks decorated with potted plants and comfortable seats. Freshly-painted for the occasion and with hired musicians to provide entertainment aboard, houseboats became a feature of regattas, lining the route at Henley and typically following the racing season as it moved downriver. Of houseboats moored at Cleeve Lock, near Streatley, *The Royal River* (1885) glowingly reported: "The little muslined windows are gaily decked with flowers, there is a miniature flower-garden upon the flat roof, and where the roof overhangs are suspended Chinese lanterns, gorgeous with many a brilliant stripe and pot." Despite being picturesque additions to the riverscape, houseboats earned the ire of river folk and local landowners alike, whether for causing blockages in and around locks or for mooring for an entire summer in a single spot, availing themselves neither of local hotels nor local eateries.

Charles Dickens Jr. (eldest son of the novelist) records in the 1898 edition of his *Dictionary of the Thames*: "House-boats have become extremely popular on the river of late years, although riparian owners are apt to look upon them, not without cause, as unmitigated nuisances... one of the first desires of the of the modern occupant of the house-boat is to show how much money they have to squander."

The Rise of the Regatta

Racing on the Thames had included, from 1716, the Dogget Coat and Badge, contested by watermen who had recently completed their apprenticeship by rowing between London Bridge and Chelsea. Just as it was unthinkable for a gentleman to row himself from one place to another rather than to pay a professional to do so, it was equally preposterous to the upper classes that true sport, including rowing, could be anything but amateur. The river's first amateur race, the Wingfield Sculls, began in 1830 and mirrored the soaring membership of rowing clubs along the Thames. A long, straight river section at Henley provided a course for the first Oxford-Cambridge University boat race in 1829 and ten years later became the site of the river's first annual regatta, quickly becoming a social as much as a sporting occasion. In *Victorians on the Thames*, R. R. Bollard quotes a nineteenth-century edition of the magazine *Punch* offering some tips for attending the Henley Regatta: "If you really wish to make a favourable impression upon everyone, be cheery, contented, good-natured, and, above all, slightly interested in the racing."

After Henley, the commercial appeal of regattas became apparent and they spread rapidly. Goring and Streatley, Marlow, Cookham, Maidenhead, Windsor and Eton, Wargrave, Chertsey, Molesey, Bourne End and other riverside communities all showed themselves eager for the business boost of such an event. Some regattas pointedly disregarded the distinction between amateur and professional and allowed full-time river men to show their prowess. Others, alongside the serious races, might include punt racing, water jousting and the climbing of a greasy pole suspended over the water to catch a pig (which itself was the prize).

The Docks and After
Being a source of pleasure contrasted with the Thames' other role as an economic linchpin of the British empire. Trade on London's river expanded dramatically through the eighteenth century and by the nineteenth had inspired a total change in the landscape and population patterns of the city. Tracts of east London became vast wet docks ringed by warehouses and enclosed by towering brick walls; some extant communities were destroyed while others were effectively corralled. Advancing industrialization transformed the riverbank in London and to the east along the Thames estuary, where long-standing boatbuilding and barge repair yards were joined, and soon outnumbered, by cement works, chemical plants, grain silos, sugar refineries, power stations,

gasworks and sewage treatment facilities. Extensive commercial usage polluted the river and its banks, and even the non-tidal river (above Teddington) bore the scars of technological advance. A book-length study, *The Thames Valley from Cricklade to Staines: A Survey of its Existing State and some Suggestions for its Future Preservation*, appeared in 1929, its authors aghast at the horrors of advertising hoardings and petrol stations steadily undermining the beauty of Thameside settlements.

For good or ill, the solution to the docks' decline (brought about from the late 1960s chiefly by the rise of containerization) came in the late 1980s when the area's regeneration became one of the many controversial features of the prime ministership of Margaret Thatcher, and was symbolized by the shrine to a deregulated economy that was Canary Wharf Tower. The sprouting of the Millennium Dome on the stagnating Greenwich Peninsula under a subsequent government also provoked loud derision, though in the years following the millennium itself, such additions were just two of the more easily recognizable features of a new London riverscape.

Of the river generally, the discovery of a seahorse in the estuary in 2004, the first such creature spotted in the Thames since 1976, was widely taken as an indicator of a cleaner river enticing back the diverse marine life that decades of industrial pollution had driven away. Some, however, suggested that global warming was responsible for the seahorse's visit and could also have pointed to the regular release of raw sewage into the river as a reminder than the waterway is still often regarded as repository for waste, despite the efforts of local environmentalists and public campaigns for sustained improvement of the Thames and its surrounds. The appearance in January 2006 of a normally deep-ocean-dwelling northern bottlenose whale as far upriver as west London, excited local residents and the global media and offered a reminder not only of the mysterious lives of whales, but also of the enduring ability of the Thames to provide sudden, unexpected spectacles.

While far from perfect, far from clean and with new structures on its banks likely to provoke excitement and disgust in equal measure, the Thames today is nonetheless more inviting to human visitors than it has been for centuries. The Thames Path, currently 183 miles from the source to the Thames Barrier, has made travelling the river without the aid of a boat easy and rewarding. Beyond the barrier too, new footpaths are being created that reveal long hidden riverside vistas of natural, historical and cultural value.

The Art of the Thames

Bird's-eye cartographic views of London and its river had been created in the sixteenth century, notably by the Flemish Anthony van den Wyngaerde (1525-71) and Ralph (Radulph) Agas (c.1540-1621). A century later came the groundbreaking work of a Bohemian refugee, Vaclav (Wenceslas) Hollar (1607-77). From an eyrie in a Southwark bell-tower, Hollar worked the eight-foot-long, *Long View of London from Southwark*, completed in 1647. That London would soon be ravaged by plague and much destroyed by the Great Fire in 1666 made Hollar's work all the more valuable as a record of the city and the river along which it spread, as were his subsequent depictions of the fire itself and the ruined city that emerged from it.

An infusion of Dutch and Flemish painters into Britain from the late seventeenth century brought greater artistry to depictions of the Thames. Peter Tillemans (1684-1734) composed river panoramas that included *The Thames at Twickenham*, while others cast the river as a backdrop to great events. These included the 1680 *Greenwich from One Hill Tree* by Johannes Vorsterman (1643-99), a view as suggested by the title but one depicting the new Royal Observatory and the restored Charles II's new palace, as royal yachts off Deptford fire a salute and a sunburst above the river bestows heaven's blessing on the king's return.

Whether geniuses or journeymen, British artists could find a regular source of income with river subjects. Shipbuilders wanted their creations recorded for posterity, captains commissioned reminders of ships they commanded, and naval ships, whether new or returning from victory in battle, provided further sources of revenue. Artists such as Francis Holman (1729-84) and his pupil Thomas Luny (1759-1837) were prominent among those working in the Dutch maritime tradition. Another was John Cleveley (1712-77), who was a Deptford-based shipwright before turning to art, a course followed by his twin sons John the Younger (1747-86) and Robert (1747-1809).

After the 1746 arrival in London of the Venetian Canaletto (1697-1768), the Dutch style became less dominant. Canaletto's river scenes were often wide-angled vistas from elegant riverside terraces but with *London: Seen Through an Arch of Westminster Bridge* (1747) he presented St. Paul's Cathedral and its surrounds through the arches of the new Westminster Bridge, linking the architectural symbol of London's recovery from the 1666 fire to the modern city's economic health, about to be improved still further by completion of the bridge. Canaletto's popularity boosted the market for river views and his style influenced many British maritime painters, including Samuel Scott (1702-72), whose subsequent work moved away from ships to studies of Thames bridges, river workers and fishermen. Similarly capturing the underbelly of river life was the 1883 pen-and-ink *Toil, Glitter, Grime and Wealth on a Flowing Tide*, by W. L. Wyllie (1851-1931), though much of the artist's renown stemmed from his paintings of naval vessels.

Jacques (James) Tissot (1836-1902), who arrived in London as a refuge from the Franco-Prussian War, found the Thames less a place of work than a fashion accessory for the Victorian society he portrayed. As Michael Wentworth suggests in his study of the artist: "for Tissot, the wonders of the river… were always as much social as nautical." Tissot's river people included the middle classes in rural settings such as with *Autumn on the Thames (Nuneham Courtney)* and *On The Thames—A Heron*. One set on a busier reach, a jungle of steam funnels and sails providing the background, was *The Thames*; its supposedly salacious content—one man, two unchaperoned women and several bottles of champagne in a small boat—provoked uproar in 1876 following its first public showing.

English artist J. M. W. Turner (1775-1851) grew up close to the river at Brentford and in 1805, as his reputation was growing, travelled upriver as far as Oxford, creating a number of etchings and subsequent paintings that provide insights into the Thames of the time as well as into Turner's own development. His early images of river workers at Walton and farmhands beneath Kingston Bridge quickly became the stuff of history. In the new age of railways, Turner returned to Maidenhead to create a painting in 1844 that showed a river and a country on the cusp of change: *Rain, Steam and Speed—the Great Western Railway*. Change was also evoked in Turner's *The Fighting Temeraire* (1838), suggestive of the end of mast and sail as the eponymous naval vessel, a participant in the 1798 British victory at

Trafalgar, is towed to its destruction by a steam-powered Thames tug.

Claude Monet (1840-1926) was already well established by 1899 when he arrived in London and began a series of paintings studying the interplay of water, buildings and (usually misty or polluted) air, including such widely-reproduced images as *The Thames at Westminster* and *The Thames below Westminster Bridge*. Monet's view of the Thames from a balcony of the Savoy Hotel was occasionally shared by his friend, the American painter James Whistler (1834-1903). Whistler created many memorable (and controversial) scenes beside the Thames, including the gritty, if impressionistic, depictions of London river life at Rotherhithe and Wapping published in 1871 as *The Thames Set*, and celebrated canvases such as *Nocturne in Blue and Gold: Old Battersea Bridge*.

Many have photographed the Thames, but few have done so as evocatively as Henry Taunt (1842-1922). Son of an Oxford tailor, Taunt was a photographer's assistant at the age of fourteen and a regular river traveller by the early 1860s. The river scenes he captured became the basis of an 1871 lecture series: *A Trip down the Thames from London to its Source*, complete with readings, live performers and Taunt's glass slides projected onto walls. The following year, Taunt published the first of what would be fifty books, *A New Map of the River Thames*, a commercial success as the river's popularity soared. While Taunt developed other interests, including writing songs and tricycle repair, his ability with the chemical processes of early film and his eye for composition made his Thames images particularly striking. Not only did he record river features now long gone: flash locks, wooden bridges, eel bucks and more, but displayed a rare ability for a photographer of his time to make his subjects, people and families for whom the river might have provided a livelihood for generations, appear entirely at ease. As Bryan Brown writes in *The England of Henry Taunt*: "most of Taunt's photographs have a remarkable freshness about them. Although not unaware of the photographic equipment, his subjects seem to take up poses natural to their age, character and occupation."

Writing the River: Taylor and Thacker
Ferryman, pamphleteer and author, John Taylor (1580-1653) proclaimed himself the "water poet" of the Thames. Apprenticed to a waterman, Taylor was soon press-ganged into the navy and reputedly

completed 16 voyages before returning to the Thames only to find its traditional skills in decline and the waterman's livelihood threatened by new forms of transport, including the new hackney carriages, which prompted Taylor to write:

Carrouches, coaches, jades and Flanders mares,
Do rob us of our shares, our wares, our fares,
Against the ground we stand and knocke our heeles,
Whilst all our profit runs away on wheels.

Taylor became a prominent member of London's Guild of Boatmen and campaigned for improvements with books such as *Thames Isis*, which also gave river historians of later eras an important source of reference (as did his subsequent account of river trade, *Carriers Cosmographie*). Taylor was known to bend a truth or two, however, and part of his income came from planning outrageous journeys and selling subscriptions to future accounts of them. For one such trip, Taylor undertook to walk to Edinburgh without "borrowing, begging, or asking meat, drink or lodging" and wrote the story up as *The Pennyles Pilgrim*. Some purchasers demanded their money back as word spread that Taylor, although he had walked to Edinburgh, had borrowed and begged the whole way. Although Taylor enjoyed celebrity and published numerous books of verse, he was not noted for his literary skills:

Some through ignorance, and some through spite
Have said I can neither read nor write.

Long after Taylor's death, however, poet Robert Southey glowingly wrote: "Kings and Queens condescended to notice him, nobles and archbishops admitted him to their table, and mayors and corporations received him with civic honours." But the *Cambridge History of English and American Literature* placed Taylor in a lesser light: "…a voluminous scribbler, possessed of irrepressible assurance and facile wit of a coarse vein. He had, however, the saving grace of acute observation of men and manners, and this has given his productions a certain value for the student of social history. The term 'literary bargee' befits him much better than his own self-styled title 'the water-poet'."

Three self-published volumes, *The Stripling Thames* (1909), *The Thames Highway* (1914) and *The Thames Highway Vol. 2: Locks & Weirs* (1920), earned Fred Thacker a reputation as an expert on Thames history. Far from seeking to promote his own stature, the beauty of Thacker's work is that it was clearly not work at all, but a labour of love for the river on which he had spent his entire career and a great deal of his leisure. Thacker's meticulous research, spanning the documents of many centuries coupled to personal insights gained from his experience of the river and its people, makes for compelling reading, despite the dated prose style and what, in other hands, might be an excess of detail and trivia. The 1920 book, for example, really does spend several hundred pages accounting the minutiae of Thames locks and weirs but holds interest simply through the author's enthusiasm and his regular discovery of river quirks and curiosities.

Even Thacker's interludes of nostalgia seem less a descent into sentiment than a cry of joy for the Thames, especially as he is keenly aware that the river and the river people he describes will not stay as they are for long. Of his discovery of an abandoned miller's cottage at Ray Mill Island, at Boulter's Lock near Maidenhead, Thacker wrote:

> I roamed and dreamed over Ray Mill close one day of March in 1912, while the new works were in progress; and discerned before it was too late what a little kingdom the island once formed for the soul and hand of a man. At the lower end was his material living, the mill: busy enough in old centuries when England was wise to feed herself; and close by stood his home. Here lay all his intercourse with the outside world. Within lay secluded what an earthly paradise, surrounded with living Thames! Still I behold shady undulating alleys leading by little bridges across artificial brooks; still ancient barns and bowers of honeysuckle and clematis; still tiny sandy capes and bays where, a long lifetime ago, you might have sat for golden hours and watched the last Thames salmon leap below the weir. Above the garden extends a triangular meadow, narrowing to the weir; which continues northward in its curve at least six centuries old. On the right main Thames flows down in tumbling foam, muttering of the sea, huddling along as though already late.

Part One

A Meandering River

For the first of the approximately 120 miles from its disputed source to Reading, the Thames disguises its importance, a trickle pressing through reeds and grasses, amounting to nothing more than a minor addition to the rural topography. Yet even weaving a narrow course through farmland and the kind of villages for whom the adjective "sleepy" was invented, the river displays its uncanny ability to reveal many millennia of English history. The Thames' first crossing is a road dating from the Roman conquest; the first sizeable town on its course is one with Saxon roots sited near a major Iron Age track.

Of the river's own history, barely a bend or secluded glade on its early course is not enlivened by tales of legendary lock-keepers or long-vanished weirs. Many of these rich veins were mined by in the early 1900s by author Fred Thacker, but where Thacker spent his working life on the river and his retirement chronicling its past, others of more elevated social rank accorded the Thames similar gravitas. For William Morris it provided a thread running through his post-apocalypse vision of England, *News from Nowhere*, and a waterway beside which to turn a declining farmhouse into Kelmscott Manor, a beacon of the Arts and Crafts movement. Other writers, as diverse as Robert Southey, Lewis Carroll and Colin Dexter, have found inspiration along the banks of the stripling Thames, while George Orwell's wish to spend eternity in a quintessentially English village was fulfilled near the river at Sutton Courtenay.

Whether navigating the Cumnor Hills, bringing views of Oxford's spires across Port Meadow, exposing the surreal isolation of Tenfoot Bridge, or the Civil War scars at Radcot Bridge, the meandering Thames rarely seems in a rush (the evocatively named Sandford Lasher an exception). Despite an overwhelmingly pastoral outlook, the young Thames holds many surprises. Water-filled former quarries link the waterway to what sometimes seems an inland sea; by the Iron Age

fortifications of Wittenham Clumps looms the twentieth-century behemoth of Didcot Power Station; the serene meadows at Culham conceal the cutting-edge physics that may yet revolutionize how the world gets its energy.

The Source(s)

Beneath an ageing ash tree in a group of fields that constitute Trewsbury Mead, a stone bears the inscription: "The Conservators of the river Thames 1857-1974. This stone was placed here to mark the source of the river Thames." A leap of imagination is required to see a dry field near the village of Kemble amid the rolling hills of the Cotswolds as the start-point of the river that charts a course not only from here to the North Sea but through two thousand years of English history and providing, on the way, inspiration for poets, novelists and artists. Robert Gibbings wrote of the scene in 1940: "I had hoped to see at the source of the river a clear brook issuing from a rock or gravelley bed but, instead, I found only a dried-up well and a series of muddy land drains. Needless to say I was disappointed." Nonetheless, the Thames officially begins here and, after prolonged rainfall, due to the porous limestone beneath ground and a position within a drainage basin, the field may resemble a small lake. For much of the year, though, including the summer when most visitors arrive, a dry field is all to be seen, other than a herd of cows grazing lazily. Fred Thacker admitted: "One's first emotion is almost to tears."

Arguments over the details of the river's source have raged from the bar of Kemble's Thames Head pub to London's Houses of Parliament. In 1937 the member whose constituency included Seven Springs, eleven miles north of Trewsbury Mead and the head of the River Churn, insisted that maps be re-drawn to show Seven Springs as the Thames' true source. He was ridiculed for his shameless opportunism by the Minister for Agriculture who pronounced that the source would remain at Trewsbury Mead: which happened to be in the Agriculture Minister's own constituency. Even today, maps convey uncertainty, if not over the source then over the name: many label the waterway as "Thames or Isis"; a few older examples mark the outpouring from Seven Springs as "the Churn or Thames".

Close to Trewsbury Mead, the river passes beneath the A433, also

Trewsbury Mead: the "source"

known as Fosse Way, a Roman route marking the western extent of the Roman occupation of Britain. The Thames emerges on the other side recognizably a river but a small one that struggles through weeds and rushes. Thomas Love Peacock wrote:

> Let fancy lead from Trewsbury Mead,
> With hazel fringed and copsewood deep,
> Where, scarcely seen, through brilliant green,
> Thy infant waters softly creep.

A soft creep was the last thing on the mind of John Pridey, who in 1781 completed the first survey for what would become the Thames and Severn Canal, intended to extend the navigable Thames to the River Severn. Within ten years, the section from Inglesham to Stroud was in operation with seventy-foot barges carrying thirty-ton cargoes. Yet the natural springs that today can seem reluctant to show themselves forced water through the clay bed of the canal following heavy winter rain and, in summer, canal water leaked through the holes. Always struggling to make a profit, the canal closed in 1933, its route still visible in the landscape. Passengers as well as cargo travelled on the canal and found the journey less bumpy than the stagecoach equivalent. C. S. Forester in *Hornblower and the "Atropos"* describes his eponymous hero making a 24-hour trip, including the negotiating of a hundred locks, from Gloucester to London: "The passage boat was making her way from Gloucester to London along the Thames and Severn Canal; going far more smoothly than the stage coach, it was very nearly as fast and decidedly cheaper, at a penny a mile, even in the first class."

Forester's traveller also noted the local building material, Cotswold stone: "Standing on his sea-chest, Hornblower could look over the canal banks, at the grey stone boundary walls and the grey stone farms." A type of oolitic limestone dating from the Jurassic period, Cotswold stone provides an excellent building material and was long used as such for cottages, churches, public houses and bridges throughout this stretch of the Thames. Stone quarrying damaged much of the landscape between Kemble and Cricklade, leading inadvertently to the creation of the Cotswold Water Park as abandoned quarries flooded and the resultant lakes were linked to the Thames. Quarrying continues in and around Waterhay Bridge where the riverside path, where it can be discerned, is marked with disturbing warnings of the dangers of quicksand.

For drivers, the water park brings the disconcerting appearance of sails behind roadside hedgerows, while nearby Ashton Keynes finds the Thames rippling through the village in a series of small channels, many of which are crossed by slender footbridges. Of Ashton Keynes' many crossings, Thacker speculated: "One is tempted to herald abroad that it possesses as many in its tiny area than in all the rest of Thames." To William Cobbett in 1826, however, Ashton Keynes was simply a "very curious place".

Cricklade

The western limit of the navigable Thames, Cricklade ("place by the river crossing") grew significantly in Saxon times, marking the Wessex-Mercia frontier with fortifications raised by Wessex's King Alfred. Signs to "Saxon ramparts" liable to excite historically-minded visitors are misleading, however. The most evident vestiges of Saxon Cricklade times are the grid-style layout and impressions of the ramparts in the landscape, best assessed by ascending the striking four-pinnacled Tudor-era tower of St. Sampson's Church, which looms above the high street.

The *Anglo-Saxon Chronicle* notes of 1015 that the Dane Cnut crossed the Thames at Cricklade intent on regaining control of the northern Danelaw, where his foe Æthelred had taken power and who had, in turn, been usurped by his own son, Edmund: "Here in this year Cnut came with his enemy army, and Ealdorman Eadric with him, across the Thames into Mercia at Cricklade, and they turned then into Warwickshire within the Christmas season, and ravaged and burnt and killed all they came across."

By the eighteenth century, Cricklade had gained an unwanted reputation as the rottenest of England's rotten boroughs, where parliamentary seats bore no relation to population and elections were won through bribery. Social reformer William Cobbett was particularly aggrieved by the conditions endured by Cricklade's farm labourers, whose work seemed only to provide food for those in urban areas. In *Rural Rides* (1830) he wrote: "I passed through that villainous hole Cricklade about two hours ago, and certainly a more rascally looking place I never set my eyes on. The labourers look very poor; dwellings little better than pigbeds and their food nearly equal to that of a pig."

Cricklade makes a doubted claim to be where St. Augustine sought to convert the Anglo-Saxons to Christianity. Better documented religious activity involves the Particular Baptists who opened a chapel here in 1852 and performed baptisms in the Thames at Hatchett's Ford. The decline of the sect saw the closure of the chapel in 1937; it now houses the town museum.

Inglesham, Lechlade and Old Father Thames

East of Cricklade, the Thames traverses a flat landscape in endless shades of green. In 1885 the authors of *The Royal River* wrote of the scene: "The river itself, so far, claims no particular notice, calls for no warmth of admiration. It makes no noise, performs no astonishing feats, inspires no terrors, but steals tranquilly through the meadows, and silently flows by the plentiful rushes which, unmolested, protect its banks in these remote reaches."

At Inglesham (where the thirteenth-century church was restored by William Morris; see p.9), overlooking the now-dry bed of the Thames and Severn Canal and almost obscured by weeping willows and creeping ivy, is a lock-keeper's round house, one of the purpose-built homes erected by canal companies for their employees. This example enjoys the distinction of a conical roof intended to allow the collection of rainwater for drinking purposes.

Although the decline of the canal threatened their livelihoods, the river's tourism boom was good news for lock-keepers. In *Thames Valley Villages* (1910) C. G. Harper wrote: "At Inglesham Round House there are plentiful facilities wherewith to refresh the body... the lockkeeper's domain includes a number of sheds and shanties devised for the benefit of picnic-parties... Here also is a greatly-patronised camping ground, generally plentifully occupied with tents in favourable summers."

From Inglesham, Lechlade and the dominant spire of its church appears across the Thames, boosted on either side of the town by the rivers Colne and Leach. Also within sight is the Halfpenny Bridge, carrying the A361 into Lechlade. Built contemporaneously with the canal, the bridge's high arch suggests the size of the cargo barges that once passed beneath it, while its name derives from the toll levied on pedestrians. Fear not if you arrive without loose change today: the pedestrian toll ended in 1839 and the toll house which sits on the bridge's eastern end is unattended.

Pleasure boats tethered on Lechlade's marina suggest little of the busy activity around what were once the town docks, the loading point for London-bound vessels. In *The Stripling Thames*, Thacker quotes an account of a 1793 Lechlade barge-master departing for London with: "Iron, Copper, Tin, manufactured and pig iron, Brass Spelter, Cannon, Cheese, Nails all Iron goods and Bomb shells" and returning with a load including "Raw Hides for Tewkesbury and Worcester and Gunpowder to Bristol and Liverpool".

Presumably such commercial bustle greeted four Thames travellers in August 1815 arriving here on a journey to the river's source. They were the poet Percy Bysshe Shelley, his lover Mary Godwin (the future Mary Shelley) and her stepbrother, and poet and novelist Thomas Love Peacock. At Lechlade Shelley proposed to abandon the quest for the source and instead embark on a two-thousand-mile canal journey around Britain. Short of the £20 necessary to pay the canal boatman, however, the four abandoned both undertakings. At some point, Shelley repaired to the yard of the fifteenth-century St. Lawrence's Church, raised in Cotswold stone, to pen what became "A Summer Evening Churchyard, Lechlade, Gloucestershire", which concludes:

> The dead are sleeping in their sepulchres:
> And, mouldering as they sleep, a thrilling sound,
> Half sense half thought, among the darkness stirs,
> Breathed from their wormy beds all living things around,
> And, mingling with the still night and mute sky,
> Its awful hush is felt inaudibly.
>
> Thus solemnized and softened, death is mild
> And terrorless as this serenest night.
> Here could I hope, like some enquiring child
> Sporting on graves, that death did hide from human sight
> Sweet secrets, or beside its breathless sleep
> That loveliest dreams perpetual watch did keep.

In the church, a small plaque records the Shelley connection but fails to mention the poet being sent down from Oxford University for co-authoring *The Necessity of Atheism*.

Lechlade's other Thames crossing, carrying the A417, is St. John's Bridge, a nineteenth-century replacement for a thirteenth-century stone bridge which, in turn, appeared on the site of a wooden crossing destroyed by flood in 1206. Close by, St. John's Lock, at 250 feet above sea level, is the highest lock on the Thames and the only one watched over by a sculptured figure of Father Thames himself. Commissioned by London merchants and crafted in Portland cement by Rafaelle Monti, Father Thames was made for the 1851 Crystal Palace Great Exhibition. Saved when the palace burned down in 1936, the statue served ignominiously as a garden ornament until a Thames Conservancy official moved it to Trewsbury Mead in 1958; after an attack by vandals, it was relocated here in 1974. Despite sentiment applied to it by some writers and the countless photos taken of it by Thames tourists, Father Thames is an ugly statue with no true link to the river and one that might well appear incongruous in any setting: the vandals of Trewsbury Mead perhaps had a point.

East of Lechlade, the riverside landscape locates another chapter of English history: a succession of ruined Second World War concrete pillboxes, originally part of the defensive line intended to stop invading German forces pressing northward into the Midlands; the pillboxes' effectiveness, of course, was never put to the test.

Onwards to Nowhere: William Morris and Kelmscott Manor

A look inside Inglesham Church reveals what David Sharp calls "a miracle brought about by William Morris", only slightly overstating the quality of the 1880s restoration of the tiny church. Focusing on its original Jacobean pulpit and medieval paintings, Morris' work sought to emphasize the church's true history and character rather than re-arranging its form to suit the prevailing affection for ecclesiastical Gothic.

William Morris (1834-96) was a founder of the influential Arts and Crafts Movement; partly a reaction to the industrialization which he saw as destroying traditional craft skills, just as urban living in factory towns separated people from nature. Morris designed furniture, fabrics, wallpaper, typefaces, and much more, and in 1871 bought (with Pre-Raphaelite painter Dante Gabriel Rossetti) the lease on Kelmscott Manor, close to the Thames beside the village of Kelmscott. The "manor", really a Tudor farmhouse, was extensively renovated by Morris. In *The Stripling Thames* Thacker quotes a Mr. Leslie recalling a visit: "Morris took us up into the attic where he delighted in descanting on the old woodwork displayed in the trussing and staying of the roof timbers. We paid a visit to the garden, and on one hedge, a clipped yew, was the form of a dragon which Morris had amused himself by gradually developing with the clipper." Of Kelmscott in the 1940s Sydney R. Jones recalled in *Thames Triumphant*: "We stalked this lovely old building from every angle; noticed the walls that Morris used to speak of, battering up slightly out of the perpendicular; saw the perky little windows with pediments, up above the mullioned ones; admired the beautiful roofs, the gable finials, and the chimneys."

With his Kelmscott printing-press, Morris published hand-bound volumes of Chaucer and his own utopian novel, *News from Nowhere*. In it, the novel's narrator wakes up in a future England where money, strife, and industrialization have vanished; its final section describes a journey along the Thames through an idyllic landscape, freed of railways and canals, to Kelmscott. Along the same route in 1896, Morris' body was carried from his home in Hammersmith to be buried in Kelmscott Church beneath a distinctive canopy-shaped tombstone.

Towards Newbridge: Buscot, Eaton Hastings, Shifford and Radcot

In 1859, with a fortune earned from gold trading in Australia, Robert Campbell bought Buscot Park Estate, running south from the Thames between Lechlade and Farringdon, and began turning its derelict four thousand acres into what he called his "great agricultural experiment". With a state-of-the-art irrigation system, a narrow-gauge railway, concrete buildings and even its own gasworks, Buscot began producing sugar beet, the spirit from which was extracted in a large distillery and exported to France to become brandy. Campbell allegedly spent £100,000 on the enterprise, but a combination of illness, the Franco-Prussian war plus the high initial outlay all contributed to his bankruptcy and in 1879 the farm's contents were sold off. The former distillery now holds a Thames Water pumping station while the rest of the estate, the former farm, a manor house and landscaped gardens, are owned by the National Trust.

Seemingly oblivious to the rise of river traffic, Hilaire Belloc in *The Historic Thames* (1907) wrote: "There are dozens of reaches upon the upper Thames with little in sight save the willow, the meadows, and a village church tower, which present exactly the same aspect to-day as they did when that church was first built." By being similarly oblivious to busy roads, new housing developments, and the intermittent presence of military aircraft using RAF Fairford, it is easy to say, a century on, that Belloc's comments hold true; snippets of local history and folklore are all that pepper the marshy route from Kelmscott to Newbridge.

Rich legends have evolved up around the weirs that once marked this section and the toll-collectors whose job involved prolonged solitude miles from the nearest village. J. H. B. Peel mournfully describes Shifford Lock as "the loneliest on the Thames". Nonetheless, the job could have its perks, not least the supply of illicit liquor carried by bargemen to ease the monotony and provide a source of additional income.

In 1909 Thacker said of Eaton (then Hart's) Weir: "The one real adventure of river life still survives at Hart's Weir; and for many years may it flourish with its white rymers and paddles, and fresh tumbling water filling the air all day with murmurous sound." Alas, it ceased to murmur by order of the Thames Conservancy in 1936, as did an earlier weir at Tenfoot, now remembered by the wooden, hump-back Tenfoot Bridge which preserves the public right of way. A suggestion of the sights and sounds that so thrilled Thacker, however, might be found at Rushey Lock, where a paddle-and-rymer weir remains.

Indications of a greater historical substance are provided in the hamlet of Shifford by a field and a rock called "Alfred's Stone", thought to indicate the site of the "first English parliament" presided over by King Alfred around AD900 with a membership that included, according to *Reliquiae Antiquae* (a nineteenth-century gathering of early English manuscripts): "Many bishops, and many book-learned. Earl's wise and Knights awful."

At Radcot, an important centre for the transport of Cotswold stone and earlier of Cotswold wool, the river divides into two channels beneath two bridges. Dating in part from the twelfth century, the older bridge, like many of the time, was raised by a religious order. Of its three arches and craftsmanship Thacker concluded: "Built wonderfully with strength for its destiny, the old fellows fashioned it a miniature of beauty." In December 1387 the bridge was the scene of a battle between Robert de Vere, Earl of Oxford, on the side of Richard II and attempting to return to London, and the Earl of Derby, one of the "Lord's Appelate" and the future Henry IV. A poet recorded:

Thy copious waters hold their way
Tow'rds Radcot arches old and grey,
Where triumped erst the rebel host,
When hapless Richard's hopes were lost;
And Oxford sought, with humbled pride
Existence from thy guardian tide.

While de Vere evaded capture by swimming his horse across the river, Derby's victory helped precipitate what became the Merciless Parliament, imposing restrictions on the young monarch. Three hundred years later, with royalist forces garrisoned at Faringdon, two miles south, the bridge saw action in the Civil War as Prince Rupert's men routed a parliamentarian force seeking to take control of the crossing. After the war, the bridge itself became a target: the Levellers are credited with lopping off the statue of the Virgin Mary which occupied a niche on the downstream side.

Radcot's newer bridge crosses a 1780s navigation cut built in anticipation of increased traffic following the construction of the Thames and Severn Canal. As evinced by the scrapes along its inner walls, the newer course proved more difficult to navigate. Thacker lamented: "many a steerman has here in mere seconds lost the sedulously acquired reputation of a lifetime."

Newbridge and towards Oxford

The "new bridge" at Newbridge is actually quite an old bridge, raised by Benedictine monks in the thirteenth century to facilitate the transport of Cotswold wool but earning its name by being younger than the bridge at Radcot. It is also distinguished by its six arches and by having sixteenth-century inns on either end: on the Oxfordshire side stands The Rose Revived; on the Berkshire bank is The Maybush. And that is just about all there is of Newbridge.

Swelled by the waters of the Windrush, the Thames continues from Newbridge to Northmoor Lock, where the desire for preservation has led to a refitting of the old rymer-and-paddle lock with fibreglass parts and Bablock Hythe, where the management of the Ferrymen Inn until recently maintained the tradition of operating a ferry at a crossing point documented since Roman times. Author and critic Matthew Arnold (1822-88) used the local landscape as the setting for his 1850s poem "The Scholar Gypsy":

> Crossing the stripling Thames at Bablock-hithe,
> Trailing in the cool stream thy fingers wet,
> As the punt's rope chops round;
> And leaning backward in a pensive dream,
> And fostering in thy lap a heap of flowers
> Plucked in the shy fields and distant Wychwood bowers,
> And thine eyes resting on the moonlit stream.

In 1894 the Thames Conservancy decided to replace the rope by which the ferry was pulled with what Thacker described as "a submerged chain for the benefit of modern degeneracy". Local opposition to distant authority soon saw the rope return.

Amid the seventeenth-century cottages of Stanton Harcourt are the older remnants of the manor of the Harcourt family (resident from the twelfth century until moving to Nuneham Courtenay), where in 1718 Alexander Pope completed the fifth volume of his translation of Homer's *Iliad*. Pope worked in a study at the top of what is now Pope's Tower, from where "there would be a splendid view… were it not for the spreading elms that screen the landscape," wrote Thacker in 1909. While here, Pope heard about two local lovers, John Hewet and Sarah Drew, "an industrious young man & virtuous maiden of this parish", who were struck by lightning and killed. Pope composed an epitaph to them at their grave in the local churchyard, dismayed at the opposition to their being given a Christian burial, writing to a friend: "They cannot get it out of their heads (that) it was a judgement of God."

The Cumnor Hills
Arnold was not alone in finding literary inspiration in landscapes that rise from meadow-coated flatlands to the richly wooded Cumnor and Wytham Hills. Oscar Wilde wrote in *Burden of Itys*:

> If it was though jasmine-cradled bird
> Who from the leafy stillness of thy throne
> Sang to the wondrous boy, until he heard
> The horn of Atlanta faintly blown
> Across the Cumnor Hills, and wondering
> Through Bagley Wood at evening found the
> Attic poet's spring...

While perhaps more affectingly, since it was written by a soldier during the First World War, Dyneley Hussey offered in "An Oxford Retrospect: May 1915":

> O'er the cloud-dappled Cumnor hills the shade
> Chases the sunlight-there I oft have strayed
> And watched dun much-cows munch the hours away.

At the foot of the hills, the privately-owned Swinford Toll Bridge continues the practice, established here with the opening of the bridge in 1777 so that the Earl of Abingdon could recoup his outlay, of collecting a toll on those who cross. Pedestrians are exempt, but drivers are charged 5p. For collecting the toll, and indeed doing a fine job of maintaining the bridge and its immediate surrounds, not least installing the toilets that make a welcome sight for Thames hikers, the long-serving lock-keeper Bill McCreadie was awarded an MBE in 2002.

Godstow and Mr. Dodgson

Turning south at Kings Lock, the river brings views of Oxford and passes the ruins of Godstow Abbey, a twelfth-century Benedictine nunnery established to provide education for the daughters of the nobility. It was here in 1176, two years after her role as Henry II's mistress had become known, that Rosamund Clifford ("Fair Rosamund") arrived, dying soon after and lying within the chapel, her tomb candle-lit and strewn with fresh flowers. In 1191 the tomb was discovered by St. Hugh of Avalon, Bishop of Lincoln, who banished her remains to the adjacent nuns' cemetery where it is popularly thought they were buried beneath a hazel tree. The popular story that Rosamund bore Henry two sons is dismissed by many historians who also give scant credence to the story that Rosamund was murdered by a jealous wife, Queen Eleanor of Aquitaine. Poet Robert Southey played on public affection for Rosamund and in his *Inscriptions* series of 1797 included "For a Tablet at Godstow Nunnery":

> Here Stranger rest thee! from the neighbouring towers
> Of Oxford, haply thou hast forced thy bark
> Up this strong stream, whose broken waters here
> Send pleasant murmurs to the listening sense:
> Rest thee beneath this hazel; its green boughs
> Afford a grateful shade, and to the eye
> Fair is its fruit: Stranger! the seemly fruit
> Is worthless, all is hollowness within,

For on the grave of ROSAMUND it grows!
Young lovely and beloved she fell seduced,
And here retir'd to wear her wretched age
In earnest prayer and bitter penitence,
Despis'd and self-despising: think of her
Young Man! and learn to reverence Womankind!

The nunnery's former hospice now forms part of the Trout Inn. A riverside setting and proximity to Oxford helped the inn acquire a clientele that included (along with the alleged ghost of Rosamund) academics and literary notables such as A. P. Herbert, Aldous Huxley and Evelyn Waugh, who gave it a bit part in *Brideshead Revisited*. Another regular, Colin Dexter, authored the *Inspector Morse* books, which were adapted into a ratings-topping TV series in the 1990s. The Trout appeared in several episodes of *Inspector Morse* and became a feature on the tourist circuit, a development which might well find the fictional Morse crying into his glass of cask-brewed ale.

In July 1862 ten-year-old Alice Liddell and her two sisters were taken along the river from Folly Bridge in Oxford to Godstow by Charles Lutwidge Dodgson, mathematics tutor at Oxford's Christ Church, where Alice's father was dean, and the Reverend Robinson Duckworth. Such outings were regular occurrences for the five, for whom Dodgson carried "a large basket full of cakes" and would make up stories with characters based on the girls cast into fantastic settings. In 1928 Alice told the *New York Times*: "The beginning of *Alice* was told to me one summer afternoon when the sun was so hot we landed in the meadows down the river, deserting the boat to take refuge in the only bit of shade to be found, which was under a newly made hayrick. Here from all three of us, my sisters and myself, came the old petition, 'Tell us a story' and Mr. Dodgson began it."

At Alice's further insistence, and for her entertainment, Dodgson began putting his stories `onto paper. The result was the 1865 publication, under the pseudonym Lewis Carroll, of *Alice's Adventures in Wonderland*, a title soon shortened to *Alice in Wonderland*, followed in 1871 by *Alice through the Looking Glass*. Both became enduring tales, enjoyed by children and adults of many generations. As "Lewis Carroll" their author gained wealth and fame, and wrote further fiction. As himself, Dodgson shunned publicity, wrote mathematical papers under his own name, and succeeded in remaining a challenge to biographers who seek to resolve the enigma of Mr. Dodgson to this day...

Oxford: the Tortured Thames

South from Godstow, the spires of Oxford come into view across the open pastures of the horse-dotted Port Meadow, where grazing rights were bestowed by Edward the Confessor on the Freemen of Oxford— who still hold them a thousand years on. On the river's east side lies the village of Binsey with its 800-year-old pub, The Perch. Retaining its thatched roof despite rebuilding following a fire in 1977, the pub was described by Thacker in *The Stripling Thames* in phrases dripping with English pastoralism: "upon the green, behind a duck pond, with pleasant lawns at the back, and an old English skittle ground, busy on Saturday afternoons."

Ahead, the river passes beneath the dainty Medley Footbridge and while its immediate surrounds encourage delusions of rural tranquillity it is soon parallel with icons of the industrial age: the railway and the Oxford Canal, running for 77 meandering miles to link the city with Coventry.

Until now, the Thames has generally been the reason for the existence of every community along its course and retains high importance, albeit an aesthetic rather than commercial one. At Oxford, however, not only does the river have to endure the indignity of being improperly named, known to locals as the Isis and to cartographers hedging their bets as "Thames or Isis", but it becomes shunted from centre stage to skirt the western edge of the city while a rival, the Cherwell, patrols the eastern side.

Oxford began as a "ford for oxen" probably close to the site of an eighth-century Augustan priory and evolved into an important trade centre due to its waterways and position at England's geographical heart. Gaining a castle in 1073 under Robert D'Oyley, a knight of William I, who recognized its strategic merits, Oxford prospered as a market town enjoying royal trading privileges on a par with those of London. To complement his hunting lodge at nearby Woodstock, Henry I raised Oxford's long demolished Beaumont Palace and Henry III held a parliament at Oxford in 1256. Nonetheless, after centuries on steady course to become a major English city, Oxford embarked on a radically different course. The *Royal River* observes: "It had its Norman castle, its Guild Merchant, its charter as good as those of London. It was a place where parliaments met. It had a palace of the kings, and a rich Jewry, and a great mind to trade. But the university sprang up and choked these things." In 1167, many of the Anglo-Norman scholars expelled from Paris as a result of Henry II's disputes with France headed for the monastic schools at Oxford to continue their learning. In 1256, University College, the first of what today are almost forty colleges, was founded and academia steadily came to dominate the old Oxford of trade and commerce.

With 18,000 students (of the "old" university, double that if one includes the newcomer, Oxford Brookes) and seemingly almost as many dons among its 147,000 population, Oxford spends the academic year as an intellectual powerhouse and the summer as a tourist attraction, drawing five million visitors annually. The latter imbibe the riot of collegiate architecture that comprises the city centre: the Gothic of Merton College; Magdalen's medieval tower; Hawksmoor's neo-classicism at The Queen's College; the stone and brickwork patterns of Butterfield's High Victorian Keble College. They inspect foibles such as the 1913 Bridge of Sighs above New College Lane linking two sections of Hertford College in imitation of its Venetian namesake, and find cerebral thrills at the Bodleian Library, among the world's oldest repository of books and manuscripts with the much-photographed Radcliffe Camera as its main reading room, and the Ashmolean Museum, which is a repository of everything else, be it ancient Greek sculpture, Viking relics, Chinese porcelain, Milton's snuffbox, Guy Fawkes' lantern or Einstein's blackboard.

Salter's and Folly Bridge

Images of carefree and straw-hatted students punting along the Oxford waterways are as much a part of the city's legend as its dreaming spires. Yet while the latter are real and punting remains popular, the image of the aristocratic oaf in plus-fours belongs to the past and as much to the Cherwell as the Thames. The Thames, however, provided the route for longer river trips; popularly north to Godstow or south to Nuneham

Courtney. Boats could—and still can—be rented from the firm of Salter's, which become the best-known boat yard on the Thames, claiming to have built the Oxford-Cambridge Boat Race winner for nine consecutive years and, from the late 1880s, running a popular steamboat trip to Kingston.

Fred Thacker, apostle of the river's joys and mysteries, was dismissive of the casual excursionist, writing in *The Stripling Thames*: "To the ordinary voyager from London, intent upon 'doing the river' in the fewest possible days, Salter's' raft is the ultimate limit and source of the Thames. He learns, if he learns anything, of mere slums above, of gasworks and railway bridges, and easily concludes that Nuneham and Iffley are the last word the River has for him..." Salter's still plies its trade today though it might not have been the yard supplying a rented craft when in Oxford to Jerome K. Jerome and companions in *Three Men in a Boat*: "The boy went, and re-appeared five minutes afterwards, struggling with an antediluvian chunk of wood, that looked as though it had been recently dug out of somewhere, and dug out carelessly, so as to have been unnecessarily damaged in the process... Was it the fossil of a pre-Adamite whale, or was it an early Roman coffin? The boy said it was THE PRIDE OF THE THAMES."

Salter's is sited close to the 1826 Folly Bridge, which earned its enduring nickname from an extra storey applied to the gatehouse of its seventeenth-century forerunner that created a topsy-turvy appearance. The bridge originated in the twelfth century with King Stephen's drawbridge, built to aid the capture of Oxford from Queen Matilda by spanning the river on the main route from Abingdon. A latter version is said to have held, above the gatehouse on the north side, the study of Franciscan scientist-monk Roger Bacon (1214?-92), inventor of the optical lens and the magnifying glass before he himself was re-invented fictionally in the twentieth century by Ian Morson. Facing the bridge is The Head of the River pub, occupying a former warehouse, and the Folly House, its exterior decorated by statuettes said to represent ladies who once worked within during the house's alleged time as a brothel.

Racing towards Iffley

If any certain statement can be made about the post-war world, it is that Eights Week has not lost its attractions. Industrial difficulties may shake society to its foundations, meetings and festivities of all sorts may be cancelled, trains may become scarcer and scarcer, but on every "night" of this unique week the traditional crowds are on the banks of the Isis. Indeed, they seem this year to be greater than ever; college barges could hardly hold another soul... the throng of punts on the towpath-side, adorned with a novel decoration of air-balloons, makes a continuous floating platform which Xerxes himself may have erected.

The Times, 23 May 1921

On the river, Oxford's big events are the inter-collegiate rowing races of Eights Week, each May, and amid slightly less hullabaloo, Torpids, held in late February or early March. Both of these events began in the early 1800s and involve the arrow-like craft stored and lovingly maintained in the boathouses beside the river, most of them downstream from Folly Bridge adjacent to Christ Church Meadows. Both are bump races in which success is measured not by crossing the finish line first, but by "bumping" (that is catching up with, not necessarily smashing into it) the boat in front, the race having started with all boats arranged beside the bank in single file. With races staged over several days, a successful crew will steadily work its way up the starting order; the year's final placings provide the initial positions for the following year's races. The best overall Eight (the number of rowers in each boat) is head of the River—hence the name of the pub.

The crowds, excitement and rituals of Eights Week that so delighted the *Times* correspondent show few show signs of abating and also provided a backdrop to *Zuleika Dobson* (1911), the only novel of wit and caricaturist Max Beerbohm. The tale's eponymous character is a beautiful conjuror invited to the races by her grandfather, warden of the fictional Judas (based on Merton) College. Such are her radiant good looks that all men fall in love with Zuleika and are then driven to suicide by their unrequited passion—their massed deaths occurring at the climax of the races.

Outside race weeks, the riverside scene is appreciably calmer. Below Donnington Bridge, Iffley Meadows provide 28 acres of unsullied, marshy greenery on the east side while, on the west, the Isis Tavern once had the distinction of being a pub with no road: supplies once arrived by river; they now come by truck along a dirt track.

Iffley Lock is a 1923 successor to one of the earliest pound locks on the Thames, built around 1620. Iffley Mill, which once stood by the lock, survives only in the canvases of innumerable painters and the comments of Charles Dickens Jr.: "Rarely indeed is there an exhibition of the (Royal) Academy or the Dudley, or any of the water-colour societies without at least one bit from Iffley." The painters might have been better advised to point their easels towards nearby Iffley Church, a fine expression of Norman beakhead and zigzag carving with a tower of perfect Norman arcades. Describing the church and its surrounds in *Oxford* (1965), Jan Morris wrote: "in a hush above the river—with a long low rectory on one side, and an old country house on another, and an owlish stump of a dead tree, and a dead yew, and a patch of shaggy walled graveyard so green, so silent and mole-heaped that you might still be far out in some distant rural backwater."

From the Sandford Lasher to the Swift Ditch

"The pool under Sandford lasher, just behind the lock, is a very good place to drown yourself in," wrote Jerome K. Jerome of the most vicious segment of the upper Thames. Those who have drowned here are remembered by an obelisk in the centre of the weir, sometimes used as a diving board by those with a devil-may-care attitude. The Lasher marks one of the biggest drops in water levels on the Thames, the frenzied scene of foaming water at odds with a landscape that becomes increasingly pastoral as Oxford recedes. Not that a placid landscape means an entirely placid past. The mill built at Sandford by the Knights Templar in the thirteenth century sucked water from the river and raised the ire of those living downstream. Thacker quotes a fourteenth-century account: "the men of Oxon broke down the locks of Sandford which 'the brethren' there raised."

From Sandford, the river passes farms, meadows and sewage works, and continues between Radley on one side and Nuneham Courtney on the other. Owned by the Courtenay family (of Sutton Courtenay) from

Iffley Church: "some distant rural backwater"

the thirteenth century, the manor and accompanying land passed into the hands of Earl Harcourt (of the Stanton Harcourts) in 1712 for £17,000, a deal described as the "cheapest pennyworth that was ever bought in Oxfordshire." The manor was demolished and the villa of Nuneham Courtney raised, gaining in the eighteenth century a Lawrence "Capability" Brown-designed 1,300-acre garden. Looming in the gardens like a mysterious hillside obelisk is the Carfax Conduit, a Jacobean-style stone cistern that originally stood at Carfax in the heart of Oxford to provide drinking water. As Carfax's traffic increased, the cistern became an obstruction as was uprooted and presented to Lord Harcourt; it now provides befuddlement for boaters unaware of its history. Of Nuneham, James S. Whitman wrote in *Down The Thames in a Birch-Bark Canoe*, published in the American magazine, *Harper's*, in 1881:

> No words could convey any adequate idea of the loveliness that gathers about the trees, the meadows, the cultivated fields and slopes, the old

homesteads, the thatched roofs. One rests his paddle, and as he drifts lazily along with the stream, the distant sound of the Oxford bells blends mysteriously with the music of the lark singing from his invisible height, the notes of the cuckoo, and the cawing of the rooks. On this side and on that man and nature have lent each other a helping hand to produce picturesqueness and beauty. There is really an irresistible desire to land and stroll about the little retreat of Radley, on the right, that lies nestled amid elms, beeches, limes, and oaks, or forest beneath the wooded slopes of Nuneham, that most beautiful of English parks.

By the early 1900s, Thames tourism was in full swing and Nuneham was more popular than ever, particularly for picnic parties who were allowed to land on Tuesdays and Thursday during the season. Not everyone approved. In 1910 Charles Harper observed: "Nuneham is the very last place to which any one who is not a fish or duck would wish to go... Truly, no more miserable experience is possible than that of sitting in one of the picturesquely thatched arbours by the waterside, and dallying over a lukewarm tea, awaiting the hour for the up-river steamer's arrival..."

Continuing in what now is a westerly direction, the river reaches the point where its course was diverted around AD960 by monks of Abingdon Abbey for their own "convenience and cleanliness". The original course was along the south side of Andersey Island towards Culham, a waterway that remained, according to Sydney R. Jones, "a secluded backwater owning every sort of Nature bounty in overgrowth and decked waters." The old course is properly called Swift Ditch but is given on many maps as Back Water.

Abingdon and Culham Bridge

At Abingdon, the Thames is crossed by an eight-arched bridge dating from the fifteenth century though greatly rebuilt in the 1920s. The abbey, founded in AD675 to house twelve Benedictine monks, filled three acres and boasted a church 300-feet-long. Ransacked by Danes, restored by King Alfred and among the richest in England when dissolved by Henry VIII, the abbey is chiefly remembered by its splendid gatehouse. Meanwhile, beneath its tall spire, the Church of St. Helens provides a fine example of the ecclesiastical architecture known as Cotswold perpendicular.

Aside from the modern outskirts and the seemingly perpetual traffic jams in its centre, Abingdon still holds much from its past. Joseph and Elizabeth Robins Pennell were sufficiently charmed to write in the August 1889 issue of *The Century*: "Abingdon is very picturesque, with its old gabled houses… its abbey gateway and St. Helens Church, whose graveyard is bounded by quaint old almshouses and whose spire is a landmark for the Thames traveler. But were I to begin to describe the endless beauty that lies near the Thames, and just hidden from it, I should never get back to the river again."

In *News From Nowhere*, William Morris wrote of Abingdon as scarred by "nineteenth-century degradation", presumably mindful of the railway and the Wilts and Berks Canal which linked Abingdon with the Thames and Severn Canal and put it at the heart of the regional transport network. But another William Morris, born in Oxford and a one-time bicycle maker, would become more closely associated with Abingdon. Switching from bicycle to motor manufacturing, Morris created such British automotive icons as the Morris Oxford and the Morris Minor and, for fifty years until 1980, a factory at Abingdon manufactured the legendary MG sports car.

South of Abingdon, Culham Bridge crosses Swift Ditch just before the old Thames course rejoins the new. Both Culham and Abingdon bridges were designed to improve Abingdon's economy, threatened during the fifteenth century by a new bridge at Wallingford which provided an easier, if longer, transport route for London-bound Cotswold wool. While Abingdon Bridge was later rebuilt to accommodate increased traffic, Culham Bridge became neglected and, with road traffic now carried by a newer span, still looks like the medieval edifice it truly is. As Geoffrey Phillips noted in *Thames Crossings*, "if the ghost of a fifteenth-century mason should walk this way, he will find much that is familiar."

Sutton Courtenay and George Orwell

Beyond Abingdon, the main navigable route of the Thames is through Culham Cut, though the old course meanders to the south to pass through Sutton Courtenay, once with 17 footbridges crossing the river

Sutton Courtenay: "a country churchyard"

and of which the 1929 *Thames Survey* wrote: "A charming and secluded village lying off the track of river-steamers, which pass through Culham Cut; it consists of one long and wide street with grass verges, and flanked by cottages of different periods, with a few larger houses that harmonise well with their environment."

Very little today renders the description obsolete. The Courtenay family gained the land on which the village sits from Henry II and raised the surviving stone Norman House around 1200. Although it serves a small community, and in various forms has done so since the thirteenth century, Sutton Courtenay's Church of All Saints holds a couple of surprises in its cemetery. One is the grave of Herbert Henry Asquith, liberal prime minister from 1908 to 1916, who lived locally. Another is that on which an inscription reads: "Here Lies Eric Arthur Blair. Born June 25, 1903. Died January 21, 1950." Eric Blair was the real name of author George Orwell, who had no connection during his life with Sutton Courtenay but willed to be buried in "a country churchyard". Sutton Courtney was near the estate of Orwell's close friend, newspaper editor David Astor, who arranged for Orwell to be buried here and who himself now lies amid the church's yew trees.

Orwell's legend as author of such emotive and enduring works as *Animal Farm* and *1984* grew after his death; through his life he was chiefly regarded as a left-wing journalist who wrote novels on the side. In *Orwell: The Life*, D. J. Taylor writes of the author's sparsely attended funeral: "This was, everyone agreed, a desperately sad affair: not some ancient literary eminence called to his eternal rest in a blaze of pomp and glory but a man of forty-six who had not survived long enough to taste the fruits of his success." For one who championed so much that was truly English, Orwell's quiet, simple grave in a tiny Oxfordshire village, visited only by those prepared to make the effort to do so, seems entirely proper: a less *1984* setting is hard to imagine.

Culham, Clifton, the Barley Mow

Close to Culham Lock and Sutton Bridge, the meandering off-shoot of the river rejoins the main Thames flowing through Culham Cut. To the north, structures usually non-committally described as "government buildings" on maps, are actually a base for the United Kingdom's fusion energy research. Since 1960, finding a controllable, safe and non-polluting form of energy through fusion (rather than fission, the messy stuff of conventional nuclear power) has been the goal pursued here, and inside these innocent-looking buildings are scientists who spend their days heating plasma to ten million degrees centigrade and fussing over spherical Tokomaks.

The Thames, meanwhile, continues beneath a 1920s railway viaduct to reach the village of Appleford. The *Thames Survey* suggested Appleford's "charming river-front (is) spoilt by the close proximity of the railway viaduct now being built." With the passage of time, however, the 167-foot-span structure has earned its place in the landscape; a landscape that *The Royal River's* authors found abounding "in rural walks, and in subjects both for the pencil of the artist and the pen of the man of letters."

Ahead, the Clifton Cut makes for speedy passage towards Clifton Hampden, while the winding older course passes the edge of Long Wittenham. The digging of Clifton Cut was partly inspired by embarrassment when the mayor of London became stranded here in

1826. Thacker quotes a contemporary account titled *The Lord Mayor's Visit to Oxford*: "The navigation here appeared to be particularly defective; for, with all the advantage of exertions that had been made by the Water-Bailiff's directions, and the expense that had been incurred for the supply of water; the country having been comparatively drained for several miles along the upper districts,—and though the City Barge and shallop drew scarcely more than two feet of water—they were detained at Clifton a considerable length of time."

Since it increased the greater water flow through Clifton Hampden and prevented farmers from fording the river with their cattle, Culham Cut inspired the building of Clifton Bridge, designed by George Gilbert Scott, who would find greater architectural fame with London's Albert Memorial and St. Pancras Station and who, legend records, first sketched a plan for the bridge on his cuff.

Close to the south end of the six-arched bridge, the half-timbered, thatched-roof Barley Mow Inn is "without exception, I should say, the quaintest, most old-world inn up the river," according to Jerome K Jerome, who wrote part of *Three Men in a Boat* while a guest. The inn was a regular stop for Victorian and Edwardian pleasure boaters but has been providing, food, ale and lodging for much longer. It celebrates its literary connection with the Jerome Rooms, which help make the Barley Mow, without exception I should say, the most over-rated feature on the Thames.

The Wittenhams, Dorchester and Shillingford

While Clifton Hampden and its thatched inn are a magnet for Thames travellers, the more intrepid find greater reward along the country lanes south of Clifton Bridge leading to Long Wittenham and Little Wittenham. At the latter, a footpath just beyond the church leads to Days Lock and a willow-fringed bridge beside a lock-keeper's cottage. It was here in 1983 that the first world pooh sticks championship was held, inspired by a game played in A. A. Milne's *Winnie the Pooh*. Each March, several hundred potential champions pay £1 to take part, the proceeds going to charity and the winner being the entrant whose stick, dropped into the river, is first to cross the finishing line.

On the river's west side rise the Dyke Hills, site of Iron Age fortifications guarding the settlement at Dorchester and accessible from the river by footpath. Strengthening the natural protection provided by the Thames and the River Thame, the defensive line nonetheless failed to hold back the Romans who established themselves here (Dorocina, as they knew it). By Saxon times, Dorchester was an important religious centre and in AD635 was made the see of the first Bishop of Wessex; on the site of its Saxon cathedral stands the partly twelfth-century abbey which dominates the village. By the 1920s Dorchester was a busy stop for coaches on the London-Oxford road, sufficiently so for the *Thames Survey* to warn that its "virtue may be impaired if advertisements, petrol-stations, and signboards are not regulated... already pink asbestos roof tiles have been used at the north end of the village." That their warning was heeded, albeit with the help of the M40 motorway, enables Jerome K Jerome's opinion to hold good: "Dorchester is a delightfully peaceful old place, nestling in stillness and silence and drowsiness."

Rising above the Thames south of Little Wittenham, Wittenham Clumps are a series of hills with more Iron Age fortifications, their defensive value clearly apparent after even the shortest climb since they afford a spectacular view over a large swath of countryside. They also offer a full panorama of Didcot Power Station, a provider of energy that has been draining water from the Thames since opening in the 1960s. J. R. L Anderson, in *The Upper Thames* (1970), described the power station as "one of the new citadels of technological strength... rising like some gaunt prison of the spirit. In a light Thames mist it can appear as a fairy castle." Readers of *Country Life*, by contrast, voted it Britain's third biggest eyesore in 2003.

Continuing south, the river passes beneath the impressive three-arch Shillingford Bridge, completed in the 1820s entirely of stone. Records suggest that a bridge existed here from 1301, probably erected to provide access to the abbey at Dorchester but later destroyed, presumably for the security threat it posed to the castle at Wallingford. Carrying the A329 as it sweeps towards Oxford from the steep, tree-shrouded Shillingford Hill on the south side, the elegance of the bridge is enhanced by its 1920s balustrades and the simple fact of it being entirely disproportional to the small community around it.

Travelling this section of the Thames in 1805, artist J. M. W. Turner painted the then wooden Shillingford Bridge and, behind it, the Bridge

Hotel, which remains in progress-defying solitude on the south side. Turner also sketched the view towards Benson, just below Shillingford, with Benson weir in the foreground; an outlook of which fellow artist Samuel Ireland noted: "the gentle fall of its waters, forming a continual cascade, connects a pleasing section of objects, highly worthy of the exertions of an artist."

Wallingford

A sixteen-arch and part-thirteenth-century bridge, a ruined castle, and the Church of St. Peter with its elegant spire, suggest that Wallingford has a past much grander than its present. The town indeed conceals a startling history: it grew as the area's lowest all-year river crossing; Sweyn ransacked it during the Danish invasion of 1006; the castle was built in 1067; a parliament was held under Henry II in 1154; Cromwell demolished the castle during the Civil War; and fire devastated the town in 1675. Some four hundred years before Cromwell, the castle provided refuge for Matilda, daughter of Henry I, after she escaped imprisonment at Oxford and crossed, it was popularly recorded, a frozen Thames barefoot. The subsequent Treaty of Wallingford solved the succession dispute that had been the reason for Matilda's incarceration, allowing for Stephen I to rule until his death and for Matilda's son, Henry, to then take the crown—which he did in 1154, beginning the Plantagenet dynasty.

Remarking in the 1940s that the town's railway station had no trains, save for a tiny steam engine that did little to lure passengers off the London-Oxford mainline service, Sydney R. Jones deduced a shrewd move: "In this way Wallingford has managed its railway affairs quite as well as Abingdon. That old puffing traveller through the cornfields saved the town; it has helped to reserve Wallingford on the Thames riverside, a remarkably pleasant town, the very place for a sensible soul to settle down to sleep in and achieve a tremendous old age."

A tiny corner of Wallingford may forever be associated with red herrings, devious servants and record-breaking book sales. For many years until her death in 1976, Winterbrook Lodge was home to Agatha Christie, the reclusive *grande dame* of country house whodunnits. Among Christie's legion of followers are those who insist that the lodge was the model for Danemead, home of Christie's fictional sleuth Miss

Marple, and that Wallingford itself is thinly disguised in Christie's work as Market Basing. They may, of course, be on completely the wrong track...

Time to ruminate on the ups and downs of Wallingford's history is provided by the river continuing south though a pleasant course untroubled by distinctive landmarks. Of Cholsey, however, it might be worth noting a *Thames Survey* entry for the village, suggesting: "the County Mental Hospital... requires screening from the river by a belt of trees." Whether to shield the inmates from the crazed antics of Sunday boaters or vice-versa is not made clear.

A short way beyond, Isambard Kingdom Brunel's brick-arched Moulsford Bridge carries the London-Oxford railway over the river and past the Beetle and Wedge, the quaintly-named hotel known to readers of H. G. Wells' *The History of Mr. Polly* as the Potwell Inn: "It was about two o'clock in the afternoon one hot day in high May when Mr. Polly, unhurrying and serene, came to that broad bend of the river to which the little lawn and garden of the Potwell Inn run down." From here, the Thames continues toward Goring Gap. Dividing the Chilterns of Oxfordshire from the Berkshire Downs, the gap formed at the end of the last Ice Age as the glacially-assisted river gouged a route through chalk hills. It now divides itself into three wide and shallow channels around two islands as it passes between the neighbouring villages of Goring and Streatley.

Goring and Streatley

Goring is the far larger of the two communities but it was not always so. Streatley enjoyed a prominence thanks to its place on the Reading turnpike, the route's former post house now the Bull Inn where, in *Three Men in a Boat*, Jerome K. Jerome and companions consume a lunch "much to Montmorency's satisfaction".

An earlier traveller was J. M. W. Turner whose 1805 *Goring* depicts grazing cows before the local mill and church. Unwittingly, Turner started a trend. George Leslie, himself an artist, wrote in the 1880s: "One cannot wonder at the number of artists who are attracted by the many beauties of Streatley and Goring; the river, the two mills, the eyots and backwaters all lend themselves to the painter's skill, the whole place abounding in rich material for his art. But my pleasure in it, I am ashamed to confess, is considerably lessened by the numbers of sketching tents and white umbrellas that meet the eye, perched on every point of vantage around this spot: in the sketching season the little coffee room at the Swan has easels and artists' traps in every corner, and the village swarms with geniuses and their wives."

A contrast to the rural idyll admired by easel-bearers arriving in Turner's wake is provided by the 1997 glass-and-steel boating pavilion that sits by the river bank, erected by architects Brookes Stacey Randall. According to the architects, the pavilion provides "a very contextual response whilst being dynamic in form… [enabling] the client to enjoy the life of the river whilst being firmly rooted in the landscape."

While some find the setting overly twee and others find the boating pavilion overly modern, the location's true worth is found at the summit of Streatley Hill and the view of Goring Gap that unfolds beyond. Elizabeth and Joseph Robins Pennell recalled: "It was the hour of sunset when we mounted and looked down on the valley, spread out like a map below, the river winding through it, a path of light between the open fields, a cold, dark shadow under the wooded banks. May the lazy minstrel another time wait to smoke and weave his lazy lay until he has climbed the hill, and then he will sing of something besides the Swan at Streatley!"

Pangbourne and Mapledurham

Running for a time parallel to the river, the railway into Pangbourne crosses a bridge "covered with a multitude of glaring advertisements that positively repel the visitor and discourage him from lingering to enjoy the many attractions," according to the 1920s *Thames Survey*. In *News from Nowhere*, William Morris refers to Pangbourne as having been "thoroughly cocknified" (the term "cockney" at the time commonly applied to middle-class Londoners relocating westwards). All of which seems a little harsh on what is a pretty, if unremarkable, Thamesside commuter town, though it might explain the retaining of the toll on the white-painted lattice girder bridge that links Pangbourne to Whitchurch, a small community on the Oxfordshire bank. A 10p charge is levied on cars (walkers and cyclists free), presumably to deter cocknified Pangbournites from disturbing the peace with their infernal horseless carriages.

A fictional Pangbourne estate of luxury homes behind high security fences formed a backdrop for J. G. Ballard's 1988 novella *Running Wild*, which begins with all 32 of the estate's adults being found murdered, the culprits eventually discovered to be their own children who killed "to free themselves from a tyranny of love and care." The tale was described by *Publisher's Weekly* as "a sharp portrait of complacent privilege in Thatcher's England."

Onward, the river negotiates a broad sweeping bend overlooked on the left by the Tudor-age Hardwick House and, soon after though slightly hidden by trees, the imposing Mapledurham House. Raised in the sixteenth century by the Bourne family in the shape of an "E", for Elizabeth I, who was an occasional guest, and still occupied by the Bournes, the house provided sanctuary for Catholics (as the Bournes were) at a time when practising the faith was illegal.

Mapledurham gives its name to the hamlet around it and is the only spot on the Thames likely to unite fans of John Galsworthy, Kenneth Grahame and Ozzy Osbourne. The house was cast as Soames' mansion in Galsworthy's *The Forsythe Saga*: "It was full late for the river, but the weather was lovely, and summer lingered below the yellowing leaves. Soames took many looks at the day from his riverside garden near Mapledurham that Sunday morning." It also inspired Toad Hall in Kenneth Grahame's *The Wind in the Willows*: "Rounding a bend in the river, they came in sight of a handsome, dignified old house of mellowed red brick, with well-kept lawns reaching down to the water's edge." And in 1970 Osbourne's pioneering heavy metal band Black Sabbath used the house's fourteenth-century windmill as a backdrop for the cover of their first album.

With indecent speed, the country landscapes around Mapledurham become the sprawl of Reading, ever-expanding alongside the M4 motorway. Like many of its neighbours, Caversham is a once-individual community now largely consumed by suburban creep. From the twelfth century, however, it was consumed by pilgrims visiting Our Lady of Caversham's shrine. A jewel-encrusted statue of the Virgin Mary provided the shrine's focal point but, among other relics, the shrine claimed a spearhead that pierced Christ on the cross, a piece of the rope with which Judas hanged himself, and the knife that killed St. Edward the martyr. The 1538 dissolution closed the shrine, its location now disputed. Caversham's early wooden bridge and a chapel that stood on an island alongside it are also long gone, the river now crossed by the concrete Caversham Bridge opened in 1926 by the Prince of Wales: one of the less controversial moments in the life of the future Edward VIII.

"Oh Beautiful World": Reading

Reaching Reading after travelling on the Thames from London in the 1960s, a nonplussed J. H. B. Peel remarked: "First, a power station appears, rearing like a poisonous fungus in the waste land; after that, shunting sheds in various shades of British Railway dirt, followed by gas-works, tin huts, and factories wreathed with pylons and cables which, if they were reproduced in little, would be acclaimed as the sculpture of the year: and above the lot, a cancerous halo." Whatever its ills, Reading no longer justifies Peel's description, not least because most riverside totems of manufacturing industries have given way to an agreeable if unexciting riverside promenade and British Railway dirt is the stuff of nostalgia.

Reading's rise was due to the River Kennet rather than the Thames and its early growth was triggered by a Benedictine abbey founded by Henry I in 1121. Lasting infamy, however, was acquired by imprisoning the writer and wit Oscar Wilde in the 1890s. For gross indecency (the then crime of homosexuality), Wilde received two years' hard labour, most of it spent in Reading Jail's cell C33. His stay inspired *The Ballad of Reading Gaol*, written in France following his release and built around the fate of another Reading inmate, Charles Wooleridge, a guardsmen executed in 1896 for killing his wife, though revealing Wilde's thoughts on prison life:

> The vilest deeds like poison-weeds
> Bloom well in prison-air:
> It is only what is good in Man
> That wastes and withers there:
> Pale Anguish keeps the heavy gate
> And the Warder is Despair.

Across the Kennet from the bleak jail stands Bruce Williams' statue of Wilde, unveiled in 2000 and forming part of the Oscar Wilde Memorial

Walk which includes the riverside railings onto which is etched "Oh Beautiful World!", the phrase uttered by Wilde on his release in May 1897.

Part Two

A River of Change

Between Reading and London flows the Thames of popular imagination: riverside pubs, rowing clubs, the Henley Regatta and scenes still reminiscent of Jerome K. Jerome's *Three Men in a Boat*. Yet look more closely and the river reveals something quite different: a story of economic, social and political change reverberating through the centuries. Jerome's perennially popular novel evoked the late-Victorian Thames and documented a new era in the life of the river as improved wages and holiday entitlements underpinned the rise of pleasure on the waterway. The three men (to say nothing of the dog) around whom the narrative evolves were themselves beneficiaries of the 1870s education acts that made their white-collar careers possible.

Nineteenth-century change was also documented by J. M .W. Turner. The artist painted from many points on the river's course but here was able to capture the railways' usurping of the river's role as the pre-eminent mover of goods and people. His early portrayals of tranquil scenes at Goring and elsewhere gave way to images of speeding trains and the river's new rail bridges: additions sometimes as artful as they were technologically innovative. Rail not only changed the river, it changed riverside settlement. Market towns such as Kingston were re-born as London suburbs; villages like Twickenham, previously best known for literary associations that originated with Alexander Pope, expanded into towns. In recent decades, rail itself has been supplanted by road and created the "corridor" of the M4 motorway, turning many Thameside towns into rural-suburban dormitory communities of London.

At first glance, the string of current and former royal residences—at Windsor, Hampton Court, Richmond and Kew—along this section of the river could be seen as signifying stability rather than change. Rarely over its long history, however, has the English monarchy been secure, and the Thames provides proof of the impermanence of power. At Runnymede, King John saw his authority lessened by the epochal Magna

Marlow Bridge

Carta; plotters in a cellar at Hurley undermined the Catholic James II and instigated his Protestant replacement; a government-destabilizing scandal of the 1960s became forever associated with a high society lair above the Thames at Cliveden; and a royal dog biting a commoner in Windsor Great Park focused public attention on the position of England's present-day monarchy.

Despite the scent of revolution, however, a person could easily traverse this route entirely untroubled by affairs of state and still discover a river with unexpected tales at every turn: Frankenstein emerging from a Marlow cottage; the truth and lies of the Hell Fire Club; counter-cultural Eel Pie Island; and the strange case of John Dee, wizard of Mortlake.

Sonning and Shiplake

Is there a spot more lovely than the rest,
By art improved, by nature truly blest?
A noble river at its base is running,
It is a little village known as Sonning

James Sadler, Sonning lock-keeper (1845-85)

East of Reading, the Thames takes a tight left-hand turn to reach the almost too-well-preserved village of Sonning, where the half-timbered cottages in a flowery location prompted J. H. B. Peel to complain: "Strong indeed is the temptation to paint a flattering likeness, but Sonning is too notorious to be camouflaged. On a summer weekend it is Hell to live in, Hell to drive through, and so hellishly hard to park at that the queue of cars may be half-a-mile long." Jerome K. Jerome suggested: "It is the most fairy-like little nook on the whole river. It is more like a stage village than one built of bricks and mortar. Every house is smothered in roses, and now, in early June, they were bursting forth in clouds of dainty splendour." The *Thames Valley* at least admired the late eighteenth-century redbrick Sonning Bridge, "one of the most beautiful across the Thames and should be preserved at all costs... an entrancing picture of river scenery." The bridge marks the spot where a ferry operated from the fifteenth century and where Sonning Mill, once producing corn and then electricity, now earns its keep as a theatre and restaurant.

After the unreal preservation encountered at Sonning, the river takes a relaxing meander towards Shiplake and encounters a quartet of islands beyond which the small village grips a bluff above the river's north bank. It was in Shiplake's church ("ruined by 'restoration'" noted a scathing Peel) in June 1850 that future poet laureate Alfred Lord Tennyson married Emily Sellwood. Neither Tennyson not his bride had any link with Shiplake beyond the fact that the poet's cousin had also been married by the vicar. Perhaps distracted by events of the day, Tennyson showed his gratitude by composing, in the vicar's honour, what might be his worst poem:

> Vicar of this pleasant spot
> Where it was my chance to marry
> Happy happy be your lot
> In the vicarage by the quarry.

Henley-on-Thames

Beyond Shiplake and a further series of islands, an oak-lined section of the Thames known as "the Fair Mile" continues to Henley, synonymous with the Henley Regatta or, more formally since 1851 when Prince Albert gave his approval, the Royal Henley Regatta. Launched in 1839 to attract commerce, the regatta quickly became part of the English social season: the 1970 *Shell Guide to England* summed it up as "fashionable and pretty girls vying for attention with the athletic prowess on the river."

Despite thousands of working-class Victorian Londoners who arrived on special trains and a current popularity spreading across a widening spectrum of the population, many aspects of the regatta seem determined to retain social divisions. Labyrinthine rules and regulations are imposed on spectators who, save for those in the proletarian enclosures entered by payment at the gate, occupy strictly segregated areas and are admitted only with the right credentials. Those using the Stewards' Enclosure require an invitation and must adhere to a dress code: for men, jacket, collar and tie (usually straw boater and a blazer); for women, dresses with hemlines below the knee. Members (there are several bodies to be members of, again with a hierarchical order of importance) indicate their right to be present with metal badges: those with "full metal jackets" are members of everything.

Over Britain's longest natural stretch of straight river, the showpiece races are the Grand Challenge Cup and the Diamond Challenge Skulls. Even on the water, however, social divisions have long played a part: foreigners and professional rivermen were originally barred from competing, and as recently as the 1960s, Peel lamented that the regatta had ceased to be "English, amateur and aristocratic", suggesting that the rot set in during 1906 when a Belgian won the Grand Challenge Cup.

Without the early July regatta crowds, Henley exudes a calm and dignified charm with a plethora of medieval pubs, a thirteenth-century church and the commendable Museum of the River & Rowing. The major river feature, though, is the 1786 bridge connecting the counties of Buckinghamshire and Oxfordshire. The bridge's architect, William Haywood, tends to be less well remembered than the sculptor who contributed its keystones, depicting the faces of Isis and Tamisis. She was Anne Damer (1749-1828), known in her lifetime not merely as the first woman in England to wear black silk stockings but for her scandalous lesbian affairs, including an enduring relationship with Horace Walpole's literary executor, Mary Berry, with whom Damer lived at Walpole's Strawberry Hill home near Twickenham after the author's death.

Start-point for the regatta's races, Temple Island lies in the grounds of Fawley Court and features an impudent 1771 fishing lodge folly. Complete with England's first Etruscan interior, the lodge can now be booked for the better class of wedding and private event. Fawley Court itself acquired a handsome makeover under Sir Christopher Wren in 1684 for Colonel William Freeman in whose hands, and those of his descendants, the house became known to royalty and was lavishly maintained. Fawley Court was requisitioned during the Second World War and, in dilapidated form, was purchased in 1953 by the Marian Fathers, a Polish religious order. Intending to instill traditional Polish and Catholic values into Polish boys in England, the school continued until 1986. The Fathers now run Fawley Court as a conference centre and retreat.

From Temple Island the river negotiates a broad right-hand bend, passing on the left Greenlands, the 1853 Italianate mansion erected on

Henley-on-Thames

the site of a seventeenth-century manor by William H. Smith, founder of the W.H. Smith retail chain and later Lord Hambledon, owner of a large chunk of the riverside. Of Greenlands, Jerome K Jerome noted "the rather uninteresting looking river residence of my newsagent—a quiet unassuming old gentleman, who may often be met with about these regions, during the summer months, sculling himself along in easy vigorous style."

Directly ahead resembling an oversized cottage, the white-timbered Hambledon Mill was mentioned in *Domesday* and remained productive until the 1950s. The interior has since been converted into river-view apartments, while the exterior, seen across the dashing white waters of Hambledon weir, remains the target of amateur painters and photographers. The adjacent Hambledon Lock was, in 1829, the start-point for the first Oxford-Cambridge Boat Race, which brought victory to Oxford by "many lengths".

Hell Fire and Medmenham Abbey

One leaves Henley, and passing islets of osier beds, arrives at a bend in the river that discloses the captivating surroundings of Medmenham. The ruined abbey lies close by the river, nestled among trees, and its ivy-grown walls are the favorite resort of boating parties from the adjacent villages. The inscription, Fay ce que voudras, conspicuous above the door, recalls the licentiousness of a band of fashionables in the last century who made the cowl the cloak of the most infamous orgies.

James S. Whitman, "Down the Thames in a Birch-Bark Canoe", *Harper's*, 1881

The ruined abbey is that of Medmenham, founded by the Cistercian order in 1200 but by 1536 able to claim only one monk and one abbot to its name. Its subsequent decline was arrested by various additions, not least a coating of eighteenth-century Gothic intended to make the ruined abbey conform to the popular image of a ruined abbey. Other sections were converted into a mansion by the landowning Dufford family.

Assuming they actually took place, the infamous orgies were those conducted by what popularly became known as the Hell Fire Club, founded in 1740 by Sir Francis Dashwood, who leased the mansion from the Duffords. Before relocating to a series of tunnels in West Wycombe (the present-day tourist attraction of the Hell Fire Caves), Dashwood and his group earned a reputation for Bacchanalian nights of wine and ribaldry in the company of naked aristocratic women, and the odd baboon, with a circle of initiates who, if some accounts are to be believed, included prominent political figures and formed part of a worldwide group of illuminati shaping world events before and since.

Hurley's Glorious Revolution

Invading Danes travelling from Essex to Gloucester forded the river at Hurley in 894, their presence hinted at by the name of the luxury Danesfield House Hotel on the river's north side, perched on a tree-covered chalk cliff with views over a large segment of Berkshire. Hurley itself held a Saxon church, a Benedictine priory and in 1929 was described by the *Thames Valley* thus: "Secluded and known only to the discerning few, this village has so far completely escaped mutilation." While since discovered by the discerning many, Hurley still bears few signs of mutilation.

In the former grounds of the priory, an Edwardian mansion called Lady Place assumed the site and name of a sixteenth-century abode raised by Sir Richard Lovelace, a seafaring colleague of Sir Francis Drake. Lovelace financed the mansion, according to Thomas Macaulay's *History of England*, "out of the spoils of Spanish galleons from the Indies." In its cellar, a descendant of Sir Richard hosted the plotters who conspired to replace the Catholic James II with the Protestant William of Orange (crowned William III): what became England's 1688 Glorious Revolution. As the flamboyant Macaulay continued: "Beneath the stately saloon, adorned by Italian pencils, was a subterraneous vault, in which the bones of ancient monks had sometimes been found. In this dark chamber some zealous and daring opponents of the government had held many midnight conferences during that anxious time when England was impatiently expecting the Protestant wind."

From the west, riverside Hurley is announced with "the huge majesty of Hurley Weir, from which you should keep well clear," suggested Graham Hayward giving tips for boaters in *River Thames* (1988); the weir forms part of a network of river channels and islands around Hurley Lock. On the north bank, the dainty 1775 Palladian-style Harleyford Manor, built for prominent landowner Sir William Clayton, is now occupied by company offices and made an unlikely setting for the World Memory Championships, one of many mind-power pursuits undertaken within its walls when occupied by the Buzan Group, here until 2002.

Ahead, the river is crossed by the arching Temple footbridge, a 150-foot span which opened in 1989 much to the relief of Thames Path walkers and those who missed the last ferry, which ceased operations here in 1953. The large but placid Temple Lock once powered a paper mill and was the site of the Temple Copper Mills which fashioned copper sheets for the hulls of Britain's naval ships, its expansion enabled by the opening of the Thames and Severn Canal which, as D. G. Wilson put it, "brought the industrial revolution into the heart of the Thames Valley."

Bisham Abbey

The Norman tower of Bisham Church rises on the river's south bank close to Bisham Abbey, its current use as a national sports centre belying a long and turbulent history. More priory than true abbey, much is Tudor although the oldest sections date from the thirteenth-century Knights Templar. Edward II ended the Knights' activities and used the abbey as a prison: Elizabeth Queen of Scots was incarcerated here as was, in a later era, Elizabeth I.

The Royal River remarks on the long list of abbey burials as "a remarkable testimony to the perilous life led by the aristocracy of those days: 'Thomas, Earl of Salisbury, who died at the siege of Orleans in 1428; Richard Neville, Earl of Salisbury and Warwick, beheaded at York in 1460; Richard Neville, "the king-maker", killed at the battle of Barnet in 1470; his brother John, Marquis of Montague, killed at the same battle, and Edward Plantagenet, son of the Duke of Clarence, beheaded in 1499 for attempting to escape from confinement.'"

Following the dissolution of the monasteries, the abbey's ownership passed to the Hoby family, who built a mansion on the site from the late 1550s. Many believe Lady Hoby (died 1609) still remains, appearing in the Tower Room during the coronation of each new monarch, "washing her hands with invisible soap in imperceptible water." Lady Hoby locked her misbehaving young son in a room and forgot about him until she returned from Court some time later, finding him starved to death, and now, it is said, spends eternity attempting to wash the blood from her hands. Lady Hoby's tomb stands in Bisham Church, her unfortunate son at her feet.

Marlow

Unlike Henley, where wide streets run parallel to the river, Marlow's riverside area is kept secret, lurking at the end of backstreets that once concluded in a sudden display of wharves and warehouses and today reveal tethered pleasure boats and the patrons of riverside pubs savouring views to Lock Island. The town's best river feature, however, is Marlow Bridge, an exceptional mix of engineering and aestheticism complemented by the spire of All Saints Church. Marlow Bridge was completed in 1836 by William Tierney Clarke, responsible nine years earlier for Hammersmith Bridge and subsequently for Budapest's first suspension bridge over the Danube. Sadly, the art and history qualities of Marlow's span tend to be lost on drivers queuing to cross its single-lane course.

Of Marlow Lock, Thacker enthused: "This beloved scene of the silvery Thames is full of old histories pertinent to my subject." He proceeded to elucidate the problems of the flash lock used here in earlier times, quoting a sixteenth-century account of a disaster: "the Streams there were so strong and the Water had such a dismal Fall that four Men within a short time were lost; three whereof drowned and a Fourth had his Brains dasht out."

Like Henley, Marlow hosts a regatta and has done so annually since 1866. Since 2001, however, the official Marlow Regatta has taken place not in Marlow but over an Olympic standard course on Dorney Lake, near Eton. In response, Marlow spends two weeks each June enjoying the similarly-named Marlow Regatta and Festival, a celebration of the town and its past with arts and crafts shows, concerts and rowing events thrown in. The latter can be watched from what the event's website promised in 2004 would be a "small grandstand and large licensed bar".

Novelist and poet Thomas Love Peacock lived in Marlow during the early 1800s, part of a local literary circle headed by Leigh Hunt (best remembered for his narrative poem, *Story of Rimini*), and encouraged his friends, the poet Shelley and his wife Mary, to join him. In 1816 the newly-married Shelleys settled into Albion House on West Street, part of the row now called Shelley Cottages and lived there for two years.

The previous summer, the Shelleys had visited another literary notable, Lord Byron, in Switzerland and in the company of Byron's doctor John William Polidori, listened to a selection of German ghost stories read by their host, who challenged those present to create a ghost story of their own by the following morning. Only Polidori succeeded, though Mary Shelley's idea of a person created from human body parts and brought to life was conceived then and the story completed in Marlow to be published in 1818 (and in revised form in 1831) as *Frankenstein*.

Her husband meanwhile used their time at Marlow to complete *The Revolt of Islam* and, using the *nom de plume* The Hermit of Marlow, to author two political tracts: *A Proposal for Putting Reform to the Vote*, advocating annual parliaments and a national referendum, and *An*

Address to the People on the Death of Princess Charlotte. Influencing Shelley's political thinking was the poverty apparent in Marlow as mechanized lace-making undercut the market for handmade lace, a staple source of income for many impoverished locals.

Cookham and Stanley Spencer
Leaving Marlow, the Thames passes the tree-clad slopes of Winter Hill with glimpses of enviably secluded homes between the branches while, on the other side, a railway embankment conceals a sewage works and water-filled quarries. As the river continues around a right hand bend, Winter Hill gives way to the wetlands of Cock Marsh, while the sewage works and old quarries give way to Bourne End. It was between Bourne End and Marlow that the steam train nicknamed the Marlow Donkey (also the name of a popular Marlow pub) travelled a single track, remembered by J. H. B. Peel as "a stirring sight, on a wintry evening... the venerable tank engine snorting like Vulcan, and its brace of Edwardian coaches miming a liner at night." And it was indeed a sight preferable to Bourne End itself: "bungalows and boathouses... tinged with suburban smut."

Few have such qualms about Cookham, just south of Bourne End and occupying the opposite bank. The riverside area, separate from the more recent growth around the railway station, still retains a village appearance and luxuriates in the distinction generated by Stanley Spencer (1891-1959), born in a cottage on the High Street, who became one of England's most fondly remembered (if much mocked) artists. For Spencer, Cookham was a "village in heaven" and so much did he sing its praises while studying in London that "Cookham" became his nickname. Many of Spencer's paintings depict Christ in an everyday English setting, not least standing in the doorway of Cookham Church, as in *The Resurrection, Cookham* and the unfinished *Christ Preaching at Cookham Regatta.* The Methodist chapel presided over by Spencer's mother now holds the Spencer Gallery, a homely setting in which to admire some of the artist's work and one which feels entirely in keeping with the artist's nature. Spencer died in 1959; a memorial stone marks his resting place in the church cemetery.

The last years of Spencer's life were spent at Clivedon View which, as its name suggests, affords a view across the Thames to the wooded hills of the Clivedon estate across the four channels into which the Thames divides to negotiate a series of islands before narrowing into Clivedon Deep.

Clivedon: Dukes, Duels and the Profumo Affair

The first house at Clivedon, set amid trees high above the river, was a hunting lodge built for the second Duke of Buckingham, a notorious rake who, though married, used the house to entertain his mistresses. His affair with one of them, the Countess of Shrewsbury, culminated in Buckingham challenging the Countess' husband to a duel which took place in 1668, leaving two of the six participants dead. Though Buckingham survived, his Court days were ended and Cliveden gained a reputation for scandal that it would rediscover three hundred years later.

Cliveden regained its links with royalty from 1737 when occupied by Frederick, Prince of Wales, son of George II and father of George III. It was then that Cliveden heard the first rendition of *Rule Britannia*, the words by Scottish poet James Thomson put to music by the English composer Thomas Arne that became an unofficial national anthem even though it was not intended as such. Cliveden acquired its present form in the 1850s, was sold to American entrepreneur, William Astor, in 1893 and subsequently passed to his son. Under Lady Astor, Cliveden became a renowned celebrity retreat, everyone from George III and Winston Churchill to Charlie Chaplin and George Bernard Shaw among its guests.

For all its long history, however, Cliveden is best remembered among present generations for its role in the 1961 Profumo Affair. Around Cliveden's pool, 19-year-old Christine Keeler, guest of society osteopath Stephen Ward, met John Profumo, the married Secretary of State for War. Keeler and Profumo began an affair, causing problems for the Conservative government after Keeler sold her story to the press and outrage as it became apparent that Profumo had lied to the House of Commons over the matter. The moral dimension was eclipsed by a security scandal when it emerged that Keeler had also been sleeping with Yevgeny Ivanov, an assistant naval attaché at London's Soviet Embassy who was known to British security services as a spy.

Profumo had no choice but to resign, ending what until then had been a meteoric political career. For supplying prostitutes, Stephen Ward was charged with living off immoral earnings. Ward's intent seemed less about making money than winning friends and influence in establishment circles; widely regarded as a scapegoat, he committed suicide during the trial. Many years later, Keeler's autobiography visited previously unexplored areas of the case, claiming that she had unwittingly become part of a cover-up for a Anglo-Soviet spy ring.

The Profumo affair did nothing to help the ailing Conservative government which lost the 1964 election and, some think, cleared the way for Britain to enjoy the swinging 1960s. One enduring mystery, however, was the identity of the "man in the mask": a fellow who attended Ward's parties naked save for a face mask and who ate his food from a dog bowl.

Maidenhead

After the duels, fires, and scandals of Cliveden, Maidenhead seems comfortable but dull English suburbia. In Edwardian times, however, the town and particularly the stretch of the Thames around Boulter's Lock was the scene of high-class frolics as straw-boatered men in white blazers and women in impractical dresses hopped in and out of boats. Maidenhead gained a resort atmosphere and promised illicit liaisons in a string of Thamesside hotels. Jerome K. Jerome described it as "too snobby to be pleasant. It is the haunt of the river swell and his overdressed female companion. It is the town of showy hotels, patronised chiefly by dudes and ballet girls."

The influx of upper-crust revellers from London went down poorly with some locals. In *The River In Our Time*, Patrick Wright refers to Boulter's Lock as "crammed with punts full of drunkenness and amorous misdemeanour," while on the banks local youths "thought nothing of tossing grape skins into the laps of genteel ladies in passing punts, then laughing into the spluttering faces of their husbands."

A century or so earlier, the forerunners of the "showy hotels" were the plethora of inns serving stagecoach travellers on the London-Bath route. A day's journey short of London, many spent the night here so as not to have to cross the open land known as Maidenhead Thicket until daylight. A notorious lair of highwaymen, the thicket, legend recalls, included one masked villain who would rob his victims and then commiserate with them in the course of his legitimate employment at the Sun Inn.

The London-Bath Road, now the A4, still passes through Maidenhead and, since 1770, has done so via the elegant stone-built Maidenhead Bridge. It was Maidenhead's other Thames bridge, completed in 1839, that brought a change in the town's character however. Isambard Kingdom Brunel's rail bridge helped turn Maidenhead into a London commuter base, and was the subject of Turner's 1844 painting, *Rain, Steam and Speed—the Great Western Railway*. Travelling the river in a small boat barely forty years before, Turner had produced such pastoral scenes as *Goring Mill and Church* on a journey described by David Hill as one where "the current of the river as it meandered its way to sea, was the measure of the true pace of things." Turner's tumultuous depiction of Maidenhead's new bridge and a train speeding over it mirrored the profound changes occurring on the river and in England: the railway was now the measure of the true pace of things; Turner's earlier images suddenly belonged to a very distant past.

Downstream from Maidenhead, the river passes Bray, a village of half-timbered cottages both real and fake, a state befitting the location of a major film and TV studio complex and, more surprisingly still, holding the two Michelin 3-star restaurants that caused Bray to be dubbed "the country's gastronomic capital" by the *Guardian* in 2004.

The river continues beneath the M4 motorway bridge and flows around Monkey Island, named either for the monks of neighbouring monasteries or, less likely, for the painted monkeys captured in the act of fishing that decorate the lodge built on the island in the 1720s for the third Duke of Marlborough. In expanded and much modified form, the lodge is now a hotel. It was on this spot that H. Schultz Wilson got caught in a rain shower and wrote in *The Royal River*:

> Now, just as we come to Monkey Island, a hush falls upon the sunshine, a soft shade overspreads the heavens; and a summer shower, dinting the glassy surface of the water with dimpling rain-drops, falls gently and ceases soon. Shine out, fair sun! And so it does again, till joy returns with sunlight and with warmth. 'Man's delight in God's works' can find rapture in nearly every phase of nature. Monkey Island is an inn built upon an islet. It comprises a pavilion erected by the

third Duke of Marlborough in which certain monkeys are cleverly depicted by one Clermont. We need not land there today.

Windsor and Eton

Surely a Princes seat cannot lightly have a more pleasant site. For, from an high hill that ariseth with a gentle ascent, it enjoyeth a most delightfull prospect round about. For right in the Front it overlooketh a vale lying out farre and wide, garnished with cornfields flourishing greene with medowes, decked with groves on either side and watered with the most, mild and calme river Tamis.

William Camden, *Britain*, 1610

After gliding between the twelfth-century St. Mary Magdalen Church at Boveney (now under the restorative care of the Friends of Friendless Churches) on the north side and a racecourse on the south, the river's approach to Windsor becomes dominated by the round tower of Windsor Castle, begun by William I on a riverside chalk hill as one of nine eleventh-century defensive positions around London. Becoming a royal palace under William's son, Henry I, the castle steadily gained strength, aided by many tons of Cotswold stone transported along the Thames. But it was as a place of relaxation within easy reach of London's Buckingham Palace that Windsor gained royal affection, compounded in 1917 when George V chose Windsor to replace Saxe-Coburg-Gotha as the family name, hoping to lessen accusations of German sympathies during the First World War.

Royals can luxuriate amid countless features designed to remind them of their divine right, if not to rule, then at least to enjoy a selection of artworks and plush rooms that belong to the nation, but which the nation's people rarely see. Among sections commonly open, however, is St. George's Chapel, an exquisite piece of late-Gothic exuberance which, amid 500-years-worth of royal artefacts, holds tombs including those of Edward IV (died 1483), Henry VIII (1547) and Charles I (beheaded 1649), and the future resting places of the current Queen and Prince of Wales.

Along with such pointers to their mortality, Windsor has provided a couple of recent episodes that today's royal family might prefer to

forget. The Queen's suggestion in 1992 that the public might like to pay for repairs following a fire at the castle caused the family's standing among the British public to plummet. In 2002 Princess Anne's bull terrier attacked two children while being walked by the Queen's daughter and her bodyguards in Great Park, an expanse of greenery between the castle and the Thames. The dog was spared execution, as was the princess, who also escaped the prison sentence sometimes accorded to such offences and was instead fined.

Just as Windsor is dominated by its castle so Eton, a few strides away across the Thames by footbridge, is dominated by its school (more properly, Eton College), founded by Henry VI in 1440, with the intention that it would supply students to King's College Cambridge, which Henry founded the following year. A jewel in the crown of the English public school system (public in the sense of private; charging around £23,000 per annum), Eton College offers what might be the best education money can buy and, for many, symbolizes a Britain still dominated by a privileged elite, an elite itself dominated by Old Etonians.

In his 1960 biography of his grandfather, Lord Curzon, Leonard Mosley wrote, "Eton College in the eighteen-seventies and eighteen-eighties was vast incubator dedicatedly engaged in the task of hatching out the future rulers of the greatest Empire the world has ever known." Few would contest that Eton bestows similar advantages on its alumni even in modern Britain, having produced eighteen British prime ministers and more than twenty per cent of its cabinet ministers since 1900; many other former students occupy exalted positions within the judiciary, the armed forces and in other influential spheres.

In school and out, Eton's 1,300 pupils wear a black tailcoat, a false collar, waistcoat and pinstriped trousers, a uniform adopted to mark the passing of George III for whom, one assumes, the school has yet to emerge from mourning. Admittedly, George was significant in the school's history and while his death is remembered by the uniform, his birthday, 4 June, is marked by Speech Day and the Procession of Boats on the river in which occupants attempt to stand while raising their oars and shaking flowers from their heads without capsizing their craft.

Eton College traditions include boys "tipping" each other by a raised finger in the street, calling teachers "beaks", and, once a year since 1766 (though probably earlier) staging the Eton Wall Game, described by Old Etonian Earl Spencer in the *Guardian* as two teams which "flounder in the mud for half an afternoon, hoping that today is going to be the one which will produce a score, idly grinding their opponents' skulls against the wall, or treading it into the oozing quagmire that is the playing field…" The college's website admits: "Few sports offer less to the spectator."

Much to the envy of every state (as opposed to public) school in Britain, not least those forced to sell their land to raise funds for staff and books, orthodox sports are played across Eton College's playing fields which encompass football, rugby and hockey pitches, tennis courts and much more across a broad green belt bordered by the river, the railway and the M4 motorway. Victor over Napoleon at Waterloo and for three years a pupil at Eton, the Duke of Wellington reputedly said: "The Battle of Waterloo was won on the playing fields of Eton." In *England Your England* (1941), fellow Old Etonian George Orwell retorted: "Probably the Battle of Waterloo *was* won on the playing fields of Eton but the opening battles of all subsequent wars have been lost there." The same fields provided the setting for M. R. James' slight but curious 1920s ghost story, *After Dark in the Playing Fields*, complete with talking owl and unexplained goings-on on the stroke of midnight that lead the protagonist to conclude: "Yes, I certainly prefer the daylight population of the Playing Fields to that which comes there after dark."

The renown of its college rather leaves the town of Eton in the shade, despite being able to boast the first modern drainage system in England and the first postbox, which, as the town website proudly asserts, "is still in service", leaving the reader to assume the drainage system is not.

Both Home Park, which wraps itself for two miles around the south bank of the river as it leaves Windsor, and Great Park, which covers 4,000 acres south of the castle, are reminders of a time when Windsor was known less for its castle than for its forest, large enough to provide the wood for numerous Thames locks and dangerous enough for William Cobbett to comment in *Rural Rides* that it was "as bleak, as barren, and as villainous a heath as ever a man set eyes on." Great Park is said to be haunted by the ghost of Herne, a fourteenth-century hunter employed by Richard II, believed to appear astride a horse, wearing antler headdress and accompanied by a pack of hounds. Herne was described in Shakespeare's *The Merry Wives of Windsor*:

Herne the hunter,
Sometime a keeper here in Windsor forest,
Doth all the winter time, at still midnight,
Walk round about an oak, with great ragg'd horns;

And there he blasts the tree, and takes the cattle,
And makes milch-kine yield blood, and shakes a chain
In a most hideous and dreadful manner:
You have heard of such a spirit; and well you know,
The superstitious idle-headed eld
Receiv'd, and did deliver to our age,
This tale of Herne the hunter for a truth.

Datchet, Runnymede and Magna Carta

From the thirteenth century, the ferry at Datchet on the river's north bank provided a conveniently inconspicuous royal route to Windsor. Control of the ferry came with the tenancy of Datchet Manor and provided a handy income: Henry VII is recorded as paying three shillings and fourpence for the queen's passage in 1502. A wooden bridge of ten arches resting on stone piers replaced the ferry in 1706 but by 1794 had become "absolutely dangerous for carriages" and was swept away by floods. Legal wrangles between counties delayed the opening of a new bridge until 1812, a two-part structure comprising "a hideous monstrosity of wood on the Berkshire side, and iron on the Buckinghamshire side." As further arguments raged over responsibility for repairs, the unloved bridge was demolished in 1851 and replaced by the identical Victoria and Albert bridges, named for the Queen and her consort, each 228-feet-long with an elliptical iron span of 120 feet. Both bridges remain, though are no longer identical.

Aside from its manor and ferry, Datchet was known in the early 1800s for its poachers, recorded as providing half the inmates of Aylesbury jail. Two more exalted residents in the 1780s were astronomer William Herschel, discoverer of Uranus, and his sister, who discovered eight comets and three nebulae during her time here.

Legal wrangles about bridges and the mysteries of the cosmos both seem far removed from the contemplative stretch of the river that lies beyond Albert Bridge and passes Wraysbury into the placid and protected meadows of Runnymede beneath the slopes of Cooper's Hill. It was at Runnymede in June 1215, after five days of negotiation inside a tent, that King John acceded to the demands of a group of well-armed barons and signed the document known as Magna Carta (more precisely he oversaw the attachment of the royal seal to the Articles of the Barons here; the Magna Carta, or Great Document, was formally drawn up a few days later). In *Three Men in a Boat*, Jerome K. Jerome imagined the scene: "And King John has stepped upon the shore, and we wait in breathless silence till a great shout cleaves the air, and the great cornerstone in England's temple of liberty has, now we know, been firmly laid." In doing so, Jerome perpetuated the myth of Magna Carta as the birth of British democracy. In fact, Magna Carta was no such thing and was never intended to be. The document provided a framework by which the nobility could legally air grievances against the crown and end royal abuses such as uncompensated seizure of goods and the imposition of unreasonable taxes and unreasonable fines. With the right to a fair trial ("to no one will we sell, deny, or delay right or justice") such matters could be challenged, thereby making the king subject to the law, rather than above it, ruling by God's decree. The king lost, the nobles gained; that anybody else benefited from the legal principles established was accidental.

Derogatorily nicknamed "soft sword" for his military failure in France, modern historians generally refute the popular view of John as tyrannical and inept, tending to see him instead as a victim of circumstance. An unfortuitious sequence of events, not least the excessive spending of his predecessor, Richard I ("the Lionheart"), forced John to raise taxes, argue with the Church, and in 1213 depart for France, allowing rebellion to grow among the English nobility. Aware that no other member of the royal family was able to seize the crown, the barons' only weapon against John was demand for reform. They forced John to negotiate by seizing control of London, not with the agreement of the city's population, the bulk of whom supported the king, but by a small group of wealthy merchants opening the city gates when most people were attending Mass. Far from being the birthplace of democracy, Runnymede might better be seen as where a landowning aristocracy, aided by merchants, forcibly limited the king's powers for their own, not the greater, good.

Magna Carta is better interpreted as a founding stone of democracy by its use in the American Bill of Rights, written to create, as John Adams put in 1779, "a government of laws, and not of men". Fittingly, it was an American heiress, Lady Fairchild, who ensured that 180 acres of Runnymede did not disappear beneath property developments but were acquired by her and given to the National Trust in 1931. The meadow's markers to the past are now the Magna Carta Temple, a grand term for a little domed monument raised by the American Bar Association in 1957, and the 1965 John F. Kennedy Memorial, remembering the slain president and the place where "the idea of human rights was born" on an acre of ground given in perpetuity to the USA.

Staines

Known to Romans as a river crossing point, a base of the barons before they met King John at Runnymede, and able to claim more bridges than any other Thames settlement, Staines was so transformed by industrialization that the *Thames Valley* commented: "If any justification were required for the need of preserving the amenities of the Thames Valley, we must refer to Staines as an example of a town badly disfigured by uncontrolled development and ill-designed bungalows above the bridge." Staines is nonetheless emerging from its recent past with some panache. The gas works that consumed a riverside meadow was demolished in 1980 and the importance of the Thames acknowledged with a replica of the original London Stone, marking the former westerly limit of the City of London's authority. For all that, navigators of the Thames Path will find themselves skirting supermarket car parks and dual carriageways, yearning for the Staines described by Walford as "one long straggling street, irregularly built."

Moving south through Staines, the river weaves around Penton Hook, an area of frequent floods and difficult navigation. Thacker wrote in 1920: "The gulls or narrows here full of sandbanks, formed an immemorial obstacle to the navigation mentioned in almost every detailed account... John Taylor found 'five Barges fast aground' here in 1632. They were still being complained off in 1789."

Peel describes the river south from Staines as "having too many bungalows and Edwardian houses" though the village of Laleham has much to admire and is rightly proclaimed in *The Royal River* as embodying such "charm as may be found in a flat landscape—and it is not small when there are trees and water, red roofs and quaint chimneys, sheep, cows, and an old church—we find at Laleham Ferry, one of the quietest and prettiest spots on the Thames."

For nine years in the early 1800s, Laleham was home to Thomas

Arnold (1795-1842), later the long-serving headmaster of Rugby School and credited with transforming for the better the English public school system. His eldest son, born at Laleham, Matthew Arnold, became a noted poet and essayist and now lies in the family plot at Laleham's All Saints Church, conspicuous for its menacing 1732 square tower. In a mark of changing times, the 83-acre plot of Laleham Abbey became a convent in 1928 and in 1981 was sold to facilitate construction of river-view apartments.

Chertsey and Chertsey Abbey

From Laleham, passing flatlands and water-filled former quarries, the river runs beneath the double-decked M3 motorway and reaches the elegant Chertsey Bridge, sculptured in stone with seven arches and completed in 1785. Few who cross today spare a thought for "Sibille, ferrywoman of Chertsey" who earned three shillings for transporting Edward II and his family across the river here in 1299.

In an account of a Thames trip published in *The Century* in 1889, Elizabeth Robins Pennell recalled: "We had arrived just in time for the Chertsey regatta, and when presently the sun struggled through the clouds, as if by magic the river was crowded with boats. The races were not worth seeing. The men sculled in their vests, poled in their suspenders. Punts at the start got so hopelessly entangled that spectators roared with laughter... we did not go into the town, which Dickens says is dull and quiet."

By contrast, *The Royal River* referred to Chertsey as "a name of imperishable renown in English annals". The renown perished along with nearly all of Chertsey Abbey, the structure with which the town might once have anticipated immortality but which now is mainly remembered by its fishponds. Founded in 666 and surviving until the dissolution, the abbey became a prominent religious centre. The Halls wrote of the abbey: "Its glory extended far and near; its jurisdiction in Surrey was almost unlimited; its abbot ranked with princes—and ruled them." In 1471 the abbey received the body of Henry VI after a midnight journey along the Thames from the Tower of London "in a barge followed by others loaded with torches and full of monks singing dirges." Alleged miracles occurring around the body drew pilgrims to Chertsey; even after 1484, when Henry was moved to Windsor, a cult developed under Henry VII who led calls for the late monarch's canonization.

A Gut, a Cut and Turner's Bridges

A footnote in the long history of Thames navigational trivia concerns the course once known as Stoner's Gut, a derivative of Stone's Gut, named after the Mr. Stone listed in 1723 as leaseholder of the Crown lands on the south bank, adjacent to the town of Weybridge. Due to regular flooding, the Gut had become the *de facto* Thames course by the end of the eighteenth century. Stoner's Gut is not a name now seen on maps; no doubt to the relief of estate agents with river-view homes to sell.

Another example of course changing came in 1935 with the opening of the Desborough Cut, providing a direct route towards Walton-on-Thames, where the river's original course was to the north between Desborough Island and Shepperton. Both island and cut are named after Lord Desborough, head of the Thames Conservancy from 1904 to 1937. The island holds fields, rugby and cricket pitches and the nineteenth-century buildings of a still-functioning water treatment works. On the north bank, riverside Shepperton holds bungalows, riverside pubs and weeping willows; to the south lies Walton-on-Thames.

James S. Whitman canoed this section of the river and wrote for *Harper's* in 1881: "The scenery was not particularly interesting at this point, and so soon as the canoe's stern was well besmeared with soap—the only expedient at hand—I paddled on toward that extremely picturesque bridge of Walton that Turner has made the subject of one of his most charming pictures."

The bridge of Turner's time was completed by James Paine in 1786 and was painted, as *Walton Bridges*, by the artist in 1805. According to David Hill's *Turner on the Thames*, Turner's depiction of the bridge was far from realistic: "(the bridge) was made of deep-coloured brick with white stone edge and must have been very distinctive. One would not know this from Turner's painting, whose golden light allows us to imagine a more classical material, such as the stone of which Paine's other bridges at Richmond and Chertsey were made. Paine would no doubt have designed his bridge with the light and spacious arches that Turner shows, with slender piers and gossamer carriageway had gravity so allowed." In 1807 Turner produced a second painting of the bridge, also called *Walton Bridges*, where he "seemed to be considering afresh what form a reflection actually took when it came to the eye from different angles… It had occurred to Turner, however, that the convention of simple inversion wanted examination and rethinking. His pictures of this time were very much concerned with conventions and the way they shape our thinking. *Walton Bridges* is an instance of his finding these conventions lacking."

Contemplation of the mechanics of painting is not something likely to be inspired by the current bridge, a generic construction often clogged with traffic. Wrote Arthur Mee in *Surrey* (1938): "It was the old Walton bridge… that Turner painted by moonlight, but we doubt he would paint the present bridge in any light at all."

Chiefly composed of farmland, sports grounds and reservoirs, the river's south bank from Walton to West Molesley still warrants J. H. B. Peel's words: "to describe this reach of the river is extremely difficult… one moment you might fancy yourself in deep country; at the next, even the trees flinch to see so many ugly houses." West and East Molesley can, however, boast significant sporting history. On the plot once called Moulsey Hurst, cricket was played as early as 1723 when the "Gentleman of London" faced the "Gentleman of Surrey" and finished the day at Hampton Court being entertained by the Prince of Wales. Golf was recorded here in 1758 and thousands assembled to watch and wager on bare-knuckle boxing. By 1890 most of the area was converted to a horse-racing course which attracted, according to Walford: "large herds of betting men from London, (who) are voted a nuisance by the neighbourhood." Much of the area disappeared beneath housing in the 1960s, only the modestly-sized Hurst Park and the local cricket ground suggest former glories.

The north bank, too, has its share of reservoirs and ugly houses but also the leafy communities of Sunbury and Hampton, where actor David Garrick commissioned Robert Adam in 1754 to build a riverside home. The result was Garrick's Villa, still standing with its riverside plot linked to the main garden (designed by "Capability" Brown, moonlighting from his job at Hampton Court) by a tunnel beneath the A308. Garrick's visitors included major cultural figures of the time such as William Hogarth, Horace Walpole and Samuel Johnson, who said of Garrick's Villa: "it is the leaving of such places that makes a deathbed so terrible." Beside the Thames, the domed Shakespeare Temple was Garrick's commemoration of the playwright and displayed a Roubiliac bust of the Bard, now replaced by a replica. The temple documents Garrick's wine-to-riches story: he came to London to sell wine, turned his hand to playwriting and made his name as a naturalistic Richard III in 1741, earning enough to buy a half share in the Drury Lane Theatre and become one of the country's leading thespians.

Continuing toward Hampton Court, the A308 is linked by bridge to Taggs Island, the only non-tidal Thames island accessible by car. Now a flourishing community-conscious settlement of houseboat owners, the island takes its name from Thomas Tagg, a boat builder who responded to the growth of river recreation by erecting a hotel here in 1873. The hotel was remodelled into the Karsino after being purchased by Fred Karno, an impresario credited with "discovering" Charlie Chaplin and Stan Laurel. Although Karno declared the island "the hub of the universe for river people", the hotel steadily declined as did the island, despite hosting a concert by rock band Pink Floyd (former Floyd guitarist David Gilmour now has a houseboat recording studio here) in 1968. Taggs Island was dramatically revitalized in the 1980s by Gerry and Gilllian Braben. They created a lagoon in the centre of the now tree-filled island, and it was their efforts which saw the addition of the bridge, its predecessor having collapsed in 1965. Gerry Braben died in 1993 and is better remembered by the well-tended island than the sundial erected in his honour on the river's north bank.

Hampton Court

Before the completion of Teddington Lock, the Thames was tidal as far as East Molesey, a site that can also claim the most visually extraordinary bridge to cross the river: Ludgator and Stevens' 1753 seven section "Chinese" wooden bridge, its ornate humps memorably etched by Canaletto before it threatened to collapse after just 25 years of use. A wooden replacement was derided as "a crazy hog-backed bridge" but earned its owner, Thomas Allen, a tidy sum in tolls. A cast-iron bridge appeared in 1865, but Allen's tolls were still resented and there was much joy in 1876 when the bridge was sold to local authorities and charges abolished; the toll gates were dismantled and ceremoniously burned. The uncontentious present bridge was designed by Edward Lutyens and opened by the Prince of Wales in July 1933. Displayed on the bridge's southern approach, the Allen coat-of-arms draws few viewers.

Despite 500 years of English pageantry, including star players such as Henry VIII, Elizabeth I and Queen Victoria, contained within its walls and elaborate grounds, Hampton Court welcomes all-comers with none of the haughtiness apparent to visitors at Windsor Castle. Hampton Court was not built as a royal palace but as a private home, albeit an exceedingly grand home, for the plump, squat fellow depicted on the sign of the Cardinal Wolsey pub on the A308 approach. As Lord Chancellor, Wolsey enjoyed 17 years of wealth and power from 1515 and commissioned Hampton Court with the intention of creating the finest home in Tudor England: a visual symbol of his importance and one particularly striking to foreign dignitaries. Wolsey's residence was more opulent than that of the king. John Skelton's 1520s poem "Why Come Ye Not to Court?" satirized the discrepancy:

Why come ye not to court?
To which court?
To the king's court,
Or to Hampton Court?
Nay! To the king's court!
The king's court should have the excellence
But Hampton Court hath the prominence

Henry VIII's lack of interest in the details of government had enabled Wolsey's rise but as head of the Church, Wolsey was tasked with convincing the pope to annul the marriage of Henry and Catherine of Aragon. His failure to do so contributed to charges of treason and he was stripped of office. Wolsey gave Hampton Court to Henry in 1529 but died the following year awaiting trial.

Although Wolsey hosted elaborate feasts for hundreds of guests, it was Henry who cemented Hampton Court's image as a place of extravagance. His expansion included three new kitchens, each with a fire large enough to roast an ox and sufficient to satiate a royal appetite such that in any 24-hour period might demand the slaughter of, according to Roy Nash, "six oxen, forty sheep and a thousand or more pullets, larks, pheasants, partridges and pigeons." Henry entertained, jousted, played tennis, listened to minstrels and seemed to have everything he wanted except a son and heir. Having created the lasting split between England and Rome to facilitate his marriage to Anne, Henry found that the new queen also failed to provide a boy and his attentions turned to lady-in-waiting Jane Seymour. Jane provided Henry with an heir, Edward (who became king aged nine but died at 16), but the price was her death through illness nine days later. Henry's marriage to Anne of Cleves followed, as did the ill-suited union with Catherine Howard and then the troubled but more enduring partnership with Catherine Parr before the monarch died here in 1547.

Among subsequent incidents at Hampton Court: James I responded to the requests of the Puritans at the Hampton Court Conference by authorizing a standardized edition of the Bible, what became the King James edition; as Civil War broke out, Charles I began his doomed escape from the palace along the Thames, leaving Hampton Court to be next formally occupied by England's first and only republican head of state, Oliver Cromwell. The monarchy restored, Charles II took his new queen, Catherine of Braganza, along the river to London in August 1662, prompting diarist John Evelyn to paroxysms of awe:

> I was a spectactor of the most magnificent triumph that ever floated on the Thames, considering the innumerable boats and vessels, dressed and adorned with all imaginable pomp, but above all the thrones, arches, pageants, and other representations, stately barges of the Lord Mayor and companies, with various inventions, music and peals of ordnace from both the vessels and the shore, going to meet and conduct the new Queen from Hampton Court to Whitehall, at the first time of her coming to town.

George I's trips to and from Hampton Court by road were acknowledged by the peeling of church bells. On the river, meanwhile, Handel's *Water Music* was composed for the monarch and first played for the king on a cruise between Whitehall and Chelsea in 1717 by fifty waterborne musicians, a sufficient number, cynics suggested, to drown out the boos of the public.

Be it buildings, gardens or the general tenor of their occupancy, successive monarchs all made a mark on the palace but the biggest change came during the reign of Mary II. Arriving in 1689 mindful of the new court architecture exemplified by France's Versailles, the queen and her Dutch husband, William III, decided that Tudor architecture was unbecoming to modern royalty and commissioned Sir Christopher Wren (although much of the design might be attributed to his assistant, Nicholas Hawksmoor) to re-shape the palace, adding what became the quadrangle around Fountain Court.

Greatly hindered by an interfering king and marred by the death of two workmen, Wren's classical symmetry might look suitably majestic in any other setting, yet here, set against the red-brick Tudor original, seems strangely misplaced. From the river, the Tudor frontage that initially defines the palace is suddenly displaced by Wren's parallel lines, making a dramatic and displeasing contrast. As *The Royal River* puts it: "There is no doubt a certain stateliness about (Wren's) East Front and the Fountain Court; but it is a heavy and monumental stateliness which ill accords with the really picturesque portions of the old palace."

For years, a perk of being Lady Housekeeper of Hampton Court was extra income from charging for visits to the State Rooms. Victoria, the last monarch to occupy the palace, upset her aides but delighted the general population by instigating free admission from November 1838. Nash records: "the invasion of the 'lower orders' was of far greater strength than anyone could have forecast. As winter turned to spring, they poured out of the fetid stews of London in droves and made their way to the palace on foot, in dog-carts and pony-traps and in horse-drawn charabancs. Before long, the annual total of visitors had topped the 80,000 mark." Thurley quotes an account given by an American visitor in 1856: "Soldiers were standing sentinel at the exterior gateways, and at the various doors of the palace; but they admitted everybody without question, and without fee. Policemen, or other attendants, were in most of the rooms, but interfered with nobody; so that in this respect, it was one of the most pleasant places to visit that I have found in England. A good many people of all classes were strolling through the rooms."

Commissioned in 1690 by William III, Hampton Court's maze draws 330,000 people annually, most of them eventually finding a route out. There is a simple way to negotiate the maze: always take the next right turn. This foolproof method is touted by Harris in *Three Men in a*

Boat: "You keep on taking the first turning to the right. We'll just walk round for ten minutes, and then go and get some lunch." His confidence is such that he gains a following: "People who had given up all hopes of ever getting either in or out, or of ever seeing their home and friends again, plucked up courage at the sight of Harris and his party, and joined the procession, blessing him. Harris said he should judge there must have been twenty people, following him, in all; and one woman with a baby, who had been there all the morning, insisted on taking his arm, for fear of losing him." Predictably, Harris gets lost. The crowd calls for a keeper who climbs in over a ladder into the maze to show them the way out only to become lost himself.

Kingston

From Hampton Court, the river passes Cigarette Island (unrelated to Ash Island, just upstream) and negotiates the broad bend around Hampton Court Park, much of which is concealed behind a brick wall. From the south bank, however, the river is overlooked by the waterside homes of Thames Ditton to which even the occupants of Hampton Court's grace and favour apartments might cast envious glances. *The Royal River* noted: "Between Hampton Court and Kingston, the river is at its most charming hereabouts. Flowing between deep banks, over which the rushes and osiers bend, in summer it is studded to just beyond Thames Ditton with the cool Bohemian house-boat, a veritable desired haven to the heated oarsman." Bohemian houseboats may now be in short supply but The Swan still sits on the Thames Ditton bank as it has for 600 years. Here in the 1840s "protest poet" Thomas Hood wrote the "Song of the Shirt", not that its sentiments would have any direct connection with the location today:

> With fingers weary and worn,
> With eyelids heavy and red,
> A woman sat in unwomanly rags
> Plying her needle and thread,
> Stitch—stitch—stitch!
> In poverty hunger and dirt,
> And still with a voice of dolorous pitch,
> She sang the Song of the Shirt!

Just as Hood reflected the lifestyles of the poor and neglected, so Turner's painting, presumably made a short way downstream, *Harvest Dinner, Kingston Bank*, depicting farmhands scraping for food on the river bank, was described by David Hill as "one of Turner's most unflinching views of the hardship of life on the land."

Few such sights can be found on Kingston's river banks today, devoted as the town appears to be to the joys of consumerism and the suburban lifestyle. The old riverside was re-cast when Bentall's department store expanded into a shopping mall in the 1980s and now, with the exception of the long-serving Turk's boatyard, sports a procession of restaurants and bars liable to incite nostalgia for the power station that once stood here. In 2004, meanwhile, Kingston University broke new academic ground by opening a Centre for Suburban Studies.

A tenuous grip on a remarkably long history is symbolized by Kingston's Coronation Stone, a chunk of grey sandstone which stands largely neglected within its protective grille of seven Victorian "Saxon-style" spear points outside the modern Guildhall. While the stone's authenticity is doubtful, more reliable documents record that from 901 to 978 seven Saxon kings were crowned at Kingston and that in 838 it hosted Egbert's West Saxon assembly. Being a fording point on the river raised Kingston's importance and it gained a fixed crossing in the thirteenth century.

The present bridge dates from 1825, improved with regular widening to accommodate the ever-rising flow of traffic with Hampton Wick. A second bridge carries the railway that facilitated Kingston's nineteenth-century change from market town to commuter base. The latter played a part in what nearly became one of the worst disasters to befall the river. In January 1928 surging flood waters caused 26 barges to snap their moorings and, some laden with 100-ton cargoes, career across the waters. The *Daily Chronicle* reported: "For two hours it seemed as though the Thames had gone mad." As barges smashed against the railway bridge, the reporter ominously observed: "Just two minutes later a train passed over this rather fragile-looking bridge at normal speed."

Beyond Kingston, Hampton Wick segues seamlessly into Teddington, enabling the authors of *The Royal River* to describe "an almost uninterrupted succession of lawns and shrubberies and coolly timbered pleasure-grounds, surrounding riparian villas." On the other bank lies Ham and a riverside parkland reaching north beyond Teddington Lock.

Teddington and Twickenham

Recording a long history of difficult navigation hereabouts, Thacker quotes a report of 1775 describing efforts to "countroul the Current so as to form one certain navigable Channel: frequently near to 20 Barges were stop'd there at one time." By 1811 the first wooden lock at Teddington was in place, despite attempts to sabotage it by local bargemen angry at the disruption; in 1818 came the first in a series of robberies of the weekly takings that resulted in the lock-keeper being issued with a "blunderbuss with bayonet attached". The 220 million gallons that pass over Teddington weir daily and the workings of the largest and lowest lock-system on the river, one that divides the non-tidal river from the tidal and marks the western limit of the Port of London Authority's jurisdiction, is best contemplated, if probably not understood, from the two-part pedestrian bridge linking the banks since 1888.

With "The Parish Register of Twickenham" (1758) Horace Walpole, resident of nearby Strawberry Hill, satirized the *literati* who had settled the area:

> Where Silver Thames round Twit'nam meads
> His winding current swiftly leads;
> Twit'nam the muses' fav'rite seat,
> Twit'nam, the Graces' lov'd retreat.

The first and most prominent among them was poet and essayist Alexander Pope (1688-1744), who moved into the then rural hamlet of Twickenham in 1714. On the proceeds of his translation of *The Iliad*, Pope raised what became Pope's Villa on a riverside site at Cross Deep. While his mind was sharp and his writing acerbic, Pope was an ungainly physical figure: "about 4ft 6 ins high, very humped backed and deformed... the muscles that ran along the cheek were so strongly marked that they seemed like small cords," according to portraitist Sir Joshua Reynolds. More derogatorily, Pope was described as "the little crooked thing that asks questions."

In contrast, Pope's Villa rose with some grace from the plain cottages that bordered it, although its precise form is poorly documented and it was demolished in the early 1800s, after which a much less distinguished house appropriated the name. Surviving, however, are the series of tunnels known as Pope's Grotto that led from the house to its five acres of grounds and were decorated with geological specimens. Pope wrote: "When you shut the Doors of this Grotto, it becomes on the instant, from a luminous Room, a Camera Obscura, on the walls of which all the objects of the River, Hills, Woods, and Boats, are forming a moving Picture... And when you have a mind to light it up, it affords you a very different Scene: it is finished with Shells interspersed with Pieces of Looking-glass in angular Forms... at which when a Lamp... is hung in the Middle, a thousand pointed Rays glitter and are reflected over the place." Not everyone was impressed with the grotto. In 1822 James Kirke Paulding wrote in *A Sketch of Old England, by a New-England Man*: "to my taste, this grotto is totally unworthy of any reputable nymphs of either wood or water. It is neither splendid by art, nor magnificent, nor solemn by nature, and is, in truth, an excellent place for keeping milk and butter cool. I felt no reverence whatever for it, and heartily wished the grotto, rather than the house, had been destroyed."

Used as an air-raid shelter during the Second World War, the grotto is now contained within St. James' Independent School for Boys. The Pope's Villa that currently occupies Cross Deep is a pub and hotel, the literary figure who inspired it remembered by an unflattering inn sign: a dismal way to remember the man who introduced to the English language such enduring phrases as: "To err is human; to forgive, divine"; "Hope springs eternal in the human breast..."; A little learning is a dangerous thing..."

Like nearby towns, Twickenham itself expanded greatly in the Victorian rail boom that put it within easy reach of London. Previously, it had been a sedate village a day's stagecoach ride from the capital with its core being a cluster of two-hundred year old cottages set around St. Mary's Church. Aside from the changing nature of river traffic, Sydney R. Jones's 1940s description still rings true: "old cottages and houses jumbled together above the ferry, boats barges, and launches lying on the strand and the water... bits of present Twickenham give the flavour of the old village known to Pope and Walpole... and the celebrities of that age who either lived in, or went to that mecca of social and literary fame, making it one of the England's most celebrated shrines for succeeding generations to ponder over."

Eel Pie Island

Miss Morleena Kenwigs had received an invitation to repair next day, per steamer from Westminster Bridge, unto the Eel-pie Island at Twickenham: there to make merry upon a cold collation, bottled beer, shrub, and shrimps, and to dance in the open air to the music of a locomotive band, conveyed thither for the purpose..."

Charles Dickens, *Nicholas Nickleby*, 1838-9

A dainty footbridge links Twickenham to Eel Pie Island. Believed to be named for an eel pie stand frequented by Henry VII as he travelled between London and Windsor, the island enjoyed renown in Edwardian times as arriving paddle-steamers deposited "great numbers of holiday folk solicitous to banquet on eel-pies".

The 1830 Eel Pie Hotel, a verandah-fronted affair looking more suited to the Mississippi, ran tea-dances during the 1920s and by the late 1950s was luring a new generation of raffish music fans over the footbridge to nights of jazz and skiffle. By the early 1960s, such musical forms had been eclipsed by the British blues boom and the hotel staged early performances by such stalwarts as Cyril Davis and future rock stars as the Yardbirds, the Who and the Rolling Stones, all of whom had to carry their equipment by hand over the bridge.

By the end of the 1960s, the hotel had become a hippie commune with, at its height, a hundred members. During winter, heating was provided by the hotel itself: the floors and staircases were chopped up to provide firewood. Cliff Harper recalls in *The Education of Desire: the Anarchist Graphics of Cliff Harper*: "We started on the ground floor, because the bedrooms were on the first and second floors, ripping it apart for wood to burn. It dawned on me it was getting ridiculous when one night I saw the banisters go from the stairs. That was OK, but when I saw the *stairs* themselves going, I thought, 'how the fuck are we gong to get to the first floor?' There was a lot of that craziness, also a lot of drugs and junkies." The Who's Pete Townshend, who lived locally and allegedly smoked dope on the bridge between the Who's sets, remembers: "the so-called hippies actually developed quickly into drug addicts and thieves... as a Rock Star I felt quite at home with them, though they often woke me at 5 in the morning for tea-bags." The island's live music ended when local authorities demanded £200,000-worth of repairs to the hotel for safety reasons, and the old structure was finally destroyed by a "mysterious" fire.

The island remained a beacon of non-conformity, a place of refuge for the unconventional. Its fifty or so homes range from ramshackle weatherboard cottages to architect-designed homes of high monetary value. Among them are the studios of artists, the homes of writers and the workshop of Trevor Baylis, a long-standing resident who invented the clockwork radio here in the 1980s. Here, too, are the yards of boat repairers doing, judged by the many vessels awaiting attention, a roaring trade.

Houses: Marble Hill and Ham

Leaving Twickenham, the river's north bank reveals the expansive Twickenham Park and the white-walled Marble Hill House, home of Henrietta Howard (1688-1767), mistress of George II, later Countess of Suffolk and among the few contemporary women to own property on her own account. Howard was sometimes referred to as "Chloe" in Pope's poems and was described by Walpole as "remarkable genteel, always dressed with taste and simplicity"—adjectives that might apply to the house itself.

Across the river, obscured by trees and a high wall that further shields it from inquisitive glances, stands the not-so-simple Ham House. The Duke and Duchess of Lauderdale once owned it, a couple who made a lot of money but few friends when they stuffed the house with showy fineries. Walpole was even worried about encountering their ghosts. In a letter of 1770, he describes a visit to his niece who had married the Earl of Dysart, a descendant of the duchess and then the house's owner: "I went yesterday to see my niece in her new principality of Ham. It delighted me and made me peevish. Close to the Thames, in the centre of all rich and verdant beauty, it is so blocked up, barricaded with walls, vast trees and gates, that you think yourself a hundred miles off and a hundred years back. The old furniture is magnificently ancient, dreary, and decayed, that at every step one's spirits sink, and all my passion for antiquity could not keep them up. Every minute I expected to see ghosts sweeping by—ghosts I would not give sixpence to see— Lauderdales, Tollemaches and Maitlands."

Richmond Hill

The terrace at Richmond does assuredly afford one of the finest prospects in the world. Whatever is charming in nature or pleasing in art, is to be seen here: nothing I had ever seen or ever can see elsewhere, is to be compared to it.

Charles P. Moritz, *Travels in England in 1782*, 1795

Immediately east, Petersham meadows are more redolent of Oxfordshire than the Surrey commuter belt, and are overlooked from Richmond Hill by the 1924 Star and Garter Home for injured servicemen and women. A Star and Garter Inn was serving ale and views of the Thames from this site in the 1700s and evolved into the Star and Garter Hotel, a destination for well-to-do day-trippers. Charles Dickens used the hotel to service his superstition of being out of London when his novels were published, and *The Royal River* described it as "a sweet, a toothsome spot... which recalls cycles of flirtation and iced champagne."

Also offering Thames views from Richmond Hill, Wick House provided a weekend home for portraitist Sir Joshua Reynolds from 1771. Reynolds was sufficiently inspired to paint a rare landscape, showing the Thames snaking into the distance. From a similar vantage point, J. M. W. Turner painted *England: Richmond Hill, on the Prince Regent's Birthday*, exhibited at the Royal Academy in 1819. The exhibition marked the end of the Napoleonic wars and the Prince Regent's birthday (coincidentally St. George's Day and Turner's own birthday), and contributed to the artist's rising reputation. Earlier, Henry Purcell (1659-95) wrote a song used in *Orpheus Britannicus* (1698) and subsequently set to music by Benjamin Britten:

On the brow of Richmond Hill
Which Europe can scarcely parallel,
Ev'ry eye such wonders fill,

To view the prospect round;
Where the silver Thames doth glide
And Stately courts are filled with pride, with erdant beauties
crown'd...

The river completes a sweeping curve into Richmond passing new
luxury waterside apartments and flowing beneath the 1777 Richmond
Bridge, the oldest Thames bridge on the tidal river, once charging a
halfpenny for pedestrians to cross; half-a-crown for six-horse coaches. In
his 1883 *London Villages, Vol II*, Edward Walford enthused about
Richmond:

> The name of Richmond is suggestive of pleasant pictures, of shining
> green meadows and silver streams, of royal splendour and gentle poesy,
> of "Star and Garter" feasts and dainty "Maids of Honour", of four-in-
> hands, and summer sunshine and buoyant holiday spirits. Which of us

has not some pleasant or happy associations with the beautiful village on the banks of the Thames?

The mansions of Richmond Hill have their share of media celebrities and rock stars, but seven hundred years ago the biggest names in town were the royalty who gathered at Richmond Palace, between the river and what were once palace grounds but which is now Richmond Green. Edward III began the palace in the thirteenth century; it was enlarged significantly by Henry II, who also gave the town its name after Richmond, his Earldom in Yorkshire. Both monarchs died here, as in the early hours of a March morning in 1603 did Elizabeth I, a scene evocatively imagined by Sydney R. Jones in the 1940s: "Taking neither food nor medicines, lying on cushions piled up on the floor, and vainly clinging to the life and time of a generation outlived, the last Tudor sovereign died, just there by the Thames, near where we stood."

Only a few walls of Tudor redbrick and the gatehouse survive of the palace, while Richmond's modern-day riverside is overlooked by Erith & Terry's "Hollywood vision of old London town", as Samantha Hardingham describes the pseudo-Georgian façades from which terraced gardens reach down to the riverbank. Directly ahead is the genuine 1711 Palladian villa of Asgill House, octagonal in shape possibly because it was built on the site of one of the palace's octagonal towers and sensitively restored during the 1970s.

Directly ahead, the A316 is carried over the river by Twickenham Bridge, one of three bridges opened on a single day in 1933 by the Prince of Wales. Of greater character is the yellow-and-green footbridge over the 1894 Richmond Lock, just downstream. Opening and closing either side of high tide, Richmond Lock, actually a half-lock, became a necessary tool to control water levels following the changing tide patterns created by the new London Bridge of 1831.

To Kew, with Views of Isleworth

Old Deer Park covers numerous acres on the east side of the river, an appendage to the palace grounds first used for hunting by James I and still Crown property. In an adjacent section enclosed by the Mid-Surrey Golf Course stand the two storeys of gleaming Portland stone forming Kew Observatory, built for George III "for the purpose of studying astronomical science with special reference to the transit of Venus." The king did indeed observe the 1769 Transit of Venus here, while obelisks set across the park enabled calculations to be made which standardized London's time and assisted in the measurement of global longitude. Greenwich Observatory eventually performed a similar function more accurately, leaving Kew Observatory to become a base for meteorological and seismological studies. Behind the observatory, the river's south bank is defined by a gravel track that arches around from Richmond towards Kew, lined by scrub sycamore with little to suggest the immediate proximity of much-visited Kew Gardens. Britain's major botanical showplace with three hundred acres of botanical exotica from around the world, the gardens evolved in part from the experimental plots of George III when he resided at neighbouring Kew Palace.

On the far bank, Old Isleworth is dominated by the fourteenth-century tower of All Saints' Church, a comparatively recent rebuilding of an original that fell victim in 1943 to the combination of mischievous schoolboys and a box of matches. Jones was approving of Isleworth: "charming, quaint, without tea-shops, cut off from the main stream of humanity, secluded behind its own backwater." Beyond Old Isleworth spread the grounds of Syon House, leased to the Earl of Northumberland by Elizabeth I and in the hands of the Northumberland family ever since, earlier serving as a mixed-sex abbey (men and women were kept apart by thick screens, the segregation overseen by eight lay observers). More recently, among a host of film and TV credits, the house provided the location for Robert Altman's *Gosford Park*. In contrast to bucolic Syon Park, Brentford for many years marked its position at the junction of the Thames and Grand Union Canal with a large railway siding and a gasworks, until post-industrial regeneration gave its riverside well-planned public housing, modernistic apartment blocks of abundant glass and a lively waterfront arts centre.

Kew Bridge's arches have special significance for aficionados of *Three Men in a Boat*, providing a pivotal moment in George's account of a hapless attempt to navigate the beneath it in an entirely unsuitable "eight-oared racing outrigger":

> A dense crowd watched the entertainment from Kew Bridge with much interest, and everybody shouted out to them different

directions. Three times they managed to get the boat back through the arch, and three times they were carried under it again, and every time 'cox' looked up and saw the bridge above him he broke out into renewed sobs.

The arches that so challenged George and his pals belonged, however, to the predecessor of the current bridge, which Edward VII opened in 1903 and after whom it was named, though use of this officially title was even shorter than Edward's reign. On the north side, Kew Pumping Station is distinguished by its 1867 tower while the hard work of pumping water to west London was (and is) done by the 1846 beam engine which sits in one of the buildings below, a still functioning part of what is now Kew Bridge Steam Museum.

Strand-on-the-Green

The strikingly well-preserved former fisherman's cottages that face the river immediately downstream from Kew Bridge might be the last vestiges of the pre-industrial working Thames before the waterway reaches London proper. Known as Strand-on-the-Green and mainly dating from the early eighteenth century, the cottages comprised "hovels for boatmen, fishermen, and field labourers; but there are a few houses of the better class," according to James Thorne in *Rambles by the River* (1847). Among the "better class" were those with royal connections, such as Lady Mary Sidney, nurse to Elizabeth I, who lived at what is now Sidney House until her death in 1583, and artist Johann Zoffany, known for his informal portraits of George III, who occupied no. 65, now Zoffany House. Among later residents was Nancy Mitford, who lived at Rose Cottage in the 1940s while writing *The Pursuit of Love*. A few years later, as their *Ticket to Ride* was topping the charts, the Beatles filmed some scenes for their 1966 film *Help!* at the City Barge pub, much to the chagrin of today's regulars whose quiet drinking sessions suffer interruptions from loud tourists on Fab Four pilgrimages.

Thacker recalled looking at the cottages from the south side of the river through the arches of the 1850 railway bridge: "I shall not easily forget beholding from below, through its black framework, one golden November afternoon, this alluring little Thames hamlet of the charming name gleaming ethereally, under some caprice of winter sunlight, at the far end of the long grey water. I saw a kingfisher here on 5 May 1918: a gloomy wet Sunday afternoon."

Mortlake

Mortlake might be the only river community with a past encompassing beer, tapestries and the occult. Gaining its first brewery in the fifteenth century, Mortlake was long known to river travellers for the distinctive aroma of hops. Today it is distinguished by the tall, ugly silos used by American beer giant Anheuser-Busch to manufacture Budweiser, using an aroma-free process and announcing the so-called "King of Beers" with loud hoardings. Sanctuary is offered by The Ship, an adjacent pub with proper ales and river views.

Flemish weavers arrived at Mortlake to work at a tapestry manufactory established by James I in 1619 under the noted German designer Francis Clyne (1582-1658). Customers included Charles I, who paid £6,000 for three sets of "gold hangings". The factory lasted until 1703, its tapestries now most likely to be found in palaces and museums throughout the world.

If it records him at all, popular history defines John Dee (1527-1608) as "astrologer to Elizabeth I", making light of the considerable influence he had on the monarch and how, from his Mortlake library and laboratory, he prepared the ground for future scientific and mathematical advances, not least the work of Isaac Newton. His interests included the occult and attempts to communicate with spirits aided by crystals and human mediums. An ill-fated trip to Europe, exploitation by charlatans and accusations of wizardry contributed to the ruin of Dee's reputation and his financial decline. Reflecting the Victorian attitude to Dee, Walford wrote scathingly: "He contrived to make himself acceptable to the vanity of Queen Elizabeth, who, on one occasion, condescended to pay him a visit at his house here, to view his museum of curiosities…" Dee died in poverty without even a stone to mark his grave. As Dee biographer Benjamin Wolley notes: "Dee himself has almost completely vanished—not just from Mortlake, but from history."

Barnes and the Boat Race

While Barnes lacks Mortlake's curiosities it has retained the marshlands

The Boat Race at Hammersmith Bridge

that now form the acclaimed Wetlands Centre, introducing the wonders of the watery ecosystem to residents who might otherwise rarely see a green field. Barnes also makes a popular vantage point each March for the Oxford-Cambridge Boat Race, first contested in 1829 at Henley and staged since 1845 over the four miles and 374 yards between Putney and Mortlake.

For reasons historians still seek to understand, the race excited a broad swathe of the public who, despite having no connection with either seat of learning, displayed with rosettes or bonnets their support for the dark blues of Oxford or the light blues of Cambridge. Walford records: "High and low, rich and poor, young and old, all seem to be swayed by one common impulse: to witness a trial of skill, strength and pluck, and endurance between the representatives of those two universities..."

On race day, the river and vantage points along it became congested. G. E. Mitton wrote in 1906: "The road along by Mortlake is lined by crowds; every window is filled, and all available roofs. On the railway bridge are loosely packed ranks of people, brought there and deposited by trains, which afterwards decorously withdraw and wait to pick them up again. The price of this first-rate position is included in the fares... A gun goes off, and then, an extraordinarily short time after, a murmur begins among the crowds on the Mortlake side. It grows and grows and swells along the Chiswick shore, as first one boat creeps around the corner, and then the other."

When in 2004 the BBC, which had broadcast the race live on radio from 1927 and on television from 1938, announced that it would no longer provide coverage, it seemed a mark of the event's declining popularity. Even with the acquisition of rights by a rival broadcaster, it seems unlikely that the event will divide society in the twenty-first century quite like it did in the nineteenth.

Hammersmith Bridge and Castlenau

Completed in 1827 by William Tierney Clarke, Hammersmith Bridge became the Thames' first suspension bridge, though one unsuitable for the rise of motorized traffic or the 12,000 people who gathered annually on its span for the Boat Race. In the 1880s, Sir Joseph Bazalgette oversaw a steel replacement that utilized the extant foundations and re-used the old bridge's piers and abutments to create a pleasingly decorative addition to the river.

Presumably attracted less by its aesthetics than its importance as a traffic artery, the Irish Republican Army (IRA) planted a bomb on the bridge in 1939. After a passer-by tossed the suitcase device into the river, the bomb exploded and produced a sixty-foot column of water. The finder was rewarded with an MBE; the bombers with jail sentences. Another attempt in 1996 was thwarted when detonators exploded but failed to ignite Semtex attached to the bridge's south side; a smaller device did explode in June 2000. Repairing the bomb damage revealed structural problems consistent with age and the bridge was closed to cars for two years, greatly reducing congestion and shortening journey times made by bus, bike and on foot. Despite a strongly-supported local campaign against it doing so, the bridge re-opened for cars and congestion returned in December 1999.

The Hammersmith Bridge Company, builders of the original crossing, laid the approach road from Barnes that became known as Castelnau, part of an area described by Weinreb and Hibbert as "among the most satisfying of early Victorian developments". Anyone who can afford to own one of these expansive residences might now consider themselves very satisfied indeed.

Chiswick

"There are few localities in the vicinity of London so interesting as the pretty and pleasant village of Chiswick," declared the Halls in the 1850s. To London commuters, Chiswick is now synonymous with a busy flyover and a congested roundabout, but the Halls' words might apply to the face Chiswick shows to the Thames: weeping willows, a secluded bandstand, a string of sports grounds and green fields. After the unprepossessing townhouses of Corney Reach, a private development offering condescending access to Thames Path walkers, comes the genteel Chiswick Mall: "a charming run of Restoration and Georgian houses, rounded bows, forecourts, straight and curly ironwork, and bits of Regency elegance," suggested Sydney R. Jones. Even today, the strip is a believable setting for Miss Jemima Pinkerton's academy for young ladies, described at the beginning of Thackeray's *Vanity Fair* as pupil Becky Sharp departs: "The carriage rolled away; the great gates were closed; the bell rang for the dancing lesson. The world is before the two young ladies; and so, farewell to Chiswick Mall."

Deeper into Chiswick, the rotunda-topped Chiswick House was completed in 1729 for the third Earl of Burlington as "a temple to the arts" and celebrated both for its architecture and its retinue of guests from the world of art and literature. A less distinguished 36 years as a lunatic asylum ended with the house's purchase by the local authority and it now stands smug amid the green spaces of Chiswick Park, enjoying what the 1970 *Shell Guide to England* described as "wedding cake cornices, velvet-covered walls, gilt decoration of fabulous intricacy… an architect's and designer's dream."

A similarly well-preserved and notably less grand structure is separated by a brick wall from one of the capital's most congested roads and the roundabout that bears an artist's name. From 1749, this was a country retreat for painter and pictorial satirist William Hogarth (1697-1764), now open as the Hogarth House. Along with artist James Whistler, Hogarth lies in the graveyard of the riverside St. Nicolas' Church with a eulogy by David Garrick inscribed on his tomb:

Farewell great Painter of Mankind
Who reach'd the noblest point of Art,
Whose pictur'd Morals charm the Mind
And through the Eye correct the Heart.
If Genius fire thee, Reader, stay,
If Nature touch thee, drop a Tear:
If neither move thee, turn away,
For Hogarth's honour'd dust lies here.

In a maze of old alleyways and pubs, Chiswick becomes Hammersmith and the riverside Upper Mall, notable on its course for Kelmscott House, no. 26, home to William Morris from 1878 to 1896 and now partly occupied by the William Morris Society, who are eager to point out that, other than for their own exhibitions, the building is not open to the public.

Part Three

London's River

It is astonishing to remember that a plot of firm soil by the river's bank made a port, and the port in turn the pre-eminent city of the world.

Alan Bell, *The Said Noble River*, 1937

Despite regular attempts by the city to congest, pollute, and ignore it, the Thames and London have been locked in symbiotic embrace for two thousand years. In Roman times, the river became a local transport artery as well as a trading conduit, linking the infant city to Europe and eventually to the world. In the heyday of imperial Britain, the Thames underpinned the economy of the world's greatest metropolis with an unrivalled dock system and a belt of heavy industry stretched along its banks. Beside the Thames, the city displayed symbols of local and national power: the Tower of London, Greenwich and Whitehall palaces, the religious centres of Westminster and Lambeth, as well as countless grand homes of bishops and nobles whose lands reached to its foreshore. Even as power switched from spiritual to secular, high-powered decision-making was still being practised along its banks, whether openly at the Houses of Parliament or clandestinely in the (current) headquarters of MI5 and MI6.

With scant regard for its traditional importance, the Thames in London spent much of the late twentieth century being neglected, which made its re-emergence through the 1980s and 1990s all the more spectacular. As London recovered from its post-industrial malaise to become a global financial centre, it again found common cause with the Thames: abandoned riverside plots offered a practical solution for architects and their corporate clients in search of new space; disused warehouses became offices, homes, shops, bars and restaurants. The aesthetic impact of the river is now the stuff of highbrow speculation; at ground level, its polluted banks are being cleaned and made accessible to

walkers, joggers, cyclists—and anyone wishing to see London from a new angle. But with more schemes than even the most adept and visionary of planners could make reality, an abiding fear is that is that no-one, be they government agencies, local communities, environmentalists, architects or property speculators, can agree on what to do or how to compromise for the best, and that ultimately, if inadvertently, they might just do the worst.

Londinium and the Tamesis

Little conclusive evidence exists to suggest a permanent settlement at what became London before that established by the Romans (who named it Londinium and the river, Tamesis). In the unsuccessful Roman invasion under Julius Caesar in 54BC the waterway at the future site of London, where it could be half a mile wide at high tide and bordered by frequently-flooded marshland, was noted as having a gravel bed and thereby being fordable albeit, as noted in *Commentaries on the Gallic Wars*, attributed to Caesar, "at one place only and that with difficulty".

A successful Roman invasion by a 40,000-strong army under Claudius in 43AD saw an advance party camp at a crossing point on the river, believed to be near the site of present-day Westminster. As the Britons were subdued, the Romans established Londinium—where the river was sufficiently deep to accommodate seagoing vessels yet narrow enough to be bridged—as a trading centre which was, by AD60 according to Tacitus, "filled with traders and a celebrated centre of commerce". Despite the uprising of British tribes led by Boudica the following year that ransacked Londinium, the invaders endured and Londinium evolved from trading post to a major administrative centre, occupying a 326-acre site (the present City of London) enclosed by stone walls. On the south bank around the sand bar on which the southern end of the early bridge stood, a community named Southwark took root.

Besides being a source of drinking water for people and livestock, and a food supply (then abundant with fish), the river was a means of transportation and a natural trade route. Wooden quays and warehouses that eventually stretched for 1,800 feet were constructed along the north bank, about three hundred feet inland of its current position. Cargoes were typically unloaded from larger boats in midstream and taken ashore by smaller flat-bottomed boats, or lighters, a process that would continue on the river until (and even after) the nineteenth-century wet docks. Along with basic foodstuffs and materials came items such as French wine, Baltic amber, Spanish pottery, Italian glassware and Portuguese marble. Exports included animal skins, corn, cattle, hunting dogs, iron, silver, gold, and slaves (common throughout the Roman empire). With the Roman road network converging on London, the settlement became a major distribution centre, heightening its commercial importance.

Saxons and Vikings: Lundenwic

As its occupation became consolidated, Roman Britain imported less and relied more on local produce, reducing Londinium's trading significance though not diminishing its role as an administrative centre. A major seat of regional government, it had a status that made its defensive imperative as new threats appeared from overseas. The final withdrawal of Roman troops in 410, however, made continued defence impossible. The country fell to Saxon invaders, but what happened to Londinium foxed historians for decades: after being documented as receiving battle-wounded in 457, the city was unmentioned in historical records for 150 years. Unlike their Roman predecessors, Saxons were not urban dwellers and did not occupy the old Roman city. Evidence discovered in the 1980s indicates Saxon occupation directly west, between the site of the future Whitehall and the Fleet River, and alongside the Thames.

Incursions by Danish raiding parties along the Thames may have been instrumental in encouraging settlement within the walled Roman city for defensive reasons, which in turn led to the development of commercial quays at what became Queenhithe. Whatever the truth, between 886 and 1215, as Francis Sheppard suggests, "London was regenerated on its Roman site and grew to become the embryonic capital of a politically united England." Such unity emerged from conflict: Saxons had battled with Vikings, Christian missionaries had converted heathens, Edward the Confessor had begun what became Westminster Abbey, the Normans had invaded and William I ("the Conqueror") had built the White Tower, the first part of the Tower of London and a work of hitherto unimagined enormity beside the river to remind both locals and assertive foreigners that it was he who held power and knew how to maintain it.

Medieval London and its River

Among the few daily descriptions of life in early medieval London was William Fitz Stephen's 1173 reference to the exotic cargo arriving on the river:

Gold from Arabia, from Sabaea spice
And incense; from the Scythians arms of steel
Well-tempered; oil from the rich groves of palm
That spring from the fat lands of Babylon;
Fine gems from Nile, from China crimson silks;
French wines; and sable, vair and miniver
From the far lands where Russ and Norseman dwell.

Fitz Stephen had been secretary to Thomas à Becket, who died in 1170 a religious martyr but who was born (around 1110) to a son of Rouen merchant, one of many foreign traders who settled in the thriving port of London and came to dominate its commerce. While imports were diverse, the chief British export at this time was wool, eighty per cent of which was transported through London to Flemish clothing manufacturers.

The new London Bridge of 1176 prevented large vessels continuing upriver, restricting them to the city, which benefited accordingly. Billingsgate, east of the bridge, became the dominant landing stage though Queenhithe, to the west, remained busy. Mercantile London grew wealthy from taxation on trade while the river became crammed with vessels from "barges and tiny rowing boats to rounded, clumsy-looking cogs with an average crew of twenty-three", according to Timothy Baker's *Medieval London*. As well as being a trade route, the Thames became a major employer. Those making a living from the water included the fishermen whose numbers were such that by the fourteenth century laws were in place to limit catch sizes. Of the great variety of river occupations, Peter Ackroyd in *London: the Biography* offers a lyrical recantation: "boatmen and chalkmen, eelmen and baillies, gallymen or garthmen, ferriers and lightermen, hookers and mariners, petermen and palingmen, searchers and shipwrights, shoutmen and piledrivers, trinkers and water-bailiffs and watermen."

The river also became a place to show off. From 1425, each newly-elected Lord Mayor of London travelled to Westminster to swear an oath to the Crown. In 1454, Sir John Norman did so aboard a carved and gilded barge, signalling the river's arrival as a stage for pomp and ceremony. The royal palaces at Hampton Court, Richmond, Westminster, Whitehall and Greenwich, and the Tower, were all accessed by monarchs in elaborate royal barges, their departure, even for a quick crossing from Westminster to Lambeth Palace, marked by peals of church bells liable to bring the curious to the riverside. A journey by Elizabeth I from Westminster to the Tower was made with "a hundred boats about her Grace, with trumpets and drums and flutes and guns and squibs hurling on high and to and fro until ten at night... all the waterside with a million people looking on."

For ordinary Londoners, too, the river was an easier means of travel than the narrow, congested streets of the old city. From the many sets of public stairs leading to the river, the cry of "Oars!" as watermen touted for fares was constant and taken by at least one visiting Frenchman as an invitation to a brothel. Allied with lightermen, watermen became well-organized and fiercely protective of their livelihood, opposing the introduction of hackney coaches in 1565 as strongly as they later would any suggestion of new bridges.

The World and the Legal Quays

London's Tudor-age development into a world centre for trade and commerce owed much to the 1576 Spanish devastation of Antwerp. Another factor was the Crown's desire to raise income by granting monopolies on trade. The foreign merchants who had previously dominated trade on London's river were eased aside by royally-chartered and joint-stock companies, established to forge new sea routes with the promise of profits arising from trade on them: they included the Russia Company (1555), the Turkey Company (1581) and the East India Company (1600).

Aided by Henry VIII's founding of Royal Navy bases at Deptford and Woolwich, shipbuilding on the Thames expanded and the production of bigger, faster vessels enabled increased business with the Americas and the Far East, which swiftly surpassed that with Europe. The new routes brought new imports that in turn created new riverside industries such as tobacco processing, sugar refining and silk weaving. These in turn stimulated rising demand for clerks and customs officials, and enabled marine insurance to emerge as a financial mainstay of the city.

Introduced in 1558, the legal quay system restricted landing and loading of taxable goods to selected wharves on the north bank between London Bridge and the Tower. The intention was to bring order to the chaos of duty collection but the impact, even with the addition of the Sufferance Quays (given temporary loading and landing rights) on the south bank, was to make the river increasingly congested as trade expanded. The value of imports and exports into London doubled between 1700 and 1770 and doubled again by 1795. Swiss traveller César de Saussure, visiting in the 1720s, found the Port of London "almost hidden by merchant vessels from every country."

During the 1790s, 1,775 vessels were allowed to moor simultaneously in a space designed for a third of that number while 3,500 smaller vessels were engaged in carrying cargo from moorings to the wharves. Not only were ships at the mercy of wind and tides but were also exposed to organized crime. Pilfering of cargoes that often lay unattended on the quayside became a major industry and one that gave rise to a rich waterside lexicon of slang to denote practitioners of such crime. Merchant, magistrate, and advocate of river police, Patrick Colquhoun (1745-1820) defined criminal types on the river in *A Treatise on the Commerce and Policing of the River Thames* (1798):

>...the 'river pirates' who were connected with the marine store shops; they reconnoitred by day and made their attacks in armed boats on dark nights, cutting adrift the lighters and barges, and taking out the merchandise. The 'night plunderers'—the watermen of the lowest class, who attacked unprotected lighters and made over the stolen goods to receivers. The 'light horsemen', comprised of mates of ships and revenue officers, who would wink at the robbery of the ship, in which coopers, porters and watermen take part. The 'heavy horsemen'—porters and labourers who wore an inner dress, called a guerney, provided with pockets therein to stow away small quantities of colonial produce whilst portering about the ships and quays. Besides these organised predators, the wine coopers pilfered while

opening and refining casks; the mudlarks picked up stolen bits, which others by concert threw into the mud; the rat catchers employed on board the ships carried away produce; the lightermen concealed goods whilst going from the ships to the quays; and the warehousemen, when the sugar reached the warehouses, pilfered and sold the stolen sugar to small dealers at public houses.

Frost Fairs

Despite the congested shipping and the high level of pilferage, the river still offered opportunities for relaxation and pleasure, most remarkably from a present-day viewpoint with its frost fairs. As the name suggests, these took place when the river froze over: the pre-Victorian London Bridge and poorly-maintained banks slowed the river's flow and allowed large sections to ice-over completely during cold weather. Impromptu but often long-running (sometimes of several weeks duration), frost fairs brought entertainment of diverse kinds—archery, dancing, bull-baiting, coach racing, and more—to the river. One such freeze in the winter of 1683-84 featured, not untypically, the spectacle of an entire ox being roasted on the river. The event, the ox, and the interruption to trade such events brought to watermen, were recorded in a section of *Trivia* (1716) by poet and dramatist John Gay (1685-1732):

> O roving muse, recall that wondrous year
> When winter reign'd in bleak Britannia's air
> When hoary Thames, with frosted osiers crown'd
> Was three long moons in icy fetters bound
> The waterman, forlorn along the shore
> Pensive reclines upon his useless oar
> See harness'd steeds desert the stony town
> And wander roads unstable, not their own
> Wheels o'er the harden'd waters smoothly glide
> And raze, with whiten'd tracks, the slippery tide
> Here the fat cook plies high the blazing fire
> And scarce the spit can turn the steer entire.

A frozen river also brought the opportunity to sell souvenirs and other ephemera. In *Frosts, Freezes and Fairs*, Ian Currie records the 1813-14

FROST FAIR ON THE THAMES IN 1683.

freeze and what became the last of the great fairs: "Gin, beer and gingerbread could be bought in booths as could books and toys and an infinite variety of bric-a-brac many labelled 'bought on the Thames'. A sheep was roasted over a coal fire and was advertised as Lapland Mutton and sold at a shilling a slice. Passageway on the ice from Blackfriars Bridge was known as City-Road and was lined with tradesmen of every description and some ten printing presses."

Docks and Dockers

Beneficiaries of the legal quays included the City of London Corporation, two Oxford colleges and the family of Lord Gwydyer, who earned a payment on every mooring chain between London Bridge and Woolwich. Such vested interests prevented any substantive change to the legal quays system for 244 years, but with the rise of industrialization came a new entrepreneurial class and growing demand for free trade. As parliament acquiesced and passed the West India Dock Act, there followed what Peter Ackroyd called the "largest single, privately funded enterprise in the history of London", which financed the creation of vast artificial lakes across sections of east London protected from tides by locks and with unloaded cargo protected within warehouses enclosed by high brick or stone walls. The first of these, West India Docks, opened in 1802 and enjoyed an initial success that inspired further dock creation: London Docks at Wapping (1805); the East India Docks at Blackwall (1806); and Surrey Docks at Rotherhithe (1807).

Yet despite over £5 million being spent on them, these facilities were quickly rendered ineffective. They lacked connections to the increasingly important railway network and were soon outmoded as steam replaced sail and ever-larger ships required ever-larger docks. Consequently, wider, deeper facilities were built further east along the river, including the Royal Victoria (1855), Millwall (1868), South West India (1870) and the Royal Albert (1880). Between them, the Royal Victoria and Royal Albert offered seven miles of quayside, compared to London's total of around 5,000 feet under the old system.

Even with a sharp increase in cargo handling, the docks' profitability was subject to fluctuations in worldwide trade and was seriously affected by the "free-water clause", a provision in the West India Dock Act made under pressure from lightermen and wharfingers (private wharf owners)

permitting lighters to enter docks, unload cargo and carry it to wharves, thereby avoiding quay and warehousing tolls otherwise payable to the dock company. For this reason, privately-owned wharfs still handled the bulk of the river's cargo throughout the 1800s despite the city having the world's largest network of enclosed docks.

The docks offered new employment opportunities, but the ups and downs of free trade that affected the dock companies affected their workers too. Most dockers were employed as casual labour with work allocated at a morning "call-on", an event described by labour leader Ben Tillet as one where: "Coats, flesh and even ears were torn off, men were crushed to death in the struggle, helpless if fallen. The strong literally threw themselves over the heads of their fellows and battled with kick and curse, through the kicking, punching, cursing crowd to the rails of the 'cage' which held them like rats—mad human rats who saw food in the ticket." While Tillet's description was justified, and workers' grievances genuine, he had reason to play up the misery of the dockers' lot as he sought their support in the growing labour movement. At the second attempt, Tillet was able form a general docks union and oversee a widely supported and well-organized dock strike in 1889—a seminal moment in British labour history—in which the dockers gained pay increases and a guarantee of minimum working hours.

As part of what Francis Sheppard called "the new mass unionism of the less skilled", the collective power of Thames dockers contrasted with the watermen and lightermen who for centuries had defined working life on the river. Unlike the growing trade unions, the Watermen's Company still operated much as a medieval guild, approving apprentices and participating in ceremonial occasions and the piloting of royal barges. The free-water clause had enabled lightermen to survive the docks and even restrict their commercial success, but watermen, who numbered around 20,000 in 1800, would find no legal remedy nor widespread support to enable them to compete with London's new river bridges and became considerably diminished as a river feature by 1900, despite being granted exclusive rights to run London pleasure trips.

Building Bridges
The spate of bridge building that sealed the fate of the watermen was driven by the needs of a changing London. In the first three decades of

the nineteenth century, the city's population rose from 865,000 to 1.5 million and gained roughly twenty per cent more inhabitants each decade until 1891. London not only grew, it refused to stand still. Whether across the city or into it from growing suburbs, movement became a requisite of life in the fledgling industrial metropolis. The Thames, which had been what Weinreb and Hibbert called "for centuries the cheapest, safest, most pleasant and most rapid means of transport", was, by the mid-1800s, as much an impediment to movement as a provider of it: railways could not cross it and the few extant bridges were unable to cope with the fast-rising vehicular and pedestrian traffic using them. London Bridge experienced a twice-daily surge of pedestrians, horse-drawn carts and omnibuses, intensified as arrivals at the adjacent London Bridge rail termini rose from 5.5 million in 1850 to 11 million by 1854.

Between 1860 and 1873 came a series of new river crossings: the rail bridges of Victoria, Charing Cross, Ludgate Hill and Cannon Street each serving a new or expanded rail termini, and Lambeth, Westminster, Albert and Wandsworth bridges meeting the demand for greater pedestrian and vehicular crossings. The London of 1750 had just one river bridge below Putney; that which entered the nineteenth century boasted four. With the 1894 completion of Tower Bridge, London reached the twentieth century with eighteen.

Barometer of Change

Throughout the nineteenth century, London's river became a barometer of social, economic and political change, both local and national. The free trade that replaced river monopolies brought the docks; the rise of organized labour sired dockers' unions; the switch from rural to urban living brought the city a soaring population and a demand for more river crossings. The established governance of London, too, was under threat as local authorities and private concerns were challenged by calls for a city-wide administration similar to those in the industrial cities of northern England.

A telling example was the urgent need for a new London sewer system eventually provided by Sir Joseph Bazalgette, a celebrated engineering feat that not only rid the Thames of its stinking waste but gave it the new embankments that thrilled Victorian society. Yet even in an era of persistent cholera outbreaks (the link with contaminated water was yet to be fully established), resistance to Bazalgette's plans came from private water companies which took their supplies in poorly filtered form from the polluted river, and a laissez-faire attitude summed up in an 1854 *Times* editorial celebrating the demise of the Municipal Board of Health: "We prefer to take our chance with cholera and the rest than be bullied into health." Only the overcoming of another strand of resistance, the view that parliament should not fund local initiatives, made possible the creation of the Metropolitan Board of Works (a forerunner of the London County Council), which in 1856 appointed Bazalgette as its chief engineer.

Another change resulted from the inability of the river's controllers, the City of London Corporation, rooted as it was in a bygone era and enjoying the profits resulting from its monopoly, to offer the necessary regulation in the boom created by Britain's global trading dominance and rapid industrialization: London's docks were busy but financially they were facing ruin. London's chief port rival, Liverpool, had been under a specialist docks authority since 1857 but the capital delayed a similar step until 1908 with the creation of the Port of London Authority, a public body given jurisdiction over the tidal Thames, from the estuary to Teddington.

The mood of the river also changed. Where de Saussure in the 1720s could take delight in its display of colourful boats and social interaction ("Nothing is more attractive and charming than the Thames on a fine summer evening; the conversations you hear are most entertaining..."), Charles Dickens would write in *The Uncommercial Traveller* (1861): "The river had an awful look, the buildings on the banks were muffled in black shrouds, and the reflected lights seemed to originate deep in the water, as if the spectres of suicides were holding them to show where they went down. The wild moon and clouds were as restless as an evil conscience in a tumbled bed, and the very shadow of the immensity of London seemed to lie oppressively on the river."

The Blitz and Post-War Decline
Despite the impact of the First World War and industrial decentralization through the 1920s and 1930s, the docks and riverside commerce continued to thrive. Such industry offered an obvious target

for an enemy seeking to inflict economic damage, however. In September 1940, a year after the declaration of war between Britain and Germany, more than a thousand German bombers and fighters formed a twenty-mile column that followed the Thames along its estuary to drop incendiaries and high explosives on docks, warehouses, railways lines, gasworks and inevitably the surrounding communities of east London. Some 448 people were killed and fires blazed for a week following the first of what would be the 57 consecutive nights of air raids that became known as the Blitz. The physical scars of German bombing marked the area for decades although the docks, essential to the war effort and post-war economic rebuilding, quickly regained their commercial importance, booming during the 1960s but later undermined by the rise of containerization, road and air haulage, and better-equipped European docks.

In his 1958 *London's Riverside Past, Present and Future*, Eric de Maré lamented: "That is the trouble with the river today—we turn our backs on it. It is too inaccessible to the pedestrian and no longer seems to belong to the town. All its great dockyards—seventy miles of wharf and quay—are hidden from us behind immense walls, and a life, mysterious and apart, is lived upon it by a select few. We cross the river as fast as we can, never pausing to enjoy the breezy views to left and right as we roar across a bridge. When we come down to its side we tear along the embankments with their heavy and interminable granite walls which cut us off too firmly from the river's alien world—rarely pausing to enjoy its visual and historical offerings."

So total was London's lack of regard for the river on which its fortunes had been founded that de Maré's comments could be applied into the 1980s. It was only then that the river began to undergo appreciable change. Canary Wharf was just one among the most spectacular and controversial projects overseen by the London Docklands Development Corporation. As London was reshaped by a Thatcher government intent on financial deregulation, derelict riverside sites presented a solution to the city's space problems.

A new home on the Thames could be high-rise and high-profile, excellent for spreading company awareness and acquiring the prestige of an architecturally significant addition to the cityscape. Architects, suggested Jerry White in *London in the Twentieth Century*, exploited the river "with a flamboyant self-belief... rarely equalled at any other time in the century." One of the prominent firms was that of Terry Farrell, responsible for such additions to the riverside as Vauxhall Cross (see p.114) and Embankment Place, stacked above Charing Cross Station (see p.130). In a comment applicable to numerous others, White continues: "The riverside buildings of the Terry Farrell Partnership... were temples to an infallible God of commerce worshipped by a corporate state."

Today's Thames

With news-making additions such as Tate Modern, the Millennium Bridge and the new City Hall, London's river reached the twenty-first century once again in the limelight. Meanwhile, along a revitalized shoreline, the expanding Thames Path ensured that London's riverside was increasingly accessible. An urban, recreational Thames where a person can walk, breath and absorb the city skyline is preferable to one of abandoned toxic plots and the fenced-off remains of gasworks. Nonetheless, riverside development and regeneration remain contentious. During 2003 Deyan Sudjic sounded off in *The Observer*: "Everything that makes London look like London is being destroyed... There are no historic views anymore... All along the river you can see a variety of ski-jumps, skateboards and pillows, applied in an ever more frantic and ever more forlorn effort to do something architecturally interesting." Though failing to define what makes London look like London, the commentator's anger was rooted in riverside projects that bear scant relation to their environment: architect's calling cards rather than products serving community need and desire.

Liquid Boundaries: Dividing London

Where does London begin and end? For the purposes of this book it starts at Hammersmith on the north side and Putney on the south, continuing east to the Thames Barrier. Anyone who suggests that such boundaries are entirely arbitrary would be entirely correct. But just as the Thames prefers to ignore human geography (why else would there be a Thames Barrier?), so this framework is imposed for convenience of writer and reader mindful that, for the river, even London itself is but a recent intrusion on its banks.

London's River: The Western Edge

East of Hammersmith Bridge, the river encounters enough urban sprawl to convince any visitor that London has indeed been reached. Until the Georgian and Victorian westward expansion of the city, however, the Thames west of Westminster remained surprisingly rural. Most communities along its banks continued to be modest fishing and farming settlements until the fruit and vegetable needs of the capital encouraged large-scale market gardening, subsequently replaced by the industrialization that spread along both sides of the river but became particularly pronounced on the south side. Post-industrial regeneration of variable merit has been a feature since the 1980s and continues to fire debate and anger.

London's bishops took an early shine to this section of the riverside, but while their country retreat of 1400 years in Fulham steadily became surrounded by the trappings of metropolitan advancement, it remains a diminutive palace and park amid well-tended open spaces and tidy streets of terraced homes. Chelsea was a quiet village even as Thomas More departed it for religious martyrdom and continued to be so four hundred years later when J. M. W. Turner arrived; its character later changed by a cavalcade of Bohemians creating one of the city's fashionable, and eventually one of its most expensive, enclaves. Neighbouring Pimlico fares poorly in comparison despite a little riverside park dominated by a statesman who met a curious end. Finally, Millbank's strange past has encompassed a nineteenth-century prison that still divides opinion despite long being demolished, a major national art collection sired by a sugar mogul, and an early London skyscraper with a claim to political fame.

Hammersmith and a Religious Route to Fulham

Where Barnes can claim the wetlands and the homes of Castlenau as indicators of west London prosperity, Hammersmith on the river's north side suggests a grittier, warts-and-all metropolis. As the most westerly inner London borough, Hammersmith is dominated by two tube stations, one of which is concealed beneath a 1980s shopping mall which also boasts an unedifying triumvirate of a bus station, a disused underground car park and the British headquarters of Coca-Cola. An earlier Hammersmith was distanced from the tumult of the capital and its residents expressed their piety by a weekly trek through fields and muddy tracks to worship at Fulham Church. They were saved the journey from 1631 when Archbishop Laud consecrated a Chapel-of-Ease that evolved into the present St. Paul's Church. In keeping with modern Hammersmith, the church seems defined less by the cross of the crucifixion than by the cross formed by congested roads encircling it, the route to heaven itself interrupted by the Hammersmith Flyover carrying the evil A4 towards central London.

Slightly calmer scenes are to be found along what is conjectured to have originated as a Roman-age track, Fulham Palace Road, which runs south from Hammersmith broadly parallel to the river, passing tidy side streets of Victorian homes and the contemporary form of Charing Cross Hospital, raised on the site of a workhouse that earned an entry in the 1868 *National Gazetteer of England and Wales*: "The Fulham Union workhouse, a modern red brick building, is in this parish, as also are four lunatic asylums belonging to private individuals…"

Around 1750, both Fulham and Putney were "more or less single street villages going back half a mile from the river's bank then thinning out with detached cottages into open fields." The fields provided the fruit and vegetables on which the local economies depended, though as London expanded, industrialized and became linked by railways, so Fulham in particular became a strongly working-class quarter. By the 1970s, however, Fulham itself was undergoing the gentrification dubbed "Chelsification" that anguished established locals but caused property speculators to rejoice.

The Fulham Football Club

Despite brief periods in football's top flight, Fulham Football Club has spent much longer spells outside it since its founding as a professional team in 1898. Nonetheless, many genuine supporters might live with poor results in return for following a football club with character and a sense of community. For many years, the club chairman was comedian Tommy Trinder and despite at times boasting players such as England's World Cup winning captain Bobby Moore and maverick genius George Best, Fulham's true heroes were home-grown stars such as England midfielder Johnny Haynes who spent 18 years at the club despite lucrative offers to move elsewhere. Fulham also enjoy the picturesque riverside setting of Craven Cottage, where a stadium re-development completed in 2004 (financed, like the current team, by the deep wallet of Harrods owner, Mohamed al Fayed) carefully preserved the 1905 stand affectionately and simply known as the Cottage, on which the indefinite article is defiantly retained in the club's name. Another quirk was the opportunity for spectators in the Riverside Stand, before it gained a roof, to watch the university boat race go by before returning to the match. The crowning glory of one of England's most charming football grounds, though, is the fact that in the 1840s Edward Bulwer-Lytton (1803-73) wrote *The Last Days of Pompeii* on a site somewhere near the centre spot.

A Bishop's Lair: Fulham Palace and Surrounds

From 691 the village of Fulham and adjacent lands were acquired by the Bishops of London in whose hands parts remain. From the eleventh century, the bishops occupied Fulham Palace, a grand in name but modest in form structure, greatly rebuilt in the nineteenth century but retaining a Tudor redbrick courtyard and nestling unobtrusively amid trees and shrubbery. Modern peace conceals a bloody past, particularly in the time of Bishop Bonner (1500?-1569), charged by Queen Mary with re-introducing Catholicism and here infamously burning the hand of Thomas Tomkins, a suspected heretic, with a candle. Although the seemingly bloodthirsty Bonner was dubbed "the butcher of London" and had to be secretly buried on his death to avoid inciting a riot, recent historians have softened the traditional view of him.

Thirteen acres of the palace's grounds form the once neglected but now splendidly revived Palace Garden, though a more striking expanse is Bishops Park, a public area studded with trees, walking trails and a river walk which brings views across a muddy foreshore to the rowing clubs of Putney. Since 1999 the park has held one of the few British reminders of the Spanish Civil War in the form of a memorial to the sixty local men who served in the anti-fascist International Brigade from 1936 to 1939: "Their eyes were open. They saw no other way."

The destination for those who journeyed from Hammersmith before the opening of St. Pauls Church was Fulham Church, or Church of All Saints. The fifteenth-century tower would once have dominated the surrounding farmland but today is secreted in a peaceful and bucolic niche, enclosed by short, winding streets and far removed in mood from the broad thoroughfares of contemporary Fulham and the traffic rushing towards the river bridge. The church was less peaceful in 1976, however, when it provided the backdrop for a key scene, the impaling of a priest, in the horror film *The Omen.*

The Hurlingham Club and Wandsworth Bridge

Having acquired a plot from the Bishops of London in 1760, noted physician William Cadogan raised a brown brick "cottage", which under a subsequent owner grew into the neo-classical mansion that now sits snugly beyond public gaze in the heart of the riverside plot constituting the private section of Hurlingham Park known as the Hurlingham Club. Earlier used for pigeon shooting, the park from 1869 became the national polo centre, an aristocratic setting for an aristocratic sport remembered by Sydney R. Jones: "Bright light and shadow, fast gallops, sudden stops and turns, the skill of the game, specks of gay colour, delicate summer finery, tea, and animated conversation in the open air, combined to make Hurlingham a real Thames jewel for those fortunate enough to be able to sun in the glitter of its rays." The Hurlingham Club offers tennis courts, bowling greens, croquet pitches, swimming pool, squash courts and a cricket ground. Would-be members, however, must first be proposed by two current members and pay £150 to join a 15-year waiting list.

Beside the river immediately east, a new pathway picks a route around modern warehouses and culminates anti-climactically amid the superstores of Hurlingham Retail Park, alongside which even such a utilitarian structure as Wandsworth Bridge assumes an air of majesty. In his *A View of the Thames* (1977), Norman Shrapnel observed:

> Going to Chelsea by way of Wandsworth Bridge has the advantage of novelty. It is a small circuit but unfashionable. No tourists will jostle you, no addicted river-wanderer even. Crossing the bridge by foot brought glances of surprise from the high cabs of lorries. Yet surprise remained normal, even here. Among the sand, cement and beer-wagons plunging across the bridge I met a very old horse pulling some scrap metal and a very young man. He (the young man) was modishly dressed and gave a theatrical wave as he passed.

A mark of the changing riverscape, Shrapnel's description of Wandsworth Bridge less than thirty years ago now seems like ancient history. The bridge today is more likely to be crossed by the Mercedes and BMWs driven by the occupants of luxury riverside apartments sprouting on either side. A 1940 replacement for an 1877 structure deemed too narrow and too weak to carry London's growing number of omnibuses, the bridge has the distinction of being the only Thames crossing delayed by a diplomatic stand-off: the 1938 Munich crisis which halted supplies of high-tensile steel and led subsequently to the Second World War—a fact perhaps contributing to what Geoffrey Phillips called its "stark, battleship appearance".

Chelsea Harbour and Lots Road

Chelsea Harbour "marks the point at which the word harbour was taken over from pilots and lightermen and passed into the sales patter of estate agents," wrote John Cunningham in the *Guardian* in 1999—with good reason. Purchasers of a Chelsea Harbour apartment (around £2 million for a penthouse) are actually the owners of a flat in Fulham, since the complex is east of the muddy tongues of Chelsea Creek, and the only harbourage is that created for residents' yachts. The ugly centre-piece of the development, the 250-foot-high Belvedere Tower, was able to rise unopposed only, many have supposed, due to the political hiatus between the Greater London Council's 1986 abolition and the local borough elections; a new administration might well have vetoed its construction.

Adjacent and looming large from the river is the almighty red brick slab of Lots Road Power Station, its windows taller than many people's homes, which opened in 1905 to power the London Underground. Consuming six millions tons of barge-delivered coal daily until changing to gas in the mid-1960s, the power station drew the attention of Arnold Bennett who wrote of it in *Paris Night* (1913): "a building which must be among the largest in London, a red brick building with a grandiose architectural effect, an overpowering affair that man creates in order to show how small and puny he himself is..." The station was decommissioned in 2002 and converted, predictably, into luxury apartments.

The river at Chelsea

Cremorne Gardens

Just east of the former power station lies Cremorne Gardens, a small riverside green space where only a set of disproportionately-sized gates suggests that this was the site of much large Cremorne Gardens, which from 1840 to 1877 was London's last great pleasure garden. Unlike earlier affairs such as Ranelagh and Vauxhall (see pp.104-5 and 113-4), Cremorne operated in a period when leisure was becoming affordable to an expanding middle class and was run on commercial lines. Amusements included fireworks, trapeze acts and, in 1861, Madame Genevive crossing by tightrope to the south bank. But Cremorne went much further than its rivals as its management sought to maximize earnings with the sensationalist stunts that took it, according to Lynda Nead, "to the brink of legality and social acceptability." By night, Cremorne offered the novelty of gas lamps, the sounds of an orchestra, and a dancing platform which pitched the garden, with its socially mixed crowds, at the barrier-breaking forefront of London nightlife.

Cremorne, Nead concludes, was "part of the popular culture and popular memory of mid-Victorian London. Its image symbolised the social and moral ambiguities, the thrilling spectacle of the modern metropolis." The present Cremorne Gardens is, the local council suggests, "an interesting and well designed garden on the riverside, suitable for picnics."

Chelsea

From 1846 until his death in 1851, the artist J. M. W. Turner lived in Chelsea, then a village distanced from the sway of London life and still meriting its seventeenth-century description in Bowack's *Antiquities of Middlesex*, which noted the "sweetness of its air and pleasant situation", attracting "persons of good fashion". At 119 Cheyne Walk (then 6 Davies Place) Turner, according to David Wilton, "retreated into a world apart from his professional life, resisting the efforts of his colleagues to discover his whereabouts." One who did visit observed that the house possessed "a magnificent prospect both up and down the river (but was otherwise) miserable in every aspect." The river view was improved by a railing-enclosed viewing platform built on the roof for the painter's use.

In Turner's wake, the Georgian buildings lining the web-like series of streets east of Chelsea Creek and between the Kings Road and the river were occupied by a who's who of London Bohemia. Artists from the Pre-Raphaelites onwards admired Chelsea for its spacious and affordable houses within easy reach of the galleries of the West End. The artists' presence in turn attracted others comfortable at the margins of mainstream society. Cheyne Walk residents included Dante Gabriel Rossetti, who spent twenty years at no. 16 with a menagerie that included, according to John Bignall, "a white bull that dug up the lawn, a kangaroo that murdered its mother, a racoon that murdered the kangaroo and a peacock that died under the sofa." Poet Algernon Charles Swinbourne lived at Rossetti's address for a time; James Whistler occupied, at various periods, nos. 29, 96 and 106; essayist Hilaire Belloc was at no. 104 during the early 1900s; and novelist George Eliot at no. 4. Elsewhere in Chelsea among a very long list of notables one could find Thomas Carlyle (24 Cheyne Row, 1834-81) and Oscar Wilde (14, now 34, Tithe Street, 1885-95), while the twentieth century found Henry James, T. S Eliot and James Bond creator Ian Fleming all, at various times, enjoying the river views from Carlyle Mansions on Cheyne Walk.

Chelsea Embankment and Albert Bridge

To facilitate Sir Joseph Bazalgette's sewers, the muddy foreshore that once lined Cheyne Walk was transformed in the late 1800s into Chelsea Embankment, at first considered a wondrous addition. *The Royal River* pronounced it "a splendid promenade between avenues of plane trees, which every season will make thicker and more umbrageous." The trees did as expected but the unpredicted rise of motor traffic put a wall of sound and fury between some Cheyne Walk homes and the river. Nonetheless, Cheyne Walk retained a certain allure, not least to the Rolling Stones in the 1960s. Guitarist Keith Richards and partner Anita Pallenburg lived at no. 3, while singer Mick Jagger occupied no. 48 from 1968 to 1975, first with Marianne Faithfull, subsequently with his first wife, Bianca.

The star among the road and rail bridges linking Chelsea and Battersea, Albert Bridge was described by Geoffrey Phillips in *Thames Crossings* as having "more the appearance of a seaside pier than a metropolitan bridge". With pastel tones, web-like latticework girders and a design mixing cantilever with suspension, the bridge, particularly when showing off its night-time illumination, seems more a river decoration than a working bridge. The dainty proportions are not deceptive: concerns over the structure's weakness led to plans for its demolition in the 1970s; furious protests ensured that strengthening was preferred to destruction.

Thomas More's Chelsea

Many of the goings-on in nineteenth-century Chelsea, not to mention those of the 1960s, might well have been anathema to an earlier Chelsea resident, Thomas More (1478-1535). The prominent English intellectual of his time, More authored the stinging, satirical and influential political novel, *Utopia*, became member of parliament, a Privy Councillor, Speaker of the House, and was appointed Lord Chancellor by Henry VIII in 1523. More's abilities, good nature and religious devotions made him widely admired, but when Henry VIII was denied papal permission to divorce his wife and set about breaking from the Catholic Church, it opened a rift with More that would lead to the latter's trial for treason and execution at the Tower in 1535.

Around 1520 More had secured a plot of land in Chelsea and raised

Beaufort House, its grounds thought to occupy the area now around Beaufort Street (crossing Cheyne Walk on the approach to today's Battersea Bridge) and including part of the riverside where More kept a barge to transport him to Westminster and Hampton Court. Of life at the house, More's biographer R. S. Chambers suggests: "Dice, cards, and flirtation were forbidden to the numerous retinue of men and women; gardening, study, music and matrimony were encouraged. There was household prayer every night that the master was at home, compulsory church going on Sundays and feast days... Usually More rose at 2am and gave the time until 7am to study and devotion."

Imprisoned in the Tower, More could have saved his life by acknowledging the supremacy of the monarch. Instead, he followed his conscience and with his final words declared himself "The King's good servant, but God's first." Remembered as England's greatest martyr, More was beatified in 1866 and is further remembered within Chelsea Old Church, close to the embankment at 4 Old Church Street, where the chapel he built was the only section of the church to survive German bombing. Outside, a 1969 statue offers a seated More with a stare still likely to send a shudder through passing atheists and agnostics—and self-regarding monarchs.

Physic Garden and Chelsea Pensioners

A slender plot with a pedigree past, the Chelsea Physic Garden, its main entrance on the appealingly-named Swan Walk, originated in 1673 to help would-be apothecaries identify plants, proximity to the river creating a warm micro-climate that enabled the growing of non-native species. Physician Sir Hans Sloane (1660-1753) bought the garden and much of the surrounding land around it, leasing a four-acre section in perpetuity to the Society of Apothecaries, provided it was maintained as a "manifestation of the glory, power and wisdom of God, in the works of creation". The gardens saw the first cedar trees to be grown in England, hold the country's largest outdoor olive tree and feature a rock garden fashioned with remnants from the Tower and lava from Iceland. The gardens remain one of the city's less demonstrative riverside treasures.

"The Chelsea Pensioner with his scarlet gabardine, flaming along the ways like a travelling fire, is a figure so peculiar to this neighbourhood that one scarcely sees it anywhere else," observed *The*

Royal River's authors in 1885, and it remains the case today of the 350 or so recipients of army pensions for whom the Royal Hospital provides accommodation, meals, healthcare and a rare chance to live in a building designed by Sir Christopher Wren. On the site of a failed theological college, Wren raised a redbrick neo-classical structure suggesting military precision: colonnaded wings line the central of three quadrangles beyond which Doric columns support a porticoed main entrance. Essayist Thomas Carlyle declared the hospital "quiet and dignified and the work of a gentleman".

The idea of a hospital for army veterans was probably inspired by Charles II's visit to the French equivalent in Paris, though a popular tale has a wounded soldier approaching Nell Gwynn for help and the king's mistress being so moved that she persuaded the king to act accordingly. In the form of statue by Grinling Gibbons (the prominent wood carver of the era; see p.183), Charles stands in the main quadrangle, each May receiving garlands of oak in commemoration of his escape from the 1651 Battle of Worcester by hiding in an oak tree, ensuring the survival of the monarchy. Pensioners are usually keen to show visitors around and a few may be willing to discuss the controversy over plans for a £20 million infirmary that may change the character of the hospital. A few more may remember, or claim to, the 1852 lying in state here of the Duke of Wellington, an event which drew so many mourners that two died in the crush.

Ranelagh Gardens

"You can't set your foot (down) without treading on a Prince or Duke of Cumberland," wrote Horace Walpole of Ranelagh Gardens, an upper-crust pleasure garden adjacent to the hospital that opened in 1742. The half-crown admission fee (five shillings on firework nights) included tea or coffee and entry to the 150-feet interior diameter rotunda, inside which the live music once included an eight-year-old Mozart playing the harpsichord.

Described by Walter Besant as "large enough to roast half a score of people at once", a central fireplace provided heat and 28 chandeliers provided light, while in alcoves around the outer wall tea was served to elegant ladies as the men could take sanctuary in a box "for gentleman to smoak in." Mostly, however, the chief pastime within the rotunda was to "walk around and stare at each other" or, as the poet Robert Bloomfield suggests at the end of each verse in "A Visit to Ranelagh" (1802): "We had seen every soul that was in it. Then we went around and saw them again."

Aside from the rotunda, the gardens offered a Chinese Pavilion, a canal with gondolas, balloon ascents and masked balls that sometimes attracted several thousand revellers. The central character in Fanny Burney's 1778 debutante-coming-out novel, *Evelina*, says of Ranelagh: "It is a charming place; and the brilliancy of the lights, on my first entrance, made me almost think I was in some enchanted castle or fairy palace, for all looked like magic to me." It was less enchanting for at least one Frenchman though, who found "the most insipid place of amusement you could imagine." Ranelagh fell from fashion surprisingly swiftly, closing in 1804 with the rotunda demolished the following year.

Pimlico

Squashed between Chelsea and Westminster, Pimlico has little of its neighbours' history or prestige, and even a local charity teaching children to canoe and kayak on the Thames calls itself the Westminster Boating Base. The discovery of buried French treasure once led locals to declare independence from British rule, though this was a fictional plot in the amiable 1949 Ealing film comedy, *Passport to Pimlico*. For today's non-fictional residents, Pimlico's Victorian streets provide a quiet refuge close to the capital's political heart. The riverside is lined by the traffic-laden Grosvenor Road, but the pocket-sized Pimlico Gardens offers a chance to view the Thames and a statue of a toga-wearing William Huskisson. Though a prominent politician and statesman, Huskisson (1770-1830) became better remembered for the manner of his death than the achievements of his life: when struck by Stephenson's *Rocket* in 1830, he became the first railway accident fatality.

Millbank and Tate Britain

Between 1821 and 1903, the north side of the Thames on the approach to Westminster was dominated by the castle-like Millbank Prison, which grew from the ideas of Jeremy Bentham (1748-1830). Founder of the influential political and moral philosophy of utilitarianism, often simplistically defined as the concept of "the greatest good for the greatest number", Bentham planned the "Panopticon" as a penitentiary constructed on a radial plan around a central tower with the intention that all prisoners could be watched at all times by a small number of unseen guards. In 1975 the French philosopher Michel Foucault wrote of the Panopticon aiming "to induce in the inmate a state of conscious and permanent visibility that assures the automatic functioning of power. So to arrange things that the surveillance is permanent in its effects, even if it is discontinuous in its action; that the perfection of power should tend to render its actual exercise unnecessary; that this architectural apparatus should be a machine for creating and sustaining a power relation independent of the person who exercises it; in short, that the inmates should be caught up in a power situation of which they are themselves the bearers."

Unsurprisingly, occupants of the prison, up to 860 of them often awaiting transportation to Australia, saw things in more earthy ways. In *The Wilds of London* (1874), James Greenwood described it: "The horrible gloom of the place made it so terrible. The victuals was neither bad nor scanty. At breakfast you got a pint of cocoa and what I should think was fully three-quarters of a pound of bread; at dinner a pint of soup, five ounces of meat, and a pound of potatoes; and at supper a pint of gruel and a slice of bread. The knife allowed at dinner was a tin knife and no fork. You can neither stab a warder with a tin knife nor use it as a pick-lock, though it is quite sharp enough to sever the meat, boiled to rags as it is at Millbank."

The prison "gave way to a curious agglomeration of art gallery, military barracks, and workmen's dwellings," according to Alfred T. Camden Pratt in *Unknown London* (1896). The gallery was the National Gallery of British Art, known subsequently as the Tate Gallery and, since the creation of Tate Modern (see p.151), as Tate Britain. With a cornucopia of neo-classicisms used by architect Sydney Scott that generate an air of solemnity, the building resembles a gigantic mausoleum, albeit one boasting an image of Britannia on its roof hailing passing river traffic. Opened in 1897, the gallery resulted from a controversy over the lack of space given to British artists at the National Gallery. The pioneer of the sugar cube, Henry Tate (1819-99), financed the building and donated his own collection of British paintings to provide the core of the early displays. The opening of Tate Modern allowed the Tate Britain to re-order its galleries and begin displaying some of the finest British art of the last 500 years, including what the 1995 *Lonely Planet* guide to Britain called "stuffy Victorian work featuring endless paintings of thoroughbred race horses."

Where the style of the Tate exemplified the taste of Edwardian England, the 1963 unveiling of the 387-foot-tall Millbank Tower brought London into the age of the glass-and-steel skyscraper. From 1997, when two floors were rented by the Labour Party and provided the base for their successful election campaign, the term "Millbank" entered the political lexicon as a synonym for media manipulation or "spin". The term endured, even though Labour, faced with rising rent, moved elsewhere in 2001.

On Millbank just prior to Lambeth Bridge stand the three stone blocks forming Frank Baines' Thames House, completed in 1931 for chemical giants ICI, which, suggested Eric de Maré, "wreck the riverside scene here with their overbearing, insensitive, false and sterile pomposity." Since 1995 Thames House has been home to MI5, the section of the British secret security service focused on domestic subversion. "For the river front, these blocks are fatal," observed Pevsner, very nearly presciently as a (non-fatal) machete attack occurred at the building's entrance during September 2004.

The Western Edge South: Putney to Vauxhall

The Putney debates could be said to have shaped England's future in the troubled seventeenth century, but its present, like much of this section of the south bank, is being shaped by on-going debates between local authorities and developers that so far have re-arranged the riverside in styles ranging from the bland to the inspired. Wandsworth experienced early industrialization thanks to its position on the Wandle River and a pre-steam-age railway; it also witnessed a recent example of community action with a mass trespass and occupation of an abandoned Thameside site as arguments raged over its future use. A section of the Thames at Battersea is framed by a major park and another marked by the four chimneys of its former power station: one of the bigger symbols of long-running indecision over the future use of London's riverside landmarks.

Due largely to the protests of watermen fearing the loss of their ferry trade, the 1729 Fulham-Putney bridge became only the first new crossing to serve the city since London Bridge five hundred years before. Though opened in the age of ferries, the bridge survived into the age of railways when it was superseded by a Bazalgette-designed crossing in 1886. It was from the wooden bridge that proto-feminist writer Mary Wollstonecraft (1759-97), author of *A Vindication of the Rights of Woman* (1792) attempted suicide in 1795 by jumping into the river. The attempt, ironically perhaps induced by her mistreatment by a man, failed and Wollstonecraft later married political thinker William Godwin, with him producing two daughters. The second daughter became better known as Mary Shelley, wife of the poet, author of *Frankenstein* and one-time Thamesside resident.

Described by Charles Dickens Jr. as "a considerable suburb grafted onto an old-fashioned high street and water frontage," Putney's High Street may have lost its allure but the water frontage west of the bridge, the Embankment, still pleases the river enthusiast with its boathouses and rowers, as well as by being the start-point for the annual Oxford-Cambridge University Boat Race.

Immediately east of Putney Bridge, St. Mary's Church provided a venue for the 1647 Putney debates, what historian Francis Sheppard called "an indelible landmark in the history of English radical thought." During 1647 Oliver Cromwell, the Puritan parliamentarian who, with the New Model Army, had defeated Charles I and now favoured a negotiated settlement with the monarch, discussed here the political future of the country with the Levellers (a name by which the group became known, but not one they themselves used). The Levellers' demands, including religious toleration, a written constitution and a major extension of suffrage, were effectively defeated when news was received of the king's escape from prison but the group came to be recognized as the country's first organized political movement, and their demands inspired later ideas of liberal democracy. Largely rebuilt following a 1970s fire, little denotes the church's historic role save for a plaque placed here in the 1980s by the Cromwell Association. The church does at least remain amid a riverside Putney steadily consumed by chic restaurants, bars and expensive waterfront apartment blocks.

Wandsworth Park and the River Wandle Delta

The twenty-acre Wandsworth Park was among the first green spaces created by the London County Council as it endeavoured to use its new regulatory powers to temper the bleakness of industrial London. On the site of a riverside brewery and ironworks, the park opened in 1903 following a night of rain, described by the *Daily News*: "Overnight Nature had washed the park with copious tears, and the scene was everywhere painted in vivid colours. Fluttering pennons waved a welcome to the brilliantly-striped marquee, where the speeches were all in terms of appreciative congratulation."

Locals had reason to be appreciative. Riverside Wandsworth in the 1850s comprised, according to Mr. and Mrs. S. C. Hall, "unwholesome looking swamps (that) divide the place the place with yards and quays, and waggon-sheds, auxiliaries to manufacture of gin, soap, starch, silk, paper, candles, beer and vitriol—the first named and the last no doubt being mutually dependent for aid and assistance." Such scenes were the legacy of an industrial heritage stretching back surprisingly far and developing around the River Wandle, powerful enough to drive sixty watermills by 1800. Huguenot refugees had much earlier developed silk dying and hat-making on either side of the Wandle, while the Surrey Iron Railway, opened in 1803, used wagons pulled by horses along a wooden track towards Wandsworth docks. The meeting of the Wandle and the Thames provided a natural transit point for industrial products and also supported the densest concentration of coal and coke companies outside north-east England.

With all the grace one would expect, a waste recycling centre now dominates the Thames at Wandsworth, but the River Wandle Trail offers a route around the unspectacular though enticingly-named River Wandle Delta, while the resumption of river access close to Wandsworth Bridge offers a view of manicured streets and new homes. A Holiday Inn adds to a sense of creeping corporate advance, as does the recent history of Gargoyle Wharf, which briefly became Wandsworth Eco Village (a.k.a. Pure Genius) when the derelict thirteen-acre site owned by brewery giants Guinness was occupied in 1996 by environmental activists. Of the site, re-named Battersea Reach, the *Daily Telegraph* in May 2002 reported the property-developing Berkeley Group's "latest foray into luxury riverside developments with the purchase of 13 acres of highly contaminated land on the banks of the Thames in Wandsworth."

Battersea

*Battersea is so far off, the roads so execrable, and the rain so incessant,
I cannot bear to take my cab over Battersea Bridge, as it seems so
absurd to pay eightpence for the sake of the half-mile on this side, but
that half-mile is one continued slough, as there not a yard of flagging,
I believe, in all Battersea.*

Matthew Arnold, letter to his wife, 1852

The image of Battersea as a distant and treacherous place, separated from fashionable Chelsea by a bridge and a wider social divide, is not uncommon even today. Occupying the riverside stretch between Wandsworth and Vauxhall, the district is typically seen as neither desirable nor interesting, with the exception of the green beacon of Battersea Park and the iconic chimneys of Battersea Power Station. Norman Shrapnel, however, struck a insightful note when he wrote of Battersea Church Street and its Church of St. Mary's as "projecting a river side atmosphere—or the ghost of one—as strong as any I found along the Thames: a village air sinuous and organic, seeming to echo the river they skirted."

Set beside an oak-studded lawn and overlooking the river, the church, like Battersea, retains its particular character in defiance of the city grown up around it. For the 1770s rebuilding of the Saxon-rooted church, local architect Joseph Dixon evoked a Dutch style—influenced perhaps by the Dutch gables of the Raven, the nearby public house where he honed his ideas—with a white-trimmed brown brick body fronted by a Doric-columned entrance and topped by a spire rising from a stunted tower. Inside, modern stained glass windows commemorate poet, painter and mystic, William Blake, who married Catherine Boucher here in 1787, and artist J. M. W. Turner, who sketched the scene from a tall chair behind the vestry's bay window. Architect Dixon was interred by a grateful vestry in the crypt "at no charge". Admirers of 1960s British cinema will remember the church for its appearance alongside Michael Caine in Lewis Gilbert's *Alfie*.

The church's place as the dominant feature of riverside Battersea has progressively been challenged by the Battersea Flour Mill on its east side, the 1960s high-rise, low-rent apartment blocks to the south and in 1999 by Montevetro, a spectacular expanse of laminated glass rising immediately behind it, offering 103 riverview apartments. Architect Richard Rogers said: "I'd like to see this project not just as a very special place for a very fortunate minority but as a model for what city housing of the future could be." Despite these words, Montevetro does stand as a special place for a fortunate minority of sufficient means (penthouses go for around £4.5 million) more likely to arrive at the nearby London Heliport than the equally near Clapham Junction railway station; for all its aesthetic prowess, the structure shows little sympathy for the location's human geography.

Much the same applies to the curvilinear Albion Riverside between Battersea and Albert bridges, another episode in the changing form of riverside London from the firm of another prominent British architect, Norman Foster. Considering the Thames' new architecture and mindful of the competitiveness between its creators, critic Adrian Searle suggested that Albion Riverside represented "architecture as novelty prize marrow".

Oddly enough, prize marrows could have been a feature of an earlier Battersea, where fertile soils earned a reputation for market gardening, including the only asparagus grown in Britain and sold as a "Battersea bundle". In *Alton Locke* (1850), Charles Kingsley sought to examine the mindsets of local agricultural labourers: "I knew every leaf and flower in the little front garden; every cabbage and rhubarb plant in Battersea fields was wonderful and beautiful to me. Clouds and water I learned to delight in, from my occasional lingerings on Battersea bridge, and yearning westward looks toward the sun setting above rich meadows and wooded gardens, to me a forbidden El Dorado."

The opening of the London–Southampton Railway in 1838, its northern terminus at Nine Elms where arriving passengers would continue on the river to the city, turned Battersea's cultivated plots into sidings, workshops and depots and helped attract an expanding population of industrial workers to Battersea. An extended franchise and the growing power of organized labour helped to make political radicalism a Battersea speciality. Prominent left-winger, John Burns (1858-1943) emerged here and became the first member of the working class to occupy cabinet office; elected mayor of Battersea in 1913, John Archer (1864-1932) was the first person of African descent voted into civic office in Britain; and for five years from 1922, Shapurji Saklatvala

(1874-1936) represented Battersea North in parliament while a member of the Communist Party.

The most obvious legacy of industrial Battersea are the four chimneys rising 337 feet from Giles Gilbert Scott's 1937 Battersea Power Station. Fuelled by coal arriving on the river, the power station was intended to generate as much electricity as London's nine extant power stations combined. At its 1950s peak, the station annually consumed a million tons of coal and daily drew 340 million gallons of water from the Thames. The chimneys issued their last plume in 1983, the building becoming an empty and steadily eroding shell as a long list of failed new ventures were mooted for the 38-acre site. One which seems destined to be fulfilled is that promising, unsurprisingly, an "entertainment, leisure and retail development", including a 2,000-seat theatre and two hotels.

Battersea Fields and Battersea Park

> *In 1750, the picturesque villages of Wandsworth and Battersea were connected by a lonely road between fields, and adjoining the Thames, known as 'Pickpocket Lane', a name it well merited.*
> Sir Hugh Phillips, *The Thames About 1750*, 1951

The edge of the pre-embankment Thames between the present Queenstown and Albert bridges formed Battersea Fields, for many decades sufficiently distanced from London proper for unlawful activities to take place with near-impunity as well holding the notorious Pickpocket Lane. High-profile incidents included the illegal 1829 duel between the Duke of Wellington and the Earl of Winchilsea over Catholic emancipation (both men deliberately fired their pistol shots wide), while a notorious tavern, the Red House, provided refreshment to visitors in search of more mundane pursuits such as horse and donkey racing, bare-knuckle boxing and Sunday afternoon fairs that provided "the occasion for disgraces of all kinds". Among occasional curiosities was the attempt, reported by *The Times* in 1838, by "Harris, the pedestrian" to walk 1,750 miles around the fields in 1,000 hours, powered by a diet of "rump steaks or roast beef, with bread and coffee."

Religious campaigning, a Royal Commission and 750,000 tons of soil from the building of Surrey Docks (see p.180-1), contributed to the transformation of Battersea Fields into Battersea Park, which Charles Dickens Jr. called "One of the youngest of London parks and certainly one of the prettiest... emphatically one of the sights which no visitor should fail to see." The 198-acre park gained an aristocratic infusion in the mid-1890s when proponents of the new cycling craze were banned from Hyde Park. In *The Queen's London: a Pictorial and Descriptive Record of the Streets, Buildings, Parks and Scenery of the Great Metropolis* (1896) it was recorded: "Someone discovered that the roads in Battersea Park were excellent and before long the cycling parade there became quite one of the sights of the 1895 season... Scores of ladies and gentlemen belonging to the upper classes could be counted on any fine morning cycling at Battersea."

In 1951 as part of the Festival of Britain, the park gained a funfair that stayed in place until 1975, educating several generations of impoverished London schoolchildren in the delights of roller-coasters and water-chutes. Along with an adventure playground, a subtropical garden, endless pathways, cycle routes and assorted statuary, the park displays a riverside Peace Pagoda, a gift in 1985 from a Japanese Buddhist order. Also in 1985, a secluded quarter of the a park took possession of the Brown Dog Memorial, a reference to a memorial originally placed above a Battersea street drinking fountain to a mongrel dog "done to Death in the Laboratories of University College... Also in Memory of the 232 dogs Vivisected at the same place during 1902." Commissioned by anti-vivisectionists, the original memorial ignited rioting and required round-the-clock police protection until its clandestine removal in 1910.

Vauxhall

Like its rival, Ranelagh, Vauxhall Gardens provided a source of relaxation, entertainment and an opportunity for the great and good to be seen by others great and good. The gardens began as New Spring Gardens in 1660 when its visitors included Samuel Pepys, who wrote: "to hear the nightingales and other birds, and here fiddles and there's a harp, and here a jews trump, and here laughing and there fine people walking, is mighty divertising."

The gardens became even more divertising following the introduction of walkways dotted with triumphal arches and intentional ruins, the opening of Chinese and Turkish pavilions and the staging of concerts. James Boswell noted that the gardens were "particularly adapted to the taste of the English nation; there being a mixture of the curious show,—gay exhibition, musick, vocal and instrumental, not too refined for the general ear." During 1749 the music included Handel's *Music for the Royal Fireworks*, a rehearsal for which drew 12,000 people and caused London Bridge to be blocked for three hours. A shilling admission fee was introduced to deter the lower orders, while those seeking carnal pleasures in the darker sections were warned by notices banning "all known whores". Even notorious womanizer Casanova was thwarted after he "offered (a woman) two guineas if she would take a walk with me in a dark alley"; the woman grabbed the money and fled.

Fanny Burney wrote of Vauxhall Gardens in *Evelina*: "The trees, the numerous lights, and the company in the circle round the orchestra make a most brilliant and gay appearance; and had I been with a party less disagreeable to me, I should have thought it a place formed for animation and pleasure. There was a concert; in the course of which a hautbois concerto was so charmingly played, that I could have thought myself upon enchanted ground, had I had spirits more gentle to associate with. The hautbois in the open air is heavenly." Henry Fielding, meanwhile, was simply lost for words, writing in *Amelia* (1751): "The extreme beauty and elegance of this place is well known to almost every one of my readers; and happy is it for me that it is so, since to give an adequate idea of it would exceed my power of description."

The gardens' later years included a fancy dress celebration attended by 61,000 people; a thousand soldiers re-enacting the Battle of Waterloo; and a parachuting balloonist falling to his death. In 1840 the owners declared themselves bankrupt and the gardens closed, only to open for a series of well-attended farewells during 1859. Today's only hint of the gardens' glories is the small Spring Park, behind Vauxhall Cross.

The site of Vauxhall Gardens and the name of the traffic junction adjacent to Vauxhall Bridge were both usurped during the 1990s by MI6, a supposedly secret branch of British military intelligence dealing with foreign affairs, which constructed a twentieth-century medieval fortress and named it Vauxhall Cross. Rising by the river in strange shades of honey and green, the building evokes the mood suggested by Samantha Hardingham: "Three main blocks… step back from low-rise

bunkers at garden level rising in cold symmetry to a bow window... crowned with menacing concrete spikes."

London's River: the Hub of Power

Between Westminster and Lambeth, two miles of the Thames form what was officially named The King's Reach in 1935, commemorating 25 years of George V's reign. The regal title also suggests the river's place in what has been the centre of religious and political power in Britain since, a thousand years ago, Edward the Confessor turned an island by the Thames into a plot of spiritual and latterly secular authority, establishing a royal seat and what became Westminster Abbey outside the then boundaries of London. Westminster drew the rich and powerful, and those who sought to be rich and powerful, gaining an importance underlined in Tudor times by Henry VIII's gargantuan Whitehall Palace and in the modern day by its continuing role at the heart of national governance and administration. Crossings of the King's Reach have included one of London's few horse ferries and Waterloo Bridge, upon which and to which poet Wordsworth wrote an ode that few chroniclers can resist repeating, rarely though do they add the caveat that the poet was on his way to France and even the wonders of Westminster failed to delay him.

The Hub of Power North: Westminster and Whitehall

The Westminster next the great Tames doth entertaine;
That vaunts her Palace large, and her most sumptuous Fane:
The Land's tribunall seate that challengeth for hers,
The crowning of our Kings, their famous sepulchers.
Michael Drayton, Poly-Olbion, 1612-22

What became Westminster was Thorney Island, washed by the Tyburn River and the high tides of the Thames when around 1040 Edward the Confessor, penultimate Saxon King of England, moved his royal residence near St. Paul's (the "East Minster") for a new one at the island's monastery which he expanded and which evolved into Westminster Abbey. Edward founded the abbey and built a palace but failed to sire a son, triggering a succession crisis and ultimately the Norman conquest of England. The abbey was rebuilt under successive monarchs between 1245 and 1517 and gained its distinctive towers, designed by Sir Christopher Wren and Nicholas Hawksmoor, from 1722 to 1745. While the site's early religious history is obscured by its twelfth-century incarnation as what Stephen Inwood calls "a factory of lies and forged charters", Edward had established the link between abbey and royalty (every coronation since Edward's successor, Harold, in 1066 has taken place inside), giving England a new seat of political power separate from its seat of commerce, the City of London around St. Paul's. For four hundred years, the Palace of Westminster served as the royal seat and, according to Christopher Hibbert in *London: the Biography of a City*, "was soon a splendid edifice with noble stone walls, painted chambers and rows of offices, kitchens and cellars along the waterfront." Gutted by fire in 1512, the palace retained administrative importance (and gave its name to the present-day Houses of Parliament) as the royal seat became the sprawling Whitehall Palace.

Whitehall Palace

Raised following Henry VIII's acquisition of Cardinal Wolsey's land in 1530, Whitehall Palace covered 23 acres and lined two miles of the Thames. It held two thousand rooms, including the royal apartments overlooking the river, gardens, orchards, tennis courts and areas for jousting tournaments, cock fighting and bear-baiting. For Thomas Macaulay, the palace "naturally became the chief staple of news. Whenever there was a rumour that anything important had happened or was about to happen, people hastened thither to obtain intelligence from the fountain head. The galleries presented the appearance of a modern club room at an anxious time. They were full of people enquiring whether the Dutch mail was in, what tidings the express from France had brought, whether John Sobiesky had beaten the Turks, whether the Doge of Genoa was really at Paris." While it may have set the news agenda, Whitehall was an architectural jumble dismissed by one foreign visitor as "ill built, and nothing but a heap of houses erected at divers times and of different models." Only the gatehouses and two other buildings stood out: the Great Hall and Inigo Jones' daring and stupendous Italianate 1622 Banqueting House.

It was from a Banqueting House window that Charles I stepped to his beheading in 1649, and it was from Whitehall's royal bedchamber that James II sought to flee the Glorious Revolution in 1688, disguising himself as a commoner in the early hours of a December morning and making off by boat across the Thames, into which he flung the Royal Seal. Installed as James' successor, the Protestant William of Orange regarded the Thames air as aggravating his asthma and moved the royal seat to Kensington. Whitehall was almost completely destroyed by fire in 1690, with the Banqueting House the sole surviving building, and perhaps the most deserving.

The palace may be long gone but "Whitehall" is synonymous with the nation's administration, being the main base of various government ministries and of the civil service. Similarly, "Westminster" has become a generic term for the daily doings of parliament, today's Palace of Westminster holding the House of Commons and the House of Lords, known collectively as the Houses of Parliament. Whitehall Palace's cock-fighting plot, meanwhile, may well now be the site of 10 Downing Street, official home of the Prime Minister.

The Houses of Parliament

Visiting in disguise (women were then barred), French radical Flora Tristan wrote of the Houses of Parliament in 1831: "In appearance nothing could be meaner or more commonplace; it puts one in mind of a shop. It is rectangular in shape, small and very cramped; the ceiling is low, the galleries above overhang and partly hide the aisles beneath; the wooden benches are stained a walnut-brown colour. The chamber has no outstanding feature, nothing to show it has a lofty function to fulfill. It could just as well serve as a village chapel or house an assembly of grocers... its architecture and furnishings have no dignity whatsoever."

The current situation could hardly be more different. The richly neo-Gothic Houses of Parliament seen across the Thames and framed by the Victoria Tower at one end and Big Ben at the other, have become *the* iconic image of both London and England. That it should be so was due to a fire in 1834 that gutted almost all the old buildings. Among those who gathered amid general merriment to watch the blaze—some in the streets, some in boats, some knee deep in the river for a better view—was the artist J. M. W. Turner, who created two vivid canvases of the scene; another was an architect called Charles Barry.

Sixteen months later, Barry (1795-1860) won the competition to design the new Houses of Parliament. Barry's penchant was for Italian architecture, but a Gothic style was dictated by parliament and by prevailing tastes, for it was seen as originating in England with its religious usage suggesting a Christian form of architecture, symbolizing order and stability in a time of social, economic and political change. Stability may have been the goal but the Houses were built, as suggested by the Duke of Wellington, alongside the river to ensure that no a mob could ever completely surround them. To apply medieval religious detail to a citadel of secular power, Barry called upon the 23-year-old Augustus Pugin (1812-52), a "zealous and excitable young medievalist". Pugin oversaw every detail of the building, whether stained glass, wallpaper, carpets, coat hangers or inkwells. The Lords' chamber was completed in 1847; the Commons five years later; the Victoria Tower, then the world's tallest secular building, was finished in 1860—also the year of Barry's death. Pugin, too, would not live to see the building's completion, dying at the age of forty partly through mental illness brought on by overwork.

In *Jottings about London* (1883), Italian writer Edmundo de Amicis

(1846-1908) admired the new-look Westminster from both sides of the river: "I entered the great street called Whitehall, and came out on Parliament Square, and thence directed my steps to Westminster Bridge. The view enjoyed thence is the most beautiful in London and is worth all the views from the bridges of the Seine. On one hand you see the delicate Gothic Parliament buildings, crowned with numberless turrets, and decorated with thousands of statues of kings and queens, beyond which rise the towers of glorious Westminster Abbey, the Pantheon of England; and on the other bank, the eight graceful buildings belonging to St. Thomas's."

Since de Amicis' time, opinions of the Houses have spanned all extremes. Pevsner thought the whole complex "the most imaginatively planned and the most excellently executed major secular building of the Gothic Revival anywhere in the world." By contrast, J. G. Ballard wrote in the *Guardian*: "I dislike the Palace of Westminster more than any other architectural atrocity in London. This huge fake Gothic pile is an enormous fantasy of self-delusion, which encourages our rulers into vast flights of self-importance." The Sex Pistols, meanwhile, doyens of 1970s punk rock, marked the Queen's 1977 silver jubilee by cruising along the river on a chartered Thames pleasure boat (the *Queen Elizabeth*) and treating the Houses to a rendition of *Anarchy in the UK* before returning to Charing Cross Pier where members of their entourage were arrested on dubious charges by waiting police.

Big Ben and Victoria Tower Garden

The clock tower of the Houses of Parliament, completed in 1858 and rising 316 feet (even though it looks strangely shorter), is better known as Big Ben, though this name applied originally to the hour bell inside the tower. The clock is accurate to within one second per day, while its chimes signalling New Year were first broadcast on 31 December 1923 and are now pre-recorded—a means to avoid a repeat of 1962 when snow on the hands made the New Year arrive ten minutes late. The tower made its cinematic debut in Will Hay's 1943 slapstick comedy *My Learned Friend* and appeared in the 1978 version of *The Thirty-Nine Steps* (despite many reports to the contrary, it does not feature in John Buchan's novel) while the Pugin-designed clock face endured the indignity of being clambered upon by Jackie Chan in *Shanghai Knights* (2003).

Stressed electors feeling over-exposed to the antics of politicians might note the Jewel Tower, a rare survivor of the original Palace of Westminster across Old Palace Yard, on the way to seeking sanctuary in Victoria Tower Gardens, between the Houses of Parliament and Lambeth Bridge. In the gardens, sculptures appear aplenty: Rodin's *The Burghers of Calais*, Henry Moore's *Knife Edge*, the *Buxton Drinking Fountain* marking the 1834 abolition of British Empire slavery, and A. G. Walker's 1928 statue of Emmeline Pankhurst. On the river, meanwhile, visitors with sufficiently long necks might look east and consider what Pevsner described as "the tense, elegant, shallow curve of the first arch of Westminster Bridge".

Westminster Bridge

Earth has not anything to show more fair!
The beauty of the morning; silent, bare,
Dull would he be of soul who could pass by
Ships, towers, domes, theatres, and temples lie
A sight so touching in its majesty;
Open unto the fields, and to the sky,
This City now doth like a garment wear
All bright and glittering in the smokeless air.
Never did sun more beautifully steep
In his first splendour, valley, rock, or hill;
Ne'er saw I, never felt, a calm so deep!
The river glideth at his own sweet will:
Dear God! the very houses seem asleep;
And all that mighty heart is lying still.

William Wordsworth, "Upon Westminster Bridge", 1803

Anyone seeking to heighten their enjoyment of Wordsworth's eulogy for the London skyline by standing in his footsteps will not only find London to be barely recognizable but also the bridge itself to be entirely different from that known to the poet (who composed the ode from the roof of a carriage on his way to France). The present crossing was completed in 1862 and formally opened with a blast of canon fire at 3.45am to mark Queen Victoria's birth precisely 43 years earlier. Its style, intended to complement the new Houses of Parliament, won few admirers: "Westminster Bridge varies very much in appearance with the state of the tide. It is always a rather cardboardy affair," wrote Charles Dickens Jr. in 1893.

With compensation paid to watermen and the Archbishop of Canterbury who owned the Lambeth horse ferry (see below), the bridge of Wordsworth's day had opened in 1750 "with a grand procession of gentleman and the chief artificers of the work, preceded by trumpets and kettledrums." Dogs were not permitted and anyone defacing the structure faced "death without benefit of clergy". The bridge had 15 arches with a semi-circular recess between each pier. In 1763 diarist James Boswell acquired a prostitute and consummated the relationship inside one such recess, recalling "the whim of doing it there with the Thames rolling beneath us amused me much."

The Hub of Power South: Lambeth Palace to County Hall

... then at noon with Mr. Wren to Lambeth, to dinner with the Archbishop of Canterbury; the first time I was ever there and I have long longed for it; where a noble house, and well furnished with good pictures and furniture...

Samuel Pepys, diary entry, 14 May 1669

As Westminster began cementing its grip on national life, the south bank was little more than marshy fields and fishing settlements. Proximity to political power became irresistible to the Church, however, and Lambeth Palace was built to accommodate successive Archbishops of Canterbury. Both Lambeth and London were considerably more developed by the 1930s when County Hall became the purpose-built and much admired seat of the city's administration. Fifty years later, the building remained but London's elected assembly had been dissolved and, like much of the riverside, County Hall strived to find a role commensurate with its stature. By contrast to the area's long traditions, the current focus of visitor attention is neither parliament nor prayer but stupendous views across London from the towering wheel called the London Eye.

While the Houses of Parliament on the north bank of the river represent political power in today's Britain, a complex of buildings on the south side enjoyed a similarly powerful role for much longer: Lambeth Palace, the seat of the Archbishops of Canterbury since the twelfth century. Hemmed in by modern buildings and encircled by congested roads, it is tempting to view the palace as a calm oasis of spiritual refuge. In fact, it was at the heart of some of the bloodiest and most contentious episodes in English history. The chancery records held in the palace library were among the targets of the fourteenth-century Peasants' Revolt; it was set ablaze and the then Archbishop Simon Sudbury was pursued to the Tower and killed. In 1640 the palace was attacked by London Apprentices seeking Archbishop Laud, as it was in 1780 by Gordon rioters. Religious reformer John Wycliffe was tried for heresy here in 1378; Thomas More (see p,102-3) was interrogated in the guardroom in 1535; and Friar Peto was imprisoned in the gatehouse for his sermon attacking the marriage of Henry VIII and Anne Boleyn.

The 1490s gatehouse remains the palace's most striking feature and it was from here that the palace dispensed food to the neighbourhood needy until 1842. Later in the nineteenth century, bishops allowed local children to play in the palace grounds and in 1901 turned a twenty-acre section into a public park, the Archbishops Garden—a suitable spot to contemplate Pevsner's comment that Lambeth Palace formed "a complex of domestic buildings largely medieval and wholly picturesque, which is of such interest and merit that (Londoners) would flock to see it if only it were not so near their homes."

With only London Bridge and several thousand watermen providing passage across the Thames east of Putney before the opening of Westminster Bridge, transit for horses and any cargo they might have been carrying was limited to the horse ferry between Lambeth Palace and Millbank, owned by the Archbishop of Canterbury. Despite being able to carry six horses and a coach, the ferry sank regularly, doing so under the weight of Archbishop Laud's possessions in 1633 and again, perhaps to demonstrate neutrality in England's political crisis, when transporting Oliver Cromwell during 1656.

St. Thomas' Nightingales

On the opposite side of the Thames, the Embankment is continued on the Surrey shore up the river, as far as Vauxhall Bridge, giving a

Parisian aspect to the whole scene. 'But what are these?' a stranger is sure to ask, as he points to a number of new buildings, extending from the Surrey end of Westminster Bridge for several hundred yards along the Embankment, and directly facing the Houses of Parliament. These buildings, I reply, are the new St. Thomas's Hospital; and here one of the oldest medical charities of London, after having been dislodged from its ancient residence near London Bridge, has found a new and costly home.

Uncle Jonathan, *Walks In and Around London*, 1895

A feature of the new Albert Embankment, St. Thomas' costly home opened in 1871 and was London's first "pavilion"-style hospital. Its architect was Henry Currey but its form was inspired by Florence Nightingale's concept of modern nursing. Nightingale established her School of Nursing at St. Thomas' and transformed the image of nurses: those of St. Thomas' became known as Nightingales. The buildings that so excited Uncle Jonathan have since been replaced by ungainly blocks and do even less than their Victorian predecessors to suggest St. Thomas' 800-year history, originating with Augustinian monks on the site of what is now London Bridge station.

An Eye on London: County Hall

On the east side of the approach to Westminster Bridge stands architect Ralph Knott's "freeform Edwardian" monument to the body that nurtured modern London: County Hall, which from 1922 to 1986 was the seat of the London County Council and subsequently the Greater London Council. The site had previous been, according to Weinreb and Hibbert, "a clutter of wharves, timber yards, and factories which formed an ugly eyesore." On County Hall's opening, a *Times* leader eulogized: "It stands proudly on the riverbank, for all the world to see, a splendid monument of municipal enterprise and municipal purpose... It should stimulate and fire the civil consciousness of all the inhabitants of London."

In May 1983, the election manifesto of Margaret Thatcher's Conservative Party put things rather differently, promising tersely: "We shall abolish the Greater London Council." As a result, from April Fool's Day 1986, London ceased to have elected city-wide government and power theoretically devolved to local boroughs, but in practice became concentrated in central government. The final days of the GLC were marked by festivities and GLC supporters wearing badges stating "We'll be back." The BBC reported on 31 March: "Thousands of people have taken part in festivities to mark the historic final hours of 97 years of local rule in London. A throng of 250,000 people have gathered on the South Bank in London, home to the Greater London Council, which will not exist from midnight tonight. Festivities will end with the largest display of fireworks ever seen in the city after a week of events costing £250,000."

The GLC's affairs passed into the hands of the London Residuary Body, its bleak title symbolizing London's fall in stature from city to commodity, and by the late 1990s the capital's former administrative headquarters had become a Japanese-owned leisure complex with such pleasures as the London Aquarium, a Marriott hotel and an exploitation of surrealism called DaliUniverse. When the Saatchi Gallery opened in 2003, however, County Hall gained a more meaningful role as a home for the art collection of advertising guru Charles Saatchi, best known for buying such epochal works as Damien Hirst's formaldehyde shark and Tracey Emin's unmade bed, though lost it again when Saatchi's dispute with the building's owner led to the gallery relocating in 2006.

Of London's democratic deficit, the GLC badge-wearers had the last laugh. In 2000 came the formation of the Greater London Assembly, its members elected to a new and no less eye-catching home on the Thames.

...and the London Eye
A welcome addition to London's river has been the London Eye (more blandly known as the Millennium Wheel), with 32 sealed passenger capsules, popularly called pods, attached to the outside of a giant wheel that rotates on a half-hour cycle giving passengers a 440-feet-high outlook across and beyond London. Conceived on a kitchen table in 1993 by the husband-and-wife architectural team of David Marks and Julia Bailey for a millennium landmark competition, the idea gained the backing of British Airways and though intended to be temporary, become a permanent addition to the south bank through popular demand. Intended to allow people to "see and understand one of the greatest cities on earth," a sharper contrast with the Millennium Dome (see p.192-3) would be hard to find.

The Eye's boost to the immediate locality brought fresh impetus to improve the adjacent Jubilee Gardens, which in June 2005 was destined to become "an organic, lush and green park with softly undulating hills" instead of the bland lawn created in 1977 to mark the Queen's silver jubilee. The gardens are overlooked by the graceless 1950s Shell Center, blocking the view of the river from Waterloo station and assessed by the *Blue Guide to London* as "a much disliked lump of Portland Stone with little windows".

Waterloo Bridge

Waterloo Bridge—the grandest bridge in London, and perhaps the world—admirably falls in with the architectural character of the Embankment and its surroundings. Nothing can exceed the magnificence of these nine broad arches, each one a hundred and twenty feet in span, and thirty-five feet high; or of the columned piers from which they spring. The whole effect is colossal yet graceful to the last degree of cultured power. Where the massive pillars meet the Embankment, they give an added grandeur to the work of Sir Joseph Bazalgette, and the triumphant arches, as they leap the channel of the river, display the happiest mixture of strength and suavity.

Edmund Ollier, *The Royal River*, 1885

Such praise was commonplace for the 1817 bridge designed by John Rennie, though its acclaimed appearance concealed a terrible truth. As Geoffrey Phillips points out in *Thames Crossings*, "No British bridge had been so praised as Waterloo. It had a patrician air, an elegance, derived in part from the perfection of its line and in part from the excellence of Rennie's masonry—the stepped extrados of the arches, the Grecian-Doric columns, cornice and balustrade. But it was only 27 feet wide and its foundations had been scoured away."

Wellington's victory over Napoleon in 1815 inspired a patriotic name change for what was originally to be called Strand Bridge, but this could do nothing to save the ailing bridge from demolition in 1936. The deprivations of the Second World War caused the construction of its replacement to be delayed until 1942, when the *Times* commented:

"The main effect of the new bridge is seen in its general lines and proportions, and not in any elaboration of detail—simplicity is one of the keynotes of the design."

The details, simple or otherwise, might well have been lost on Bulgarian dissident Georgi Markov who, while waiting for a bus on the bridge in 1978, was injected in the leg with a fatal pellet of the poison ricin from the tip of what the press gleefully called a "poisoned umbrella". The Bulgarian secret services were the suspected culprits but no arrests were made, though in 2005 the *Guardian* reported on the likely murderer being a Bulgarian agent who had travelled to London under the guise of being an antique dealer.

London's River: Commerce and Culture

Flowing east, the Thames leaves the thousand-year old Westminster for the two-thousand-year-old City of London, the self-governing enclave within the bigger city largely within the boundaries of the original Roman settlement. Just as the river made Londinium a trading centre, so it underpinned London's later rise into an international centre of commerce. The ancient quays at Queenhithe and Billingsgate had enabled London's trade to expand and spread around the globe; by the late nineteenth century, the engineering and architectural daring of the river's new embankments were commensurate with the city's place at the heart of the British empire. From 2000, the new Millennium Bridge linked the north bank's commerce to the south bank's culture, for decades restricted to the predominantly brutalist auditoria of the South Bank complex but now invigorated and expanded by a riverside strip crowned by the power station-turned-contemporary art showplace of Tate Modern.

Commerce and Culture North: Victoria Embankment to the Tower

For Michael Jenner, the Victoria Embankment's dolphin-entwined lamp-posts were "delightful signs of a highly confident urban culture". Certainly, the embankment and it accoutrements—from Boudica's statue to Cleopatra's Needle—forged a new relationship between London and the Thames, reclaiming 34 acres of foreshore and creating a thoroughfare of such grandeur to befit an imperial Britain while simultaneously solving the problem of moving the city's sewage. East of

Blackfriars Bridge, by contrast, the waterside suggests a much older London, holding the historic landing stages of Queenshithe and Billingsgate, the majestic Custom House, the emotive landmark of St. Paul's Cathedral and the no less emotive Tower of London, site of royal beheadings and repository of the crown jewels.

Announced by the triumphal chariot pose of Boudica (known on this 1902 bronze statue as Boadicea) about to waste Roman London and the Battle of Britain Memorial commemorating those who prevented Germany from doing something similar to 1940s London, the tree-lined Victoria Embankment between Westminster and Blackfriars bridges excited the imaginations of Victorian writers. *The Royal River* was typical in proclaiming "a magnificent work, containing the finest effects of architecture, mingled with trees and shrubbery that is to be found in the metropolis."

But an aspect less befitting an imperial city soon emerged and it was discovered by H. G. Wells on an evening stroll described in *New Worlds For Old* (1908): "Along the Embankment, you see there are iron seats at regular intervals, seats that you cannot lie on because the arm-rests prevent that and each seat, one saw by the lamplight, was filled with crouching and drooping figures... These were the homeless, and they had come to sleep here. I remember one particularly ghostly long white neck and white face that lopped backward, choked in some nightmare, awakened, clutched with a bony hand at the bony throat, and sat up and stared angrily as we passed... One crumpled figure coughed and went on coughing."

James Bone took a more arch view in *The London Perambulator* (1926), connecting the embankment to the city's most high-profile police station, the Scotland Yard headquarters of the Metropolitan Police: "a noble promenade from which the citizens could enjoy the beauties and humours of their river... but although bordered in parts by public gardens and adorned by statues, it always looks like it was really the avenue to Scotland Yard."

A Strand by the Thames

> *I send, I send here my supremst kiss*
> *To thee my silver-footed Thamasis.*

No more shall I reiterate thy Strand,
Whereon so many Stately Structures stand.
Robert Herwick, *His teares to Thamasis*, 1648

Connecting the power centres of St. Paul's and Westminster, the medieval Strand ran parallel to the river and became lined with bishops' palaces and homes of aristocrats seeking proximity to Court. Titles in residence included dukes of Norfolk, Suffolk and Buckingham, earls of Arundel, Essex, Northumberland and Salisbury, and the Marquesses of Dorset, Exeter and Worcester. Their gardens reached to the river where the Thames provided both a means of daily transport and an escape route should a rioting mob threaten. The Great Fire of 1666 put paid to the grand homes, and the pressing housing needs of late seventeenth-century London saw abodes of lesser stature rise in their place. Victorian embanking distanced the Strand, now known for its offices, shops and theatres, from the river, leaving only the names of streets, Arundel, Essex and Surrey among them, as memory pricks for historians.

Also remembered by street naming but more tangibly by the Savoy Hotel, luxury accommodation and a high society rendezvous since 1889, was the Savoy Palace: "the most palatial private home in England... the finest jewel in the necklace linking (the City of) London with Westminster," according to Timothy Baker. Already a grand home, a fortune amassed from the Hundred Years War enabled John of Gaunt (1340-99, a powerful though unpopular son of Edward III), to fund the creation of a building of such opulence that it became widely loathed and was duly burned down during the 1381 Peasants' Revolt. The land became a hospital for the poor during the sixteenth century and subsequently a military barracks before being demolished in the early 1800s to clear the approach to the new Waterloo Bridge.

Old Hungerford Market and new Charing Cross
Destruction of another Thames landmark came with the removal of the seventeenth-century Hungerford Market to accommodate Charing Cross Station, opened in 1864 as the first rail terminal close to London's West End. Hungerford Bridge ("the ugliest thing seen on the Thames", thought Arthur Mee) was built to feed the terminal, replacing the still infant suspension bridge of Isambard Kingdom Brunel. Brunel's

suspension chains were re-used on his more famous Clifton suspension bridge in Bristol, while the abutments and landing piers, though sadly not the Italianate towers, were incorporated into the new crossing. Above the station sprouts Terry Farrell's Embankment Place, a vertical extension that created 100,000 square feet of new office space in 1992. A daring attempt to fuse modern technology with references to Victorian rail terminal architecture, the adornment is hard to love by day but fares better when viewed by its night-time illumination.

Embankment Gardens

Created to fill an awkward gap, Embankment Gardens became a lush triangle of trees, shrubbery and plants framed by neat lawns and connected by curving pathways. Over time, the gardens have acquired a eclectic range of monuments including commemorations of composer W. S. Gilbert, Scottish poet Robert Burns and the army Camel Corps; more recently, they gained a memorial to the 52 people killed in the London bomb attacks of 7 July 2005. Another feature is the 1626 Buckingham Gate, originally an entrance gate from the Thames to York House, then home of the Duke of Buckingham. To the north is the alluring Shell-Mex Centre looking, according to Bryan Fairfax, "like a titanic mantelpiece clock".

The area held scant appeal for the twelve-year-old Charles Dickens who supported his family by attaching labels to bottles at Warren's Blacking Factory on the site of the present-day Embankment station, adjacent to the gardens. Dickens' miseries were fictionalized in *David Copperfield*, in which the eponymous character recalls Murdstone and Grinby's warehouse: "…it was the last house at the bottom of a narrow street, curving down hill to the river, with some stairs at the end, where people took boat. It was a crazy old house with a wharf of its own, abutting on the water when the tide was in, and on the mud when the tide was out, and literally overrun with rats... No words can express the secret agony of my soul as I… felt my hopes of growing up to be a learned and distinguished man, crushed in my bosom."

Sad and Suggestive: Cleopatra's Needle

For late-Victorian Londoners, an Embankment Gardens picnic might well have been accompanied by a stroll across the then tranquil road to inspect Cleopatra's Needle. Older than any other object in London and the most incongruous addition to the riverside, the sixty-foot-high granite obelisk with no link with Cleopatra was, as Barker and Jackson put it, "deviously acquired, grudgingly received, and curiously delivered."

Quarried around 1475 BC for Pharaoh Tethmosis III, the obelisk was gifted to King George IV by the Viceroy of Egypt in 1819 ostensibly to mark the British victory at the Battle of the Nile in 1798. The high cost and technical difficulty of its transportation resulted in the piece staying in Egypt until the 1870s. Noted surgeon Sir William James Erasmus Wilson put up the funds to have the obelisk raised from the sands it had occupied for two thousand years and placed in a specially-constructed floating container for the tug-drawn sea journey to London. In a storm on the Bay of Biscay the tug-rope snapped, leading to six deaths and the needle being cast adrift, eventually being rescued and reaching London in 1878. The 186-ton obelisk finally regained its vertical posture beside the Thames with a time capsule buried in its base containing, among other things, cigars, newspapers, coins and pictures of the twelve women deemed the most beautiful of the day. Continuing the Egyptian theme, two bronze faux sphinxes were placed alongside, figures that on a smaller scale decorate the armrests of nearby benches.

Unrepaired damage to the one of the sphinxes is a reminder of the first air raid on London, by German planes during September 1917, the same month that a letter regarding the Needle appeared in *The Times*: "I was looking today at Cleopatra's Needle, that fascinating symbol of England's Oriental Empire that rises on the bank of the Thames amid the fog and grime of London so full of poetry and suggestiveness." Just a few decades later, H. V. Morton would say of the needle: "Sad, cold stone—the saddest monument in all London."

Somerset House

Looking very much like a baronial seat as it appears with great conspicuousness east of Waterloo Bridge, Somerset House was actually the first building in England constructed solely to provide administrative space for public offices. Completed in 1801 in dolphin-decorated Portland Stone to the design of William Chambers, the building originally had the Thames lapping against its 800-foot river frontage, its central arch, now obscured by embankment trees, allowing entry to the royal barge. Early occupants included the Royal Academy, the Royal Society, the Society of Antiquaries and various naval departments. Somerset House later became the national archive of births, death and marriages, something which inspired satirist Anthony Pasquin (pen name of John Williams, 1765-1818) to write: "In these damp, black and comfortless recesses, the clerks of the nation grope about like moles, immersed in Tartarean gloom, where they stamp, sign, examine, indite, doze, and swear…"

Through the 1980s, the use of the central courtyard as an employees' private car park epitomized the lack of public access to the building. During the late 1990s, however, Somerset House was transformed, with three galleries staging temporary exhibitions and all-comers welcome to the fifty-five "orchestrated water jets" that spurt around the courtyard's statue of Charles I. The same site during the winter holds London's largest outdoor ice rink and in summer hosts concerts. In 2002 the *Guardian* reported a performance by trance band Orbital: "The courtyard of Somerset House was an architecturally grand spot for a gig, but the fluttering union flag and the bizarre sight of a late worker at the Inland Revenue… gave off a strong whiff of establishment, cut with a strong whiff of spliff."

A previous Somerset House, on this site from 1550, provided a "residence suitable to his high rank" for the Duke of Somerset, also known as Edward Seymour, oldest brother of Jane Seymour and uncle to Edward VI, the "boy king" over whom Somerset wielded sufficient influence to effectively run the country. Despite his exalted office, the need to demolish churches and chapels to make space to create his riverside residence annoyed the Privy Council to the extent that the duke was briefly incarcerated in the Tower. His occupancy of the house was similarly short: convicted of treason, he was executed in 1552. The house became Crown property and was used by Princess Elizabeth to bide her time before her accession in 1558; Oliver Cromwell lay in state here in 1658; and architect Inigo Jones briefly lived in the house before his death in 1652.

The Lawless and the Law: Alsatia and Temple Gardens
By the seventeenth century, the area between the Strand and the Thames just west of the City became known as Alsatia (mentioned in Thomas Shadwell's 1688 play *The Squire of Alsatia* and subsequently applied to

areas of high criminality and low repute), where villains erroneously believed they could avoid arrest through the medieval law of sanctuary. Described by Hugh Phillips as "the dwelling place of cut-throats, highwaymen, footpads, pilferers, debtors and prostitutes", Alsatia ironically stood adjacent to London's most law-abiding section: the Temple, holding the four Inns of Court where student barristers received board, lodging and training.

As Arthur Mee put it in the 1930s, the legal profession "owns the land it stands on, governs itself, it gives the police no trouble, and it allows us all to enjoy its beautiful domain." The beautiful domain was earlier owned by the Knights Templar, an order of religious fighters whose members had taken monastic vows of chastity, poverty and obedience, and undertook to protect pilgrims headed for Jerusalem, thereby taking a leading role in the Crusades. Their distinctive Round Church, consecrated in 1185 by the Patriarch of Jerusalem, is among the few medieval survivors in the Temple precincts; much is Victorian-style remodelling constructed following the Blitz. The Templars were suppressed in 1312, but barristers are as plentiful as they were in the 1920s when James Bone wrote of the Temple: "where the flagstones become gravestones engraved with the names of old lawyers; busy men flit by you with the same kind of wig and gown as men wore in Queen Anne's day to please with instances far older than their costume, using phrases such as 'only as recently as 1750'..."

Once reaching to the river's foreshore but ending now at the Embankment, Temple Gardens developed from fields where knights would take contemplative strolls and was re-styled in the early 1600s to include "large and lovely walks... curious knots and beds of fragrant flowers and sweet herbs of sundry scents." The gardens were connected to the river by Temple Stairs, from which many generations of barristers departed by barge for Westminster Hall, the departure spot now occupied by the gleaming white paintwork of HQS *Wellington*, permanently berthed as a venue for social functions, dinners and presentations.

Blackfriars and the Fleet River
Immediately before the road and rail bridges of Blackfriars, two silver dragons on the Embankment denote the western boundary of the City

of London. Less obvious is the route of a once-dashing tributary of the Thames, the Fleet, which defined the eastern boundary of Roman Londinium, became an open sewer in Elizabethan times, was reinvented as the Fleet Canal after the Great Fire and was ridiculed in Alexander Pope's 1728 *The Dunciad*:

> To where Fleet-ditch with disemboguing streams
> Rolls the large tribute of dead dogs to the Thames.

By contrast, around 1750 following a partial canalization of the river, Samuel Scott painted "a most vivid impression of this half-Flemish, half-Venetian Canal which greatly helped to bring the Thames up to the artistic level of continental waterways," noted Hugh Phillips. A Thames with a continental flavour was short-lived, however. The canal failed commercially and the Fleet was covered and now discharges into the Thames beneath Blackfriars Bridge.

In June 1982 a man was found hanged from a noose beneath Blackfriars Bridge, his feet lapped by the Thames, his body weighted with bricks. The man was identified as an Italian, Roberto Calvi, an employee of the private Banco Ambrosiano with such close links to the Vatican that he had earned the nickname "God's Banker". A member of the secretive P2 Masonic lodge, reputedly connected to the Sicilian mafia, Calvi's apparently corrupt dealings had left his bank, and the Vatican, facing billion-dollar debts. As theories abounded, a verdict of suicide was returned only to be quashed as evidence emerged supporting murder, though a subsequent coroners' jury declared themselves undecided. As years passed, the evidence for murder grew stronger, and, in April 2005 four people, two with alleged links to the mafia, were arrested and charged with the killing.

Bridewell Palace and Baynards Castle
On reclaimed land bordered by the Thames and the western bank of the Fleet, Henry VIII's Bridewell Palace was completed in 1523. Five years later, it hosted the papal delegation that began discussions on the king's divorce from Catherine of Aragon, a dispute that would lead to England's momentous break with the Roman Catholic Church. The palace, too, experienced a dramatic turn of fate. By 1550 the royal

residence had become a refuge, and very quickly a prison, for the destitute: prostitutes and vagrants who were whipped on arrival and in twice-weekly sessions open to the public. Partly destroyed in the Great Fire, the prison was demolished in 1803. The site has been occupied since 1931 by Unilever House, its curving and colonnaded form described by *The Times* as "simple, masculine and well-proportioned", its exterior decoration summed up by Pevsner as "monstrously big pieces of sculpture".

Originally a Norman fortification given to an order of Dominican monks (the Black Friars, who gave their name to the locality), Baynards Castle was completely rebuilt in 1428 by the Duke of Gloucester and became one of London's most notable riverside houses, so much so that Henry VII made it his main London residence. His successor, Henry VIII, gave the castle in 1509 to Catherine of Aragon who lived there following her divorce, as at various times did Richard III and the Duke of York, before the entire castle, save for one of its octagonal towers that endured as a private dwelling, succumbed to the Great Fire.

The Great Fire and the River

Fanned by an easterly wind and fuelled by the combustible materials stored in shops and warehouses, a small fire in a baker's shop on a Sunday morning in September 1666 became a four-day blaze and a pivotal moment in London's history. The fire destroyed 13,200 homes and 89 churches, left around 200,000 destitute and marked the end of the medieval city. As the fire gathered power and people vacated their homes, some rushed to high ground to the north while those with access to boats gathered their possessions and cast themselves onto the Thames. Pepys described the scene: "Everybody endeavouring to remove their goods, and flinging into the river or bringing them into lighters that lay off; poor people staying in their houses as long as till the very fire touched them, and then running into boats, or clambering from one pair of stairs by the waterside to another…"

In his own boat aiming for the safety of Woolwich, Pepys joined those on the river: "…all over the Thames, with one's face in the wind, you were almost burned with a shower of firedrops. This is very true; so as houses were burned by these drops and flakes of fire, three or four, nay, five or six houses, one from another. When we could endure no more upon the water; we to a little ale-house on the Bankside over against the Three Cranes, and there staid till it was dark almost, and saw the fire grow; and, as it grew darker, appeared more and more, and in corners and upon steeples, and between churches and houses, as far as we could see up the hill of the City, in a most horrid malicious bloody flame, not like the fine flame of an ordinary fire."

As Pepys discovered, Southwark provided a prime vantage point for viewing the conflagration and it was from here that the Prague-born engraver and draughtsman Vaclav (Wenceslas) Hollar (see p.xxvi) constructed a visual record of the blaze, showing St. Paul's Cathedral engulfed in the flames that reached from London Bridge in the east to Baynards Castle in the west.

Wren's Plans for London and the Thames

Even before 1666, London was falling to pieces. The maintenance of the city and its buildings had been neglected through the tumult of civil war and the overthrow and subsequent restoration of the monarchy. Also, as architect Sir Christopher Wren (1632-1723) discovered on his continental trips, London was losing ground to its European rivals, which were eagerly embracing architectural modernity.

Aided in various ways by John Evelyn and Robert Hooke, Wren devised a plan for a radically new London, one that would turn the city's narrow byways into a grid-style layout of grand avenues and boulevards meeting at elegant wide squares with a replenished St. Paul's occupying a central plot. Yet the reticence of the recently restored monarch, Charles II, to impose wide-scale compulsory property purchases and enforce boundary changes on the people who had earlier beheaded his father, saw Wren's vision unfulfilled. Even after the fire had taken its toll and the king clearly favoured a new royal city, parliament was deterred by the cost and an underlying suspicion of absolutism.

One aspect of Wren's plan was the Thames Quay, a straightening of the river bank where it bordered the City and the building of state-of-the-art cargo handling areas. The vested interests of riverside landowners foiled the scheme but Wren's plan to canalize the Fleet River was partially implemented. Another aspect of Wren's plan was a new St. Paul's Cathedral.

St. Paul's Cathedral

We were just saying how little time we had to reflect on life and death when we rounded the corner to face the massive walls of St Paul's. There it was once again—as big as a mountain towering over us, gloomier, colder and more silent than ever. And barely had we stepped inside than when we felt utterly freed from the hustle and bustle outside—more so than in any other building in the world.
Virginia Woolf, Abbeys and Cathedrals, 1932

Despite being several streets distanced from the river and surrounded by high-rises of much more recent eras, St. Paul's Cathedral and its unmistakable dome dominate the skyline from both the waterway and the far bank. Founded in 604 supposedly on the site of a Roman temple to Diana, St. Paul's had regularly been rebuilt and expanded to become England's longest church and, with a city-dominating spire, one that confirmed London's place as the national capital. Like the rest of the city, however, St. Paul's was in decline before the Great Fire took its toll. In 1561 the spire collapse following a lightning strike, recorded in a contemporary account: "between one and two of the clock was seen a marvellous great fiery lightning, and immediately ensued a most terrible hideous crack of thunder as seldom hath been heard, and that by estimation of sense, directly over the City of London…" For a hundred years the cathedral remained in a damaged state, its middle aisle becoming St. Paul's Walk, site of a daily market and "an ordinary lounging-place for the wits, gallants, and disreputable characters of the time." During the Commonwealth the cathedral was used as a cavalry barracks.

Built between 1675 and 1710, Wren's new St. Paul's was fraught with controversy and disagreement. Only Wren's close relationship with Charles II (and subsequently Queen Anne) allowed him to bypass the clergy's demands for a more conservative architectural style and to acquire the funds needed to finish the job. Concealed behind scaffolding throughout its construction, the new St. Paul's was eventually revealed crowned not with a spire, but a dome, the first of its kind in England. By 1885, *The Royal River* could remark: "For nearly two hundred years Sir Christopher Wren's Cathedral has been the central monument of

London. Round its significant mass the waves of the great city beat day by day in feverish unrest… there is something in its ponderous bulk, its countless reduplication of arch and column, and its soaring cupola, which seems to image the stability of English life in the midst of constant agitation and perpetual change."

The idea of St Paul's representing a strong and secure England gained strength during the Blitz, when the image of the cathedral remaining intact as all around was consumed by flames and smoke became a symbol of war-time defiance as powerful as Winston Churchill's V-sign. American newspaper correspondent Ernie Pyle recalled an air raid: "St. Paul's was surrounded by fire, but it came through. It stood there in its enormous proportions—growing slowly clearer and clearer, the way objects take shape at dawn. It was like a picture of some miraculous figure that appears before peace-hungry soldiers on a battlefield."

Queenhithe

South of Upper Thames Street between Blackfriars and London bridges, a succession of short, warehouse-lined streets lead to the river's edge and form Queenhithe, of which Norman Shrapnell observed in 1977: "This primal beach, the cradle of mercantile London, is much frequented during breaks from work by young men with trowels and small picks, hunting for treasure."

Though digging on the foreshore is now forbidden without written permission of the Port of London Authority, river users from near and far have been dropping things into the Thames here at least since Saxon and probably from Roman times, when a wooden quay was accessible to sea-going ships and served as the main commercial strip of London's river, later becoming part of the Elizabethan system of legal quays (see p.84-5). The dock was named Queenhithe in honour of Queen Matilde, wife of Henry I, perhaps to acknowledge her funding of a public toilet here for "common use of the citizens" in 1237.

After London Bridge made access difficult from downriver, Queenhithe developed as a market for corn, salt, flour and more carried on barges so large that Daniel Defoe exclaimed: "The vessels which bring the malt and meal to Queenhithe are worth the observation of any stranger that understands such things. They are remarkable for the length of the vessels and the burden they carry, yet the little water they draw... some of these barges carry above a thousand quarter [around 100 tons] of malt at a time, and yet do not draw two foot of water."

Worshipful Fishmongers and Vintners

The Worshipful Company of Fishmongers are not to be sniffed at, being one of the foremost of the City of London's liveried companies and able to trace their origins back at least to the thirteenth century. Business in medieval London was dominated by the livery companies, each with a monopoly in a particular trade and each organized on strictly hierarchical lines. Able to train apprentices and often supporting charities, the companies were fiercely protective of their dominant position. Regulating the supply of fish into a city where it formed a staple part of the ordinary person's diet, the Fishmongers became exceptionally rich and powerful. In 1834 the company moved into Fishmongers Hall on the new approach to London Bridge, where they remain to this day, still absorbed in tradition and protecting curiosities such as the dagger that William Walworth, worshipful fishmonger and Lord Mayor of London, used to kill Wat Tyler, leader of the 1381 Peasants' Revolt.

Lower down the livery pecking order, the Vintners Company acquired a monopoly on the wine trade in 1364, overseeing the import and exports of a commodity that once accounted for a third of Britain's international trade. From 1671 the company occupied the elegant Vintners Hall, a feature of the riverside absorbed during the 1990s into a pseudo-classical slab of office space known as Vintners Place.

London Bridge

The bridge at London is worthily to be numbered among the miracles of the world.

Fynes Moryson, *Itinerary*, 1617

The present London Bridge might be visually unexciting but at least offers a blank canvas onto which two millennia of history, lore and legend can be projected. Occupying Romans built the first London Bridge, a medieval version lasted for 600 years, a Victorian replacement was sold to an American in 1960s, and over the centuries the bridge has inspired a nursery rhyme, displayed the boiled heads of thieves and traitors and held a prefabricated house shipped here from Holland.

Roman occupiers of Britain used the site of the future London as military supply base, eventually choosing a point between two hills for a fixed wooden crossing, previously fording the river with pontoon bridges. Engineering techniques tested on the Rhine were used and the bridge was built, probably of English oak and around 50AD, on a site a just east of the present bridge. The only fixed crossing below Staines, the bridge became a contributor to and a symbol of a prospering London, which soon replaced Colchester as the Roman capital. By the Anglo-Saxon period, Roman power had waned but a London Bridge, in frequently rebuilt form, endured through the period's turbulent power struggles, gaining its first known written reference—an account of the drowning of a woman convicted of witchcraft—in the *Anglo-Saxon Chronicle*.

Around 1013, in an effort to divide the forces of the Dane Svienn "Fork Beard" Haroldsson, the bridge was attacked by Olaf of Norway, an event inspiring Norse poet Ottar Svarte to compose a paean to the pagan God Odin that might in turn have inspired the nursery rhyme, *London Bridge is Falling Down*:

> London Bridge is broken down.
> Gold is won, and bright renown.
> Shields resounding,
> War-horns sounding,
> Hild is shouting in the din!
> Arrows singing,
> Mail-coats ringing—
> Odin makes our Olaf win.

From 1176 a new London Bridge was constructed of stone under the leadership of a cleric, Peter of Colechurch. The bridge comprised nineteen irregularly sized arches and included a wooden drawbridge that could be raised to enable the passage of ships to Queenhithe. The bridge also held a chapel which became a home for priests and which for centuries held Peter's remains.

Between them, the bridge's piers blocked half the river, causing a surge of water beneath it and, over time, a build up of waste that made the current notoriously uneven. Watermen referred to navigating the stretch as "shooting the bridge", while passengers often alighted on one side and crossed to the other before retaking their place in the boat, assuming their waterman had not drowned (as many did) in the meantime. The treacherous waters gave rise to a proverb, attributed in 1670 to John Ray: "London Bridge was made for wise men to pass over, and for fools to pass under."

Wise or not, anyone crossing the medieval bridge on foot might believe themselves on a regular London street, lined as it was by shops and houses that overhung the sides of the bridge by several feet and left only a narrow passage way for passing traffic. In *London in 1710*, German traveller Conrad von Uffebach wrote of the bridge: "We had gone twenty yards over it without being aware that we were on the bridge, when I asked our interpreter how soon we should reach it. He then told us we were really almost over the centre of the Thames..." Though constantly threatened by fire, bridge residents could fish from their windows and, as Hugh Phillips put it, "no houses in London had such a magnificent view." And none was as distinctive as Nonsuch House, which arrived in prefabricated form from Holland in 1577 complete with sculptured wood and gilded pilasters.

Another feature of London Bridge was the array of boiled heads of traitors and criminals displayed from pikes above Drawbridge Gate and later from the Great Stone Gate at the Southwark end. The practice began in 1305 with the head of Scots rebel William Wallace and continued for over three hundred years. A 1592 account by Jacob Rathgeb noted 34 heads "of persons of distinction" on the bridge and some regarded the head of an ancestor so displayed as a mark of social rank. Thomas Platter observed in 1599: "the young earl of Suffolk, grandson to the Duke of Norfolk, in order to raise the honour of his family, showed that he was so well connected that his forefather's heads... were on the tower of London Bridge for having coveted the English crown." Another use was found for the heads in 1560 when Dutch and German workers at the Royal Mint became ill and were told to drink from a dead mans' skull; those on the bridge were adapted as drinking vessels though failed to remedy the arsenic poisoning the workers were actually suffering from. Other notable heads included those of Jack Cade, Thomas More, Thomas Cromwell and finally, in 1678, banker William Stayley, innocent but caught up in the Catholic "plot" fabricated by Titus Oates.

By the mid-1750s, London Bridge was clearly failing to provide an adequate river crossing but the political power of watermen and the interests of riverside businesses prevented the construction of new bridges. Welsh naturalist Thomas Pennant (1726-98) wrote of the bridge as: "narrow, darksome, and dangerous to passengers from the multitude of carriages; frequent arches of strong timber crossed the street from the tops of houses, to keep them together, and from falling in the river. Nothing could preserve the rest of the inmates, who soon grew deaf to the noise of the falling waters, the clamors of watermen, or the frequent shrieks of drowning wretches." With a temporary wooden bridge erected alongside and despite the objections (and arson attacks by) its residents, London Bridge was eventually shorn of its buildings and strengthened with a fresh layer of masonry. By 1776 Sir John Fielding was able to comment: "London Bridge is now rescued from the hideous deformity of old ruinous houses that so long rendered it a disgrace to the city, and a horror to the eyes of all curious spectators."

Nonetheless, the bridge continued to be congested and the creation of a single central arch caused rushing water to erode the piers fast enough to threaten the structure's stability. For a growing port, the bridge was increasingly seen as an obstacle to trade, and momentum for a new London Bridge became unstoppable. Chosen from an architectural competition that included Thomas Telford's monumental single span of cast iron was the 928-foot-long, five-arch granite bridge proposed by Scottish engineer John Rennie (1761-1821). Connected by new approach roads and river steps to enable access to steamers and other river craft, Rennie's bridge opened in 1831 with a ceremony, which, according to *The Times* in its full-page account, "presented the most splendid spectacle that has been witnessed on the Thames for many years." Three years later, the old bridge, which had stood just to the east, was completely demolished, the ignominy of its demise epitomized by the bones of Peter of Colechurch being tossed without fuss into the river.

Rennie might have hoped that his bridge would emulate the longevity of its predecessor. In fact, the new bridge began to slowly sink soon after completion and had to be widened in the early 1900s to cope with increased traffic. In the 1960s the decision was taken to erect yet another bridge and, in an unexpected twist, the British government sold Rennie's crossing to an American for $2,460,000. Popularly thought to have made the common tourist error of mistaking London Bridge for Tower Bridge, the American was actually an oil tycoon and property developer who moved the bridge piece-by-piece to an island on Lake Havasu, Arizona, where it was reassembled and continues to live a charmed post-Thames existence in a holiday resort, adorned with Union Jacks and adjacent to a group of shops known as the "English Village".

Opened in 1973, the current London Bridge fulfills its purpose without daring to emulate its forbears. Some of its merits are less than obvious: hollow caissons allow passage for emergency services; pedestrians are stabilized by a full-length stainless handrail; heated pavements prevent ice on winter nights. Another of the bridge's under-acknowledged qualities is that it allows nothing to detract from its greatest feature: the river passing beneath and the unhindered view of London all around. That is as true of this bridge as it was of Rennie's, on which in *London by Day and Night* (1852) David W. Bartlett wrote:

> We turned away and walked to the centre of London Bridge. The day had dawned, and the east was full of crimson streaks. London lay before us—and asleep. Looking eastward, we saw a dense forest of shipping from the four quarters of the globe; there rose the vast Custom House with its walls tinted over with London smoke; still further down the stream rose the turrets of the Tower into the clear, cold sky. To the northwest, looking, we saw great St. Paul's dome, a beacon for the lost in the Great Wilderness of London. There was the tall column in memory of the great London fire, when for whole days the flames raged and the sky was black as night with smoke. It was a splendid sight; and then we thought how it must look on a summer's morning, when the sun rises long before the people wake.

Billingsgate

...we arrive at Billingsgate, now a fine and convenient market, but a few years since a collection of dirty hovels and stalls, disgraceful to a civilised community.
Mr. & Mrs. S. C. Hall, *The Book of the Thames*, 1859

Billingsgate Market sold fish and much more on the same riverside site from 1016 to 1982, operating in sheds and makeshift booths along the quay until 1877 when the market moved into a vaguely French Renaissance style building topped by a fish-shaped weather vane. The frenzied scenes of the building's interior were described by Charles Dickens Jr. in *Dickens' Dictionary of London* (1879): "There are hundreds of baskets and hampers of herrings, of mackerel, boxes of soles and of flat fish, tons of cod, thousands of lordly turbot, and any quantity of whiting, plaice, and mullet. Besides all these there are quantities of shrimps, and, if it be the season, baskets upon basket of delicate smelt and whitebait. The river fish are represented only by salmon, and perhaps a few trout, but what a magnificent representation it is!"

Proximity to the Coal Exchange also made Billingsgate the favoured landing site for colliers from Newcastle, as many as 700 liable to be awaiting docking during busy times, and passengers, too, passed through, Billingsgate being the departure point for ferries to Gravesend where international travellers would transfer to sea-going vessels. As a first or last experience of London, Billingsgate might have been a memorable one since the market was as renowned for its foul language, often perpetrated by its women, as much as for its fresh fish. Satirist Ned Ward found at Billingsgate a "Crowd of Thumb Ring'd Flat Caps, from the age of Seven to Seventy, who sat Snarling and Grunting at one another, over their Sprats and Whitings like a pack of domestic dogs over the Cook-Maids kindness, or a parcel of hungry Sows at a trough of Hogwash."

In 1982 the Billingsgate plot was sold for £22 million and a new Billingsgate Market opened across a thirteen-acre site on the Isle of Dogs. Given a make-over by architect Richard Rogers and an intensely yellow façade, the old market is now touted as a venue for fashion shows, product launches and other events of the kind that fill the diaries of media functionaries and lower-ranking celebrities. Anyone attending such a shindig might consider how far the words of James Greenwood in his 1875 *Low Life Deeps* could still apply: "It is not unlikely that after having been jostled, trodden on, plentifully besprinkled with fishy water, sworn at, chaffed, and utterly deafened, you will be sorely tempted to spurn the mud of Billingsgate from off your feet and rush impetuously from the scene of your tribulation up one of the many narrow lanes which lead out of it."

Custom House

Duties imposed by Edward I in 1275 on wool, leather and hides exported through London became the basis of the modern customs system, symbolized on the Thames by the grand 488-foot riverside frontage of the Custom House, its spectacular size and grandeur offering an awesome warning to would-be smugglers. That said, the building's history is the stuff of smugglers' dreams: since the first Custom House was erected on a nearby plot in the thirteenth century, the building burned down or was severely damaged with regularity. The 1723 incarnation was the first to incorporate a Long Room, a voluminous interior space where clerks would calculate custom fees and complete the relevant paperwork. Spanish visitor Don Manuel Gonzales was impressed: "a wainscoted magnificent room, almost the whole length of the building, and fifteen feet in height, (in which) sit the commissioners of the customs, with their under officers and clerks."

As early as the nineteenth century, Custom House Quay was developed as a riverside walk between London Bridge and the Tower. The 1844 *Mogg's New Picture of London and Visitor's Guide to its Sights* wrote of the quay: "enlarged by a substantial embankment, forms in fine weather a beautiful promenade;—and the view of the Thames from thence is considerably enlivened in the summer by the passage of steamboats and other vessels that are perpetually navigating this noble river." In the 1940s, Sydney R. Jones concurred in *Thames Triumphant* but with a surprising caveat: "The Custom House stands classic and dignified, superior to smells and smoke. It rises up from its own broad and pleasant plot, a most attractive spot for a promenade and views over the Pool, though one best avoided on New Year's morning, for then the Jews used to assemble to wail on the captivity and remember their ancestors who sat down by the waters of Babylon and wept. This performance came to be viewed with disfavour by the authorities, so may now be extinct…"

The Tower of London

Absorbing a ceaseless daytime procession of tourists seeking a Beefeater to be photographed alongside and parties of schoolchildren receiving instruction in the legend of the ravens, the Tower of London emerged from a blood-soaked past as what Weinreb and Hibbert call "the most perfect medieval fortress in Britain" to become what Norman Shrapnel termed "the most invincible of tourist attractions".

As narrators of guided Thames cruises eagerly point out, Traitors Gate, a part of the Tower adjoining the river, was where those about to be incarcerated, and perhaps beheaded, would step ashore and savour what might be their last breaths of freedom. When a princess, Elizabeth, arrived here in 1544, suspected of plotting against her half-sister Mary, she reputedly declared as she stepped from her barge: "Here landeth as true a subject… as ever landed at these stairs; and before thee O God! I speak it, having no other friends but thee alone." Elizabeth, of course, kept her head and later had it crowned; those whose heads were lost at the Tower include William, Lord Hastings (1431); Anne Boleyn (1536); Catherine Howard (1542); Lady Jane Grey (1554); the Countess of Salisbury (1541); Jane, Viscountess Rochford (1542); and Robert Devereux, Second Earl of Essex (1601). Those who lacked royal blood, among them Thomas More (see pp.102-3), were executed on Tower Hill, just outside the Tower's boundaries.

The eighteen-acre complex of the Tower grew from the White Tower, beside the river, begun under William I in 1078 and utilizing a mound that formed part of Roman London's wall. Besides being a place of execution and imprisonment, the Tower has been a mint, an armoury and the site of a royal menagerie that once included a polar bear which fished for its meals in the river and the tiger that inspired William Blake's poem "The Tyger". The Tower's ravens were never part of the menagerie but are part of its folklore, their presence giving rise to the legend that if they should ever leave, England will be invaded. Since they are housed and fed at Crown expense, however, their departure seems unlikely.

Sandcastle competitions, rowing boat trips and deckchair hire were all features of Tower Beach, created with 1,500 tons of imported sand

in July 1934 that turned the north bank of the Thames between the Tower and St Katharine's Steps into an urban beach. Intended to create a holiday experience for Londoners unable to afford a trip to the real coast, the beach stayed in place, with a brief war-time disappearance, until 1971, when an increasingly polluted river rendered it a health hazard. Much was made of Tower Beach in the 1990s as urban beaches became the talk of metropolitan sophisticates and activists alike: through 2003, under the banner of Reclaim the Beach, beaches were created on a monthly basis at Festival Pier, adjacent to the South Bank's Festival Hall.

Commerce and Culture South: The South Bank to Tower Bridge
Facing the City of London but separate from it and outside its legal jurisdiction, the south bank around Southwark tempted medieval Londoners across the river with theatre, bear-baiting and brothels. It was from here that Chaucer and Shakespeare reshaped English literature and here, centuries later, that Charles Dickens visited his father in one of the area's numerous jails. The cultural quarter east of Waterloo Bridge, known simply as the South Bank, was, by contrast, a product of post-war municipal optimism, a desire to develop an abandoned riverside plot into a cultural centre of national significance that succeeded with its content but failed with its buildings.

As recently as the mid-1990s, those arriving for South Bank opera, theatre or film seasons would be unlikely to venture further east along a Bankside bedevilled by declining river industries and overlooked by the disused hulk of Bankside Power Station. Curiously, the roles are now reversed: the South Bank complex seems dated and lacklustre compared to the redeveloped Bankside, anchored by the same power station that is now Tate Modern, one part of a immensely strollable riverside taking in such distinctive landmarks of diverse eras as the Oxo Tower, City Hall and Tower Bridge.

In 1943, as the war continued, the London County Council eyed a section of the south bank between Westminster and Blackfriars bridges and planned its future: "equipped with a continuous strip of grass and a wide esplanade, this area might well include a great cultural centre embracing, among other features, a modern theatre, a large concert hall, and the headquarters of various organisations." The area is now simply "the South Bank", a collective term for a cultural complex where split-level walkways and circular staircases link assorted auditoria: the earliest addition was the Festival Hall (1951), taking its name from the short-lived but long remembered Festival of Britain, subsequently joined by the National Film Theatre (1956), the Queen Elizabeth Hall (1967), the Haywood Gallery and Purcell Rooms (1968) and the National Theatre (1976). Not only did the scheme take far longer than the LCC planners hoped, but it took shape in a form they would never have envisaged. Instead of continuous grass, the effect is continuous concrete and a prevailing 1960s brutalism that renders the area depressing. Afflicted by long running problems over funding and appropriate modes of design, the South Bank become what critic Jonathan Glancey called "the Bermuda Triangle of architectural reputations".

The Festival of Britain
A hundred years after the Great Exhibition displayed Victorian Britain's industrial might to the world and following six years of austerity enforced by a war-weakened economy, the governing Labour Party offered up the Festival of Britain as "a tonic to the nation". Exhibits across the 27-acre site beside the Thames reminded visitors of the roots of Britain's prosperity—the land and the sea—but focused on the future with such delights as the "stereoscope" films shown in the Telekinema (the forerunner of the National Film Theatre), a radio transmitter bouncing waves off the moon, and a 74-inch telescope allowing views into the heavens. Overhead, the aluminum and steel Skylon rose 290 feet while works by the then barely known sculptors, Henry Moore and Barbara Hepworth, decorated the pathways. Declared open by King George V in the hope that "the vast range of modern knowledge which is here shown may be turned from destructive to peaceful ends so that all people, as this century goes on, may be lifted to greater happiness," the festival was a huge success with the public but offered an easy target to the Conservative opposition for its cost when British industry required investment and homes required building.

A balance of payments crisis triggered an October general election that brought a narrow victory for the Conservatives. The new government cleared the festival grounds with barely concealed glee; the Skylon was demolished and turned into souvenir ashtrays, its humiliation matching that of the Labour Party, which would not regain power until 1964.

Lambeth Marsh: LWT, Gabriel's Wharf, the Oxo Tower

East of the South Bank complex on part of what used to be Lambeth Marsh ("an unwholesome and unprofitable locality, frequently overflowed in high tides") a major British television company occupies a minor Thames landmark, described by Bryan Fairfax as "shimmering in white mosaic." Completed in 1972, the building was the base of London Weekend Television (LWT), a company that marked its new setting with an animated image of the Thames snaking across the screen in three colours as their station logo until 1979. A changing broadcasting era saw LWT subsumed into the national ITV franchise in 2002, and the building is now called London Studios.

Offering an alternative to the grand architectural statements appearing along London's twenty-first-century river, the mock-ramshackle shops and *trompe l'oeil* decoration of Gabriel's Wharf are a reworking of an industrial site by the Coin Street Co-operative, locally based and seeking to regenerate the waterfront without neglecting the needs of the local community. Another of the Co-operative's projects has been the Oxo Tower, saved from demolition in the 1980s to become a symbol of the imaginative regeneration of the immediate area.

The tower was constructed by the Liebig Extract of Meat Company, which bought riverside land here in the 1920s and created the world's biggest meat packing and storage centre to manufacture their best-known product, the Oxo stock cube. On all four sides of the tower, which rose from their warehouse, architect Albert W. Moore, spelt out "OXO", publicizing the product while circumventing advertising restrictions on what was then, at 220 feet, the city's second-tallest commercial building. Designer shops and a top-price restaurant now share the tower's interior with 78 apartments and a welcome, if tokenistic, public viewing area squeezed between the restaurant's tables.

Bankside: the Power of Art

Arthur Mee's view of Bankside in the 1930s was of "a strange region of cobbled streets, curious old wharves and dark alleys, with an occasional glimpse of shipping on the river", a scene that could hardly be more removed from that of today. Expanded and improved by the imaginative conversion of the disused Bankside power station into the Tate Modern, opened on May 2000 and joined by a new pedestrian bridge spanning the Thames, Bankside eclipsed the South Bank as a popular hotbed of culture and forms part of a riverside path reaching to Tower Bridge and beyond.

That admission to Tate Modern is free (save for special exhibitions) encourages all-comers to the site, making for a welcome mix of art lovers and bluffers, day-trippers and tourists. Exhibitions within 36,000 square feet of gallery space span the twentieth century and onwards, and are arranged thematically rather than chronologically; something copied with much less success by major art museums around the world. Also lacking elsewhere are spectacular views across the Millennium Bridge to St. Paul's Cathedral and, for those for whom the Thames is greater than all art, a large horde—clay pipes, old keys, 1970s office phones, shoes with tales to tell—unearthed from its banks during construction. The only major noticeable change to the exterior of the 1952 Giles Gilbert Scott-designed power station is the two-storey glass roof which forms part of the night-time illumination called the Swiss Light, a gift from the Swiss government in recognition of the achievements of the Tate's Swiss-based architectural firm, Herzog & de Meuron.

When the first new bridge to span London's river since Tower Bridge had to be closed after two days due to "synchronous lateral excitation", the £5 million Millennium Bridge seemed as doomed as the Millennium Dome (see pp.192-3). However, the "excitation"—the technical term for the wobble caused by massed footsteps of users, around 80,000 crossing on opening day, of the pedestrian-only bridge moving in time with one another—was cured by improved damping and allowed the bridge to re-open during 2002. With a thirteen-foot-wide deck suspended from stainless balustrades and cables, the bridge allows unimpeded river views from the centre where the cables intentionally dip below the sightlines and, from the south, fosters the illusion of leading directly into St. Paul's Cathedral. At dusk, photoelectric cells trigger illuminations and the bridge achieves what its designers (engineers, architects and sculptor Anthony Caro) call its nocturnal "dematerialization," appearing as a 1,080-foot blade of light across the river.

Wren's View

A rare survivor from Mee's time, and indeed from much earlier, is the small cluster of houses that form Cardinal Cap's Alley. At no. 49, Catherine of Aragon, on her way to become the first wife of Henry VIII, is believed to sheltered on her arrival in London, and Sir Christopher Wren is said to have lived here as his great cathedral took shape across the river, though no documented evidence supports either claim. The spot nonetheless offers an opportunity to count the spires of ten Wren churches across the river that "spike the scene like exclamation marks, commanding attention," according to Norman Shrapnel.

Shakespeare's Southwark: Bear-baiting, Brothels and the Globe

Of a visit to a bear-baiting venue immediately east of today's Blackfriars Bridge, Pepys wrote: "… with my wife and Mercer to the Beare-garden, where I have not been, I think, of many years, and saw some good sport of the bull's tossing of the dogs: one into the very boxes. But it is a very rude and nasty pleasure. We had a great many hectors in the same box with us (and one very fine went into the pit, and played his dog for a wager, which was a strange sport for a gentleman)…"

Brothels were known as "stews" and the women therein as "Winchester geese" after the Bishop of Winchester, the landowner to whom Southwark businesses of all kinds paid tax and by whom they were regulated: prostitution was regarded as a means to calm potentially rebellious spirits. Of the women, an Italian visitor wrote: "They kiss each other a lot. If a stranger enters the house and does not first of all kiss the mistress on the lips, they think him badly brought up. At the dances, men hold women in their arms and hug them very tightly. And before each dance, they kiss them in a very lustful way."

During his ten years in Southwark, Shakespeare wrote *King Lear*, *Hamlet* and *Othello* among others, becoming wealthy enough to build his own theatre, the Globe, which opened in 1599. Globe performances drew audiences of up to 3,000, either standing or occupying bench seats, and often as loud as the actors themselves. Though rebuilt after a fire during *Henry VIII*, the Globe was closed by the Puritans in 1642 and soon after demolished. After an unlikely interlude of some 350 years, the theatre re-opened in the 1990s in reconstructed form about 600 feet from the site of the original, just east of Tate Modern. The theatre stages

Shakespearian and contemporary drama during the summer; audiences markedly more subdued than their Elizabethan counterparts.

Dickens' Southwark: the Clink and Marshalsea

Such was Southwark's lawlessness that the area held five prisons; the oldest, established around 1161 by the Bishop of Winchester, was the Clink, the name of which, by the eighteenth century, had become a generic term for jails and incarceration. According to Stow, the Clink was: "a goal or prison for the trespassers in these parts; namely, in old time, for such as should brabble, frey, or break the peace on said bank, or in the brothel houses, there were by the inhabitants thereabout apprehended and committed to this goal, where they were straightly imprisoned." The Clink was attacked and its inmates freed during the 1381 Peasants' Revolt and again during the 1451 Jack Cade Rebellion, but fell into disuse and was burned down during the 1780 Gordon Riots. By all accounts, the prison was as miserable as the tourist attraction now bearing its name.

Another Southwark prison, Marshalsea, enjoyed less enduring infamy but more significance during its lifetime, being, after the Tower, the most important place of incarceration in England. Its Tudor-era inmates included Bishop Bonner (see p.97), while among Marshalsea's nineteenth-century intake was John Dickens, father of the novelist, Charles. The prison became a key feature of Dickens' 1850s novel *Little Dorrit*, described as

> an oblong pile of barrack building, partitioned into squalid houses standing back to back, so that there were no back rooms; environed by a narrow paved yard, hemmed in by high walls duly spiked at top. Itself a close and confined prison for debtors, it contained within it a much closer and more confined jail for smugglers. Offenders against the revenue laws, and defaulters to excise or customs who had incurred fines which they were unable to pay, were supposed to be incarcerated behind an iron-plated door closing up a second prison, consisting of a strong cell or two, and a blind alley some yard and a half wide, which formed the mysterious termination of the very limited skittle-ground in which the Marshalsea debtors bowled down their troubles.

Religious Southwark: a Cathedral and *The Canterbury Tales*
The east end of Clink Street meets Cathedral Street and contains the remains—a rickety-looking wall bearing the hole once occupied by a rose window—of Winchester Hall, the residence of the Bishop, beyond which lies the *Golden Hind* (see below) and Southwark Cathedral, formally, the collegiate church of St. Saviour and St. Mary's Overie, an abbreviated form of "St. Mary's over the water". On a religious site founded by Augustinians in 1106, the cathedral was spared the Great Fire that raged across the river and consequently become London's oldest Gothic church. In 1663 Pepys could write: "...so over the fields to Southwarke. I spent half an hour in St Mary Overy's church, where are fine monuments of great antiquity." A nineteenth-century rebuilding and twentieth-century additions have resulted in a voluminous though underwhelming interior, despite a display of relics from much earlier times.

South of the cathedral off Borough High Street, Talbot Yard held the Tabard Inn, a medieval meeting place for pilgrims headed for Canterbury. The inn and its innkeeper played a pivotal role in *The Canterbury Tales*, being the device that allowed author Geoffrey Chaucer (c.1343-1400) to weave the pilgrims' tales into a portrait of English life. Of the tavern which stands here now, Harry C. Shelley warned in *Inns and Taverns of Old London* (1909): "no twentieth century pilgrim to the Tabard inn must expect to find its environment at all in harmony with the picture enshrined in Chaucer's verse. The passing years have wrought a woeful and materializing change."

A Golden Hind
Mere replica it may be but the model of Sir Francis Drake's ship, the *Golden Hind* that stands in St. Mary Overie Dock, once part of the estate of Southwark Cathedral, sailed the seven seas in the 1970s, emulating the voyages of its sixteenth-century namesake. Chiefly serving as an educational resource, the ship might encourage future adventurers, or it may have the effect that the rotting original had on the Venetian diplomat Orazio Busino: "we likewise passed along the banks of the Thames in sight of some relics of the ship of the famous captain Drake, which looked exactly like the bleached ribs and bare skull of a dead horse. In that ship he sailed around the world, passing through the straits of Magellan, and returned home freighted with much gold and with

fragrant spices. Truly such gain and glory sound highly attractive, but when one reflects upon the dangers of the sea the desire vanishes."

The *Marchioness* Disaster

A birthday party turned to tragedy in August 1989 when a chartered pleasure boat, the *Marchioness* with 132 people on board, was struck by a two-thousand-ton dredger and sank close Cannon Street rail bridge, claiming 51 lives. Subsequent months brought further anguish for victims' relatives, denied permission to see the bodies and eventually campaigning until 2000 before an enquiry was set up to investigate the incident. Among the outcomes were recommendations for improved river safety and the creation of the Thames' first lifeboat service. A memorial to the dead stands in Southwark Cathedral.

Around London Bridge

On the west side of London Bridge where the 1970s span utilized a small part of Rennie's nineteenth-century predecessor, a plaque marks "Nancy's Steps", an otherwise anonymous flight employed by Charles Dickens in *Oliver Twist* as Nancy's death site and earlier where Nancy inadvertently reveals Oliver's whereabouts to Fagin's spy: "The steps to which the girl had pointed, were those which, on the Surrey bank, and on the same side of the bridge as Saint Saviour's Church, form a landing-stairs from the river... These stairs are a part of the bridge; they consist of three flights. Just below the end of the second, going down, the stone wall on the left terminates in an ornamental pilaster facing towards the Thames. At this point the lower steps widen: so that a person turning that angle of the wall, is necessarily unseen by any others on the stairs who chance to be above him, if only a step."

Passing London Bridge and skirting London Bridge Station, in 1836 London's first rail passenger terminal and a contributor to the demise of the river as the city's main transport artery, leads toward a dramatically re-cast section of the river called London Bridge City. What becomes a public riverside area is first occupied by the private London Bridge Hospital. Even an exclusive room with a Thames view provided little succor for former Chilean dictator General Augusto Pinochet who was arrested at the hospital in 1998 on the extradition warrant that led to his eventual return to Chile.

Where wharves and cobbled streets once defined the river east of London Bridge and Anne Saunders could write as recently as 1984 in *The Art and Architecture of London* of this "isolated community, separated from the rest of London," the new outlook is piazzas, atriums, bistros, sculpture, fountains, expanded river views and the start of an unbroken Thamesside walk to Tower Bridge with views to the City of London. London Bridge Pier provides a departure point for pleasure cruises, while the monstrously large HMS *Belfast*, a Second World War naval veteran permanently berthed at Morgans Lane Wharf, serves as a competent and occasionally provocative museum of naval warfare. The community, meanwhile, is less isolated and less separate but also, perhaps, less of a community.

City Hall

If a drunken glass-blower sought to create a life-sized model of the leaning Tower of Pisa, the result might be something like City Hall, a building of uncertain shape which, since 2002, has housed the Greater London Authority, the elected London Assembly and the separately elected Mayor of London (not to be confused with the Lord Mayor). The structure employs what Ken Allinson termed "the kind of difficult circular geometry that First Year architecture students are told to avoid like the plague" and symbolizes a municipal determination to regenerate the former industrial sections of London's riverside. A spiral ramp rises through the building's interior, culminating in a so-called public viewing gallery often commandeered for corporate functions. At night, according to a fawning article in *Architecture Week*, City Hall's lighting is such that the building acquires "an aesthetic of molten gold". Underground routes connect City Hall to surrounding buildings and transport facilities, allowing cynics to conclude that City Hall's occupants reach their desks in a manner appropriate for politicians and administrators: by emerging from subterranean depths.

Tower Bridge: Symbol and Sham

With a central span dividing in two to allow tall ships to pass, pedestrian walkways 142 feet high, and a faux-medieval form intended to match the Tower of London by which it stands, Tower Bridge was a striking new addition to the riverscape in the 1890s and quickly became a symbol of the city, a mark of its booming economy and the seemingly endless growth of the Port of London. To the bridge's opening ceremony, *The Times* bestowed a gravitas more suited to a coronation: "The decorations, both by land and water, were brilliant and profuse, the uniforms and robes splendid and varied, while the glorious sunshine brought out in full relief the many beauties of the great display and of the noble river which all true Englishmen love with a proud affection as the chiefest glory of their ancient capital."

Yet Tower Bridge was a sham as well as a symbol. The bogus antique cladding concealed a steel frame within which operated the world's most advanced hydraulic system to power to raise and lower the bascules and in so doing, wrote Michael Jenner in *London Heritage*, "perfectly reflected the confusion between architecture and engineering, historicism and technology, so characteristic of the (Victorian) age." On its opening, *The Builder* magazine insisted: "the whole structure is the most monstrous and preposterous sham that we have ever known of, and is in that sense a discredit to the generation which has erected it." It continued by bemoaning the fortune spent on "elaborate and costly make-believe". Taking double the projected four years to complete and costing the lives of ten of its 432 workmen, the bridge became a tourist attraction even before it was finished and opened with a sense that its time had gone: the square-rigged sailing ships for whose masts clearance had been required were heading for extinction.

For all its fame, the bridge leads a fairly dull life save for being raised around 900 times a year and experiencing sporadic events such as the three planes which have flown beneath it, the double decker bus that was caught mid-span when the bascules began to rise in 1952, and a performance by rock band Texas in September 2005. In 1910 the elevated public walkways were closed due to, depending on which account one reads, the activities of pickpockets and prostitutes, frequent suicide attempts, the antics of "publicity seekers", or simply because, as the bridge museum which now occupies one of the walkways suggests, "not many people used them."

Where Tower Bridge carries traffic over the river, the 1870 Tower Subway became the world's first underground railway carrying up to twelve passengers a time on seventy-second journeys beneath it. Claustrophobia and limited passenger numbers contributed to the tunnel's swift financial demise, however, and the subway, minus its tracks but with gas lamps, became a busy pedestrian route with 20,000 people a week paying a halfpenny toll to cross. Tower Bridge's opening ended the subway's viability and, after several decades of disuse, it found a role as a conduit for the pipes of the London Water Company and is now used to carry fibre-optic cables.

The subway elicited one of the earliest recollections of a London tourist travelling by underground train when the Italian author Edmundo de Amicis recorded in 1883:

> ...I went down and down between two dingy walls until I found myself at the round opening of the gigantic iron tube, which seems to undulate like a great intestine in the enormous belly of the river. The inside of this tube presents the appearance of a subterranean corridor, of which the end is invisible. It is lighted by a row of lights as far as you can see, which shed a veiled light, like sepulchral lamps; the atmosphere is foggy; you go along considerable stretches without meeting a soul; the walls sweat like those of an aqueduct; the floor moves under your feet like the deck of a vessel; the steps and voices of the people coming the other way give forth a cavernous sound, and are heard before you see the people, and they at a distance seem like great shadows; there is, in short, a sort of something mysterious, which without alarming causes in your heart a vague sense of disquiet. When then you have reached the middle and no longer see the end in either direction, and feel the silence of a catacomb, and know not how much farther you must go, and reflect that in the water beneath, in the obscure depths of the river, is where suicides meet death, and that over your head vessels are passing, and that if a crack should open in the wall you would not even have the time to recommend your soul to God, in that moment how lovely seems the sun! I believe I had come a good part of a mile when I reached the opposite opening on the left bank of the Thames; I went up a staircase, the mate of the other, and came out in front of the Tower of London.

London's River: the Working Thames

In the mid 1970s the view from the top of a no.5 bus as it drove eastwards into Docklands from Tower Bridge was a profoundly depressing experience. Urban dereliction marked nearly every stop, and the view over the rooftops to the old dock basins of Shadwell and Millwall showed the near terminal state of advanced obsolescence... In 1981, the situation was as hopeless as at anytime since the Blitz.
Brian Edwards, *London Docklands*, 1992

From the Thames below Tower Bridge, adventurers mapped the world, settlers colonized it and modern London made a fortune from international trade. Little of the wealth, however, reached the hands of those who assisted in its creation and lived along this section of the river. Similarly, the tax-break-fuelled developments that have characterized the area since the 1980s (nowhere more controversially than on the Isle of Dogs) have rarely brought sustained prosperity to the established population.

Geographically close to the City of London but economically and socially distanced from it, this east London precinct has long been marked by insular and tight-knit communities, a fact known to nineteenth-century social investigators. Charles Booth noted that around Bow Creek was a settlement where "many of the families have been here for four of five generations... and the place is as full of scandal and gossip as a village," while Beatrice Webb recorded that the inhabitants of Cubbit Town were so "cut off by their residence in the interior of the Isle of Dogs from the social influences of the East-end, they have retained many traits of provincial life."

All the more reason, then, for locals to oppose outside interference and view the upheavals and regeneration initiatives of the 1980s as yet another destructive wave of the kind first experienced with nineteenth-century dock building and subsequently by wartime bombing. But while the worst recent excesses blot the landscape literally and metaphorically, there has been much to applaud as the riverside has steadily become more accessible and less polluted than at any time since the industrial revolution: the entire region a more attractive place to live, for residents of all incomes, than perhaps ever before.

The Working Thames North: St. Katharine's Dock to Blackwall

A whisker breadth's east of the Tower, St. Katherine's Dock set the tone for regeneration as early as the 1970s when its decline was halted by a transformation into shops, homes and office space. Wapping, of which St. Katharine's forms a part, was a haunt of salty dogs long before the docks arrived and retains the riverside landmarks, from two ancient pubs to one of the city's most barbaric sites of execution, to prove it. Docks crushed the local spirit as their high walls divided the population, and recent widespread regeneration has created an uneasy mix of ageing local authority housing and new warehouse accommodation rarely affordable to the indigenous population. Much the same applies to neighbouring Limehouse, multi-cultural before the term was invented, and it applies particularly to the Isle of Dogs. Insular even by local standards, the Isle of Dogs became a focus of 1980s change, Canary Wharf both a siren call for deregulated design and a symbol of outside exploitation of a long-standing, if economically declining, local community.

St. Katharine's Dock

From Tower Stairs the view, looking either way, is very striking; the river is crowded with shipping and steamers, and from this point begins the succession of vessels which affords the voyager so grand an idea of the vast trade of the British metropolis. There are, perhaps, few sights in the world more striking—certainly none more calculated to make an Englishman proud of his country.
Mr. and Mrs. S. C. Hall, *The Book of the Thames*, 1859

A sprawling hotel, a yacht marina and legions of tourists now fill the view east from the Tower, the effect on an Englishman's pride only to be guessed at. When the Halls visited, however, they stood within a few minutes' walk of the westernmost of the capital's nineteenth-century wet docks, St. Katharine's, completed in 1828. In the dog-eat-dog capitalism of the times nothing was allowed to stand in the way of the dock companies' need for land: a twelfth-century religious foundation, a hospital and 1,250 homes were all destroyed, as 11,000 people were made homeless without compensation. Where the land acquisition was vicious, the docks' construction, under engineer Thomas Telford (1757-

1834), was inspired. Composed of three bodies of deep water over a 24-acre site with warehouses built flush to the quayside, the dock allowed cargoes to be unloaded and stored with hitherto unknown speed and efficiency. While St. Katharine's initially flourished with sugar, tea, rubber and luxury goods such as ivory, feathers and shells, it was an economic failure, soon congested and remote as navigation this far upriver became unfeasible for newer generations of ships. Merged with London Docks in 1864 and badly damaged by wartime bombing, St. Katharine's closed in the 1960s and became the first of the city's docks to be remodelled—as a marina surrounded by office, retail and residential spaces gouged from the former warehouses. Among the present visitor attractions are an aquarium, the pseudo-Victoriana of the Dickens Inn and a colonnaded Starbucks.

Wapping

Evolving from a Saxon settlement, Wapping grew from marshlands into a market garden, having been drained by a Dutchman and shielded from the river by an eight-foot-high wall. Easily accessed from the sea and within walking distance of the City, Wapping became a natural stop for seafarers through the seventeenth and eighteenth centuries and subsequently a major cog in the machine that was the Port of London. Naturalist Thomas Pennant described eighteenth-century Wapping as a "long narrow street, well paved and handsomely flagged on both sides, winding along the banks of the Thames... inhabited by multitudes of seafaringmen, alternately occupants of sea and land; their floating tenements lie before them."

Such seafarers were well catered for. Amid the timber buildings lining the waterfront were the shops and workplaces of boat builders, mast makers, instrument-makers, and even the nautical tailors where Nelson himself is said to have purchased his first seagoing wardrobe. Baser needs were serviced by taverns, thirty-six in Wapping High Street alone, off which alleyways could lead to further pleasures—or dangers. In *Unknown London* (1919), Walter G. Bell suggests of Wapping: "It was the foulest, most loathsome spot in all London... Men, armed with knives and loaded bludgeons, lurked in dark corners to attack and rob the seamen, already well plied with drink." Women, meanwhile, "plied with fiery spirit and quickly quarrelsome, stripped to the waist and fought with fist and claw to make a holiday for the sailors ashore, ringed about in the open streets by a throng as debased as themselves."

The scene changed with the coming of the docks, which included four massive, warehouse-lined basins whose walls made the High Street resemble a canyon. Bell lamented: "The one paved street runs beneath the sheer walls of huge warehouses that shut out all sight of the river, low-lying as though at the bottom of a deep cutting… Can this be the famous Wapping High Street?… The narrow road twists awkwardly around gasworks and stores a few workmen's tenements."

Similarly disappointed was essayist Nathaniel Hawthorne, who described a Thames pleasure cruise for *The Atlantic Monthly* in 1863: "…we landed in Wapping, which I should have presupposed to be the most tarry and pitchy spot on earth, swarming with old salts, and full of warm, bustling, coarse, homely, and cheerful life. Nevertheless, it turned out to be a cold and torpid neighborhood, mean, shabby, and unpicturesque, both as to its buildings and inhabitants: the latter comprising (so far as was visible to me) not a single unmistakable sailor, though plenty of land-sharks, who get a half dishonest livelihood by business connected with the sea."

Where dock construction had generally swelled the population of east London's riverside, the opposite applied at Wapping, which became what Weinreb and Hibbert termed "an island surrounded by high walls, with few exits." Wapping remained isolated and excluded from London life until the 1980s when a section became a conservation area of which the upbeat James Bentley in *East of the City* called "a honey pot for devotees of urban architecture". By this standard, the sweetest finds might be the two rows of Georgian terraced houses completed at Wapping Pier Head for high-ranking officials of the London Dock Company. Now divided into apartments suited to deep-pocketed City high flyers, the houses are part of a "new Wapping", forming, suggests Ed Glinert in *The London Compendium*, "an unlikely magnet for the rich, albeit one devoid of conspicuous life or community."

Before Wapping attracted property speculators, the main reason for any outsider to visit were its pubs, none better entrenched on the tourist circuit than the Prospect of Whitby. Known as the Devil's Tavern until 1777, allegedly on account of its villainous clientele, the pub is squeezed between riverside warehouses and is commonly described as London's oldest pub. River views from the rear inspired Turner and Whistler as well as later generations of holiday photographers.

Similarly steeped in Wapping history, another pub, the Town of Ramsgate, was named for the fishermen from the Kent town of Ramsgate who would unload their catches here to be transported to Billingsgate. A flimsy legend holds that Captain Bligh and Fletcher Christian drank here together before setting sail on the *Bounty* in 1787; stronger evidence supports the story of convicts bound for Australia being chained awaiting transportation in the cellar, and of the apprehension of Judge Jeffries (1648-89). Well known in Wapping and a national hate figure for sentencing 320 men to death or transportation following the 1685 Monmouth Rebellion (an attempt to overthrow the Catholic King James II), Jeffries was seeking to flee the country following James' fall in 1688 and disguised himself as a sailor before being recognized in the pub and apprehended, narrowly avoiding being torn to pieces by an angry mob as he was taken to the Tower.

Like other British ports, Wapping provided a fruitful hunting ground for Royal Navy press gangs in the seventeenth and early eighteenth centuries. Paid per capture, the gangs provided the crews for British warships until the end of the Napoleonic era. Those forcibly recruited could expect years of ship-bound misery risking their lives for the king. One such unfortunate hanged himself from the door catch of his room in Wapping's still-extant Bell pub in 1736.

The Murdoch Press Gang

Through the 1980s Wapping's disused docks were covered. Tobacco Dock became a two-level shopping mall beset with financial problems, Wapping Basing became Wapping Sports Centre, while another former dock became the base of Rupert Murdoch's News International, publishing and printing *The Times*, *The Sunday Times* and the *Sun*. Murdoch's move to Wapping was intended to escape the power of journalists and printers' unions. In protest, six thousand employees went on strike, received immediate redundancy notices and picketed the new plant. The conflict brought mounted police to Wapping's streets and the plant was nicknamed "Fortress Wapping". In 2004 it was announced that News International would again relocate, to a site in North London.

Execution Dock

The "E" painted onto a section of the Wapping bank is not a leftover of a late-1980s rave party but denotes the site of Execution Dock where, until 1830, the lives of pirates and mutinous seamen were regularly brought to a premature and prolonged end. Wapping's executions were even more theatrical than most: the condemned man would be carried to the scaffold in a cart fronted by mounted admiralty officials bearing a ceremonial silver oar. The scaffold itself, standing in the river alongside the bank, was built without a dropfloor, ensuring that the condemned would die from slow strangulation rather than a broken neck, bringing maximum discomfort for him and maximum spectacle for the audience. Incoming tides were allowed to wash over the hanged man three times before the body was cut loose, the remains of the most notorious being displayed along the Thames as a warning to others. In his 1844 *London*, Charles Knight recalled "the bodies of pirates opposite Blackwall wavering on the wind... (was) one of the first sights that were wont to greet the stranger approaching London from the sea."

Wapping Old Stairs

One of eight public stairs that served the Wapping waterfront, Wapping Old Stairs have an unprepossessing appearance unbecoming of their place in history. Here convicts took their last steps in England before transportation to the colonies, and in 1671 Captain William Blood was captured attempting to flee with Charles II's coronation crown. Nor do they evoke their contribution to nineteenth-century culture with a popular song that began:

Your Molly has never been false, she declares,
Since last time we parted at the foot of Wapping Old Stairs...

The stairs today are unlikely to encourage anyone to break into song, but the tune was sufficiently well-known to be mentioned in Thackeray's *Vanity Fair* ("finally they went down to dinner, Amelia clinging to George's arm, still warbling the tune of "Wapping Old Stairs") and in M. E. Braddon's *Run to Earth* (1868): "The captain stopped, with the bell-rope in his hand, to listen to the sound of music

close at hand. A woman's voice, fresh and clear as the song of a sky-lark, was singing 'Wapping Old Stairs,' to the accompaniment of a feeble old piano."

Wapping Police Station

The squat riverfront building of brown brick laced with white Portland Stone, usually fronted by high-speed river police launches, is the 1910 Wapping Police Station, the base of London's earliest organized police force. Founded in 1798 to combat the excessive theft from the docks, the private forces of the dock companies became affiliated to the Metropolitan Police in 1837 and were united under the Port of London Authority in 1909. A grim notice board of bodies recovered from the river once occupied the station's front wall; inside today is a police museum, its exhibits including the "saddest book in the world", a list of attempted suicides on the river with a narrative of events leading to them.

The Thames Tunnel

One way disillusioned Wapping residents could escape was under the river through the Thames Tunnel, opened in 1843 between Wapping and Rotherhithe. Marc Isambard Brunel (1769-1849), French-born engineer and father of the more famous Isambard Kingdom, pioneered a shield drilling method by which a tunnel could be constructed through soft ground. Nicknamed the "Great Bore" for the inordinate duration of its construction (it was begun in 1825, beset by floods, fires and noxious gases, and abandoned for seven years due to lack of funds), changing times rendered the tunnel redundant for its original purpose: intended to allow cargo to be moved beneath the river by horse, it was finished with stairs rather than a ramp, making it inaccessible to horses, and after railways had become the docks' main form of transport. The tunnel spent its first years as a pedestrian conduit and venue for spring fairs, becoming a domain of pickpockets and prostitutes before being sold to the East London Railway Company in 1866, eventually forming part of the East London tube line. The tunnel is documented on the south side in Brunel's Engine House (see p.181).

Shadwell and Limehouse

Warehouses form an almost unbroken line from Wapping east to Shadwell, uninhabited marshland until the seventeenth-century shipping boom and, like Wapping, carved up to create docks in the early 1800s. The conversion helped to create some of Victorian London's worst slums, which recorded some of the worst fatality statistics during the city's regular cholera outbreaks. Such social deprivation fostered a Shadwell that Henry Walker could describe in *East London—Sketches of Christian Work and Workers* (1896) as "the 'dumping ground' for the moral and social debris of the kingdom—wild harum-scarum lads who run away from home, half-witted ones who no-one cares to employ, profligate prodigals who have spent their substance and have not even pigs to tend, 'broken-down' and 'ne'er do wells' who naturally sink down as the sediments of the great backwaters of London life." The 1980s redevelopment successfully reshaped much of Shadwell, the 1922 King Edward VII Memorial Park a rare survivor from earlier times.

Anyone headed west towards London in the eighteenth century might well have considered that they had reached the city when they reached Limehouse, its houses terraced rather than spaced and Hawksmoor's imposing 1720s St. Anne's Church such a powerful feature of the local landscape that "a sailor might be deceived... supposing it a very large ship coming towards him, under easy sail, with a flag flying at her main top," wrote J. P. Malcolm in *Londinium Redivivum* (1802).

Limehouse took its name from the lime kilns established at least from the fourteenth century with the largest standing by the river at the end of Three Colts Street. Trade was boosted by the Limehouse Cut, a canal across the Isle of Dogs that linked the Thames to the River Lea, and much more so by the Limehouse Basin, also known as the Regents Canal Dock, connecting the Thames to the Grand Union Canal. Opened in August 1820, the route linked London's docks to central England, moving coal, timber and Norwegian ice, a valuable commodity for well-to-do homes in the pre-refrigerator age.

Sea trade on a far greater scale followed the opening of the West India Docks on the Isle of Dogs in 1802 and brought Limehouse an ethnically mixed population: "in and about Limehouse we should have little difficulty in finding the Persian, the Arab, the Egyptian, or even the South Sea Islander," wrote one Victorian commentator, a fact much to the delight of journalists who seized the chance to explore foreign cultures and compose lurid reports without leaving London. Of Limehouse's Chinese population, George R. Sims wrote in 1905: "There is no mistake about the Chinese element. The Chinese names are up over the doors of the little shops, and as we peer inside them we see the unmistakable Celestial behind the counter and Chinese inscriptions on the walls. At the back of one little shop is an opium den. If we enter we shall find only a couple of clients, for this is not the hour. The 'den' is dark and dirty and reeks unpleasantly."

Sims' expedition resulted in nothing more extraordinary than the accidental purchase of firecrackers, but Count E. Armfelt's 1902 article, *Oriental London*, took a closer look: "There are mysterious looking shops in Limehouse with little or nothing in the windows, and which have curtains to shut off the street. Now and again a Chinaman or other Asiatic will push the handle and disappear. It is an opium-smoking room. Enter and you will see a counter, a pair of small scales, a few cigars, some tobacco, and other *et ceteras*. The shop has a back parlour with a dingy yellow curtain. It is furnished with a settee, chairs, and a spacious divan, or wooden structure with one or two mattresses and half-a-dozen hard pillows or bolsters. It is there that the Ya'pian Kan—the prepared opium—is smoked, and the *majoon*, made of hellebore, hemp, and opium, is chewed, eaten, and smoked."

Legal and widely prescribed as a painkiller, opium nonetheless became inextricably linked with Limehouse and gave rise to Billy Bennett's music hall song, *Limehouse Liz*, recounting in the xenophobic terms of the day, the story of country girl drawn to the bright lights of London:

Then she drifted down to china town
And you all know where that is
Where slitty eyed chinks take 40 winks
And she's known as Limehouse Liz
And she lives on dope and tarry rope
She'd never have started the racket
But one day she went on a charabanc ride
And 'One Lung' gave her a packet!

Sax Rohmer's popular Fu Manchu novels, the first published in 1913, similarly employed Chinese stereotypes and dockland settings. Less sensationalist but received with some uproar was Thomas Burke's 1916 *Limehouse Nights*, a collection of fictional tales drawn on the author's own experiences. Tame by comparison was the Limehouse section of the river described by Charles Dickens in *Our Mutual Friend*, which included a pub, the Six Jolly Fellowship Porters, probably based on the Bunch of Grapes. One of a surprising number of seventeenth- and eighteenth-century remnants, the Bunch of Grapes stands on the half-mile-long Narrow Street, a riverside artery which, amid much maritime history, held the former home of Captain James Cook, demolished in 1956 and its site marked by a plaque. Evidence of changing times includes the new homes inching their way along Limehouse Cut and the "urbane and sophisticated" apartments of Watergarden, a prissy 1980s development neighbouring the Bunch of Grapes built around a garden on the site of a former power station.

The Isle of Dogs
While it became synonymous with spectacular and controversial docklands redevelopment in the 1980s, the Isle of Dogs was already no stranger to change. Long undeveloped marshland, the isle entered the nineteenth century with a single dwelling and a proliferation of windmills using the "high winds that blew unimpeded over the dismal peninsula" to assist in draining its wetlands. The opening of the West India Docks in 1802 expanded the local population to 4,000 by 1851; with the 1860s creation of Millwall Docks, the population reached 21,000 by 1901.

As its population grew, the isle's banks became lined by wharves, warehouses, factories and shipyards. In 1911 George R. Sims wrote in *The Strand*: "The island is no dreaming place. It is a land of labour. From morn till eve the streets are deserted; the inhabitants are behind the great walls and wooden gates—husbands, wives, sons and daughters, all are toiling. The only life in the long, dreary roads and desolate patches of black earth that are the distinguishing notes of the side streets is when the children come from school." While the docks lasted longer than shipbuilding and recovered well following the war, trade declined with the rise of containerization, and both the West India and Millwall docks closed in 1980. The Isle of Dogs had become, according to *The Times*, "empty waterfronts and rusting cranes", where 15,000 people had a thousand jobs between them.

Although jobs were few with the docks' decline, islanders showed little desire to leave. In *London Perceived* (1962), V. S. Pritchett wrote: "the (war-time) destruction on the Isle of Dogs was terrible, and no-one could get the inhabitants to move." In 1970 the 11,000 islanders declared unilateral independence in an attempt to highlight the area's failing economy, public transport and schools, and the lack of interest shown among politicians both local and city-wide. Activist Ted Johns, one-time watermen and harbour master, was among those behind the declaration and became an early critic of redevelopment, fearing, as happened at St. Katharine's Dock, that the benefits would not be felt by local people.

The Peninsula of Dogs; the Isle of Ducks

How the Isle of Dogs got its name is unclear. One tale holds that when Charles II occupied Greenwich Palace, the royal hounds were kept on the isle, their barking being audible to passing sailors. Another suggests that a waterman murdered a man whose dog then remained by his masters' body until forced to by hunger to swim to Greenwich, there finding the murderer and sounding an alert with loud barking. Due to the preponderance of waterfowl in its marshy days, yet another story suggests that the original name was the Isle of Ducks. A further twist is the fact that the isle is really a peninsula, or at least it was until the early 1800s when the Isle of Dogs Canal was cut to link shipping directly with the West India Docks.

Canary Wharf

Canary Wharf: It will feel like Venice and work like New York.
1987 advertising slogan

Under Margaret Thatcher's Conservative government, the new London Dockland Development Corporation was charged with regenerating the eight-mile stretch of ailing Thamesside London below Tower Bridge. Declared an Enterprise Zone with a raft of commercial incentives for developers, the Isle of Dogs became a central part of the scheme, epitomized by Canary Wharf Tower, eventually rising 843 feet above the old West India Docks. The tower instantly became a landmark and a symbol, though quite what it symbolized depended on whether one had greater empathy with locals such as Ted Johns or investment bankers such as Micheal von Clem, an excited advocate of docklands redevelopment in 1984 when head of the bank, Crédit Suisse First Boston.

In contrast to the nineteenth-century free-traders who had to fight both parliament and established practices for the right to build London's docks, their late twentieth-century Isle of Dogs counterparts were effectively handed all they wanted. Matters raised by residents and the Greater London Council fell on deaf ears, as did criticism over a major London development being dependent on North American money (Canadian developers Olympia and York from 1988) and design, notably US architect Cesar Pelli, who shaped Canary Wharf Tower.

The Docklands Light Railway, an over-ground connection to the London Underground network, ended decades of isolation for the Isle of Dogs, but motivation stemmed not from public need but from developers' demands for better public transportation being in place before they committed their funds. The early 1990s property crash bankrupted Olympia and York and left Canary Wharf with just 13,000 workers. With the decision to save money by switching off lights on its unoccupied floors, Canary Wharf Tower became a literal beacon of LDDC folly as the now clearly half-empty tower glowed in the evening skyline. It was a turn of events that made the 1987 advertising slogan seem surprisingly apposite: Venice, after all, was sinking and how well New York worked depended not on its own efforts but the vagaries of world financial markets.

With support from a new Labour government and a completion of a new tube station, however, Canary Wharf grew and by 2006 had 64,000 employees and a large complement of new buildings, including the dismal HSBC and Citibank high-rises, a shopping mall, the Museum of Docklands and tidy pavements adorned with public art.

Alongside the river just south of Canary Wharf's high-rise cluster, the Cascades is a yellow-and-blue apartment block adorned with nautical affectations: portholes, funnels and crows-nest balconies. The 171 apartments were the stuff of 1980s yuppie dreams and became a speculators' joy until the early 1990s property crash when prices dropped and the numerous flats were left unoccupied. Like much of Canary Wharf, the Cascades is heavy with political symbolism. Private home ownership was a major policy prong of the Thatcher government and it was put into practice even on the Isle of Dogs, which held the highest concentration of local authority housing in London. Just as Canary Wharf job creation became focused on outsiders, housing developments were typically beyond the reach of locals, including the office cleaners who took industrial action in 2005, an action described by the *Guardian* as revealing "a modern day tale of two cities".

Burrells Wharf, Brunel's Great Eastern and Millwall

Whether imaginative, inventive or simply bland, redevelopment is a constant feature of the Isle of Dogs riverside and becomes increasingly low-rise away from Canary Wharf. It even evokes a scene more redolent of a Berkshire rowing centre than a former hub of the British economy in the form of the Docklands Sailing and Watersports Centre, with its canoes and kayaks, at the entrance to the former Millwall Docks. Further on, Burrells Wharf now offers "blocks of flats of industrial strength", but acquired nautical fame as the building and launching site of Isambard Kingdom Brunel's *Great Eastern* in the 1850s.

With six masts, five funnels, a length of 700 feet and space for 4,000 passengers, the vessel, also known as the *Leviathan*, was the largest ship ever built. What could have been Brunel's greatest achievement was, through the financial misdealings of others, in some respects his greatest failure. The ship's size necessitated it being launched sideways, as the conventional stern-first method would have driven the vessel into the river's far bank. Against Brunel's wishes, spectators were admitted to the launch in November 1857 and witnessed the great vessel, due to under-powered hydraulic pumps, snap its mooring chains and kill a worker. Successfully launched the following year, lack of funds delayed its completion and, once seaworthy, the vessel spent most of its working life in the important but unglamorous work of laying cables, including the first across the Atlantic, before spending its retirement berthed in Liverpool as an entertainment centre.

At the south-western quarter of the Isle of Dogs, Millwall was named for the windmills that once lined the riverbank, though became better known nationally for the football team formed by workers at a local jam factory in the 1880s, which in 1910 left for a new home across the river. The team has been noted less for its success on the field than for its fans' recurrent hooliganism, said to have begun in the 1920s when an opposition goalkeeper was punched to the ground, and a defiant chant, apposite of the findings of Beatrice Webb, of "No-one likes us, we don't care."

Cubitt Town

While the Isle of Dogs' western side is generously endowed with the developments of contemporary architects, Cubitt Town, on the isle's south-eastern quarter, retains many council blocks from post-war rebuilding. The area was earlier developed by William Cubitt, a one-time Lord Mayor of London, who ensured that it acquired sawmills, cement works and timber wharves to complement employment opportunities at Millwall docks. Walter Besant remarked of Cubitt Town in his 1911 *London*: "It is for the working men of these factories that the streets of small houses have been erected; there are no houses for the better sort at all." Cubitt originally hoped that the "better sort" would be attracted to the isle's southern tip and its views of Wren's Royal Naval Hospital in Greenwich. As it turned out, they were not and the plot was bought by the hospital's commissioners who fashioned Island Gardens as a vantage point to admire the hospital's architectural grandeur—and subsequently to access the northern end of the Greenwich Foot Tunnel (see p.189).

Blackwall and a Whitebait Supper

The Blackwall Pier is, I think, the best from which the Londoner may see the traffic of the Thames. It is certainly reached by a railway which has some of the dirtiest and shabbiest stations and carriages to be found anywhere, and thus the contrast presented when the door of the Blackwall Terminus has been passed is the more striking. You exchange in a moment its dingy interior for the view of a grand bend in the river, alive with a crowd of red-sailed barges and other craft, through which a few big ships proceed slowly, like oxen among sheep. To the right the masts of the vessels in the West India and Millwall

Docks show like a larch plantation in the winter time. Both ways there is a long view down the Thames.

Reverend Harry Jones, *East and West London*, 1875

The Blackwall of the Reverend Jones' time was soon to disappear. Both it and parts of neighbouring Poplar were destroyed in the 1890s to facilitate the Blackwall Tunnel. Today's vista of oil storage containers and a traffic-laden elevated roadway suggests that little human settlement has returned, and bizarrely neither does the much more recent riverside addition of Richard Rogers' Reuters Building, a streamlined and strangely sinister growth from a toxic plot of which Stephanie Williams observed: "Glazed stair towers are the only clue to human habitation."

A sense of humanity departing does, however, chime with aspects of Blackwall's past: it was from here that nineteenth-century emigrants left with hope and assisted passage to new lives in New Zealand (the Reverend Jones recorded over a thousand a month during 1874). And it was from Blackwall in 1606 that the three ships carried 104 men and boys to what became the Jamestown settlement, the first permanent British colony in North America ("we had built and finished our Fort which was triangle-wise, having three Bulwarkes at every corner like a halfe Moone"), an event recorded beside the river by a 1920s monument which stands in front of the much more recently founded colony of Virginia Quay ("24 hour porterage and allocated parking").

People did come to Blackwall for reasons other than onward travel, though, and one was to feast on whitebait, a tiny fish abundant in this section of the river. John Timbs wrote in *Curiosities of London* (1867): "To the large taverns at Blackwall and Greenwich *gourmets* flock to eat whitebait, a delicious little fish caught in (Blackwall) Reach, and directly netted out of the river into the frying pan. They appear about the end of March or early in April, and are taken every flood-tide until September. Whitebait are caught by a net in a wooden frame, the hose having a very small mesh. The boat is moored in the tideway, and the net fixed to its side, when the tail of the hose, swimming loose, is from time to time handed in to the boat, the end untied, and its contents shaken out…"

Blackwall Docks and the East India Company
With a monopoly of trade with the East Indies, which included India

and China, the merchants who founded the East India Company in 1600 quickly amassed large fortunes. Such was the company's stature and wealth that it built its own ships from 1614 at Blackwall, the first wet dock to have a gate on the Thames. The docks later expanded into the eight-acre Brunswick Dock, subsequently replaced by the 1806 deep water East India Docks. The East India Company's ships were of such a size that they could travel no further upriver than Blackwall, where they were given permission to unload and attended by a specially appointed customs official; their cargo continuing west by barge and lighter.

Thames Ironworks

The rise of free trade enabled rival shipbuilders to challenge the supremacy of the East India Company; one that did so successfully was Thames Ironworks, evolving from the firm of Ditchburn & Mare and crossing the river from Deptford to open a yard on Bow Creek, just east of the East India Docks, in 1838. Manufacturing most of the Royal Navy's warships and many major ocean liners, Thames Ironworks became one of east London's biggest employers. Under a patriarchal managing director, the company created leisure activities for its staff including the formation in 1895 of a football team, the club crest showing two crossed riveting hammers. Following a merger with another club in 1900, the team turned professional and, as West Ham United, outlasted the company and went on to provide three members of England's 1966 World Cup winning team as well as gaining a reputation for open attacking football. The club's century of under-achievement has not lessened its fans' enthusiasm nor the popularity of their shouts rooted in a bygone age: "Come on you Irons!" and "Up the Hammers!"

When the Duchess of York arrived at Thames Ironworks in June 1898 to launch the *Albion*, a 6,000-ton cruiser built for the Royal Navy, she found that around 30,000 spectators—yard workers and local schoolchildren had been given a day's holiday—had arrived for the twin attractions of the mighty vessel's launch and the rarity of a royal visit. Such was the scarcity of good vantage points that several hundred people clambered onto an adjoining slipway, despite warning signs and the protestations of yard workers that doing so was unsafe. As the immense ship threatened to slip its dogshores, the launch was brought forward by ten minutes, but after the traditional bottle of champagne failed to break three times against the hull, the dogshores were released and the ship raced into the waters. The resultant waves smashed the flimsy slipway, tossing spectators into the water where some were trapped beneath timbers and others knocked unconscious by falling debris. Unable to see bodies in the muddy waters, police believed that all had been rescued, but the death count would eventually reach thirty-eight. Such was the widespread poverty of the area that costs of funerals and mourning clothes were met by the Ironworks' owner, Arnold Hills, though the loss of a breadwinner left some families unable to support their children, who were passed into the care of charities.

Blackwall Tunnel

Remembered for his embankments and sewers, Sir Joseph Bazalgette also persuaded the Metropolitan Board of Works of the need for a road tunnel beneath the Thames to link Blackwall with Greenwich. The Board of Works agreed the plan at their final meeting much to the annoyance of the elected members of the new London County Council who opposed it. The tunnel, opened in 1897, shifted half a million tons of earth, used seven million bricks, and at 4,400 feet became the world's longest underwater tunnel. Included on its course were bends rumoured to have been inserted to prevent horses bolting at the sight of daylight. In its first year, 335,000 vehicles, four million pedestrians and an undocumented number of horses used the tunnel, which was enlarged (and straightened) with a second passageway in the 1960s and still, with its congested approaches, looms large in rush-hour traffic reports.

The Working Thames South: Bermondsey to the Thames Barrier

Some of the most imposing contributions to the new architecture of London's river can be found in and around Bermondsey, spreading across former industrial waterfront and to the site where one of Charles Dickens' most infamous foes lurked. To the east, Rotherhithe, like Wapping, has a nautical heritage much older than its docks. Departure point for the *Mayflower* on its seventeenth-century voyage to America, Rotherhithe also fostered a distinctive local culture, epitomized by its timber-carrying deal porters. Further on, a royal dockyard once defined the waterfront of a currently resurgent Deptford while neighbouring

Greenwich is dominated by a royal palace-turned-hospital-turned-naval college that is now a university—but still one of the great sights of the Thames in London. Also a great sight, in a very different way, is the Thames Barrier, regarded as the last word in flood defences on its 1980s opening but nearing the end of its usefulness earlier than expected.

Bermondsey

Monks of Bermondsey Abbey, founded by the Cluniac Order in 1082 and surviving until the sixteenth-century dissolution, turned marshland into market gardens and embanked a section of the waterside to create St. Saviour's Dock, where the River Neckinger meets the Thames. In the aftermath of the Great Fire of 1666, London's wealthier stratas were drawn to Bermondsey to imbibe its "fine air" and visit Cherry Gardens, a scene of refined entertainment as well as cherries, visitors to which included an enraptured Pepys who recorded in his diary that he departed from Cherry Garden Pier "singing finely."

By the 1870s, the rise of river trade had given Bermondsey a predominantly working-class population and, with Butler's Wharf between Tower Bridge and the Neckinger, the largest wharf complex on the Thames. The area was described in *The Royal River* as: "the London that really works with a will. To the right are tanneries and tallow-chandleries–their odour loads the atmosphere as if it were a thick fog incapable of any effort to rise–to the left are vast granaries and wharves; and between them the narrow spaces are filled up with hurrying vehicles and toiling men."

From the mid-1980s, Butler's Wharf underwent extensive regeneration under Conran-Roche (an architecture and town planning company headed by high profile design guru and restaurateur Terence Conran), turning cavernous abandoned warehouses still scented with exotic spices into luxury apartments and offices now scented by takeaway gourmet coffee. A cobbled and pristine street, Shad Thames, is still crossed by the latticework iron bridges that originally connected the warehouses and lined by estate agents with expanding property lists as more local buildings undergo conversion. The presence of the "white Corbusian box" of the Design Museum notwithstanding, the mood of the riverside, encouraged by the terrace tables of pricey restaurants, is one of money being possessed—and conspicuously spent.

Over the Neckinger: Bill Sikes' Lair

Crossing a gated footbridge over the Neckinger leads towards the pink flourishes of China Wharf, one among many examples of flamboyant recent architecture found on and around New Concordia Wharf. Seekers of intense sensory experiences should detour inland to visit The Circle on Queen Elizabeth Street where, Samantha Hardingham suggests, they will be "ceremoniously engulfed in a vat of cobalt blue" on entering the enclosed space formed by the walls of an apartment complex occupying a former brewery. Residents of China Wharf, The Circle or any neighbouring apartment block, are unlikely have much in common with their Victorian forebears who occupied what were then some of south London's worst slums. In *Oliver Twist* (1837), Charles Dickens made the seething streets, then known as Folly Ditch (latterly as Jacob's Island), a lair for the villainous Bill Sikes:

> Crazy wooden galleries common to the backs of half a dozen houses, with holes from which to look upon the slime beneath; windows, broken and patched, with poles thrust out, on which to dry the linen that is never there; rooms so small, so filthy, so confined, that the air would seem too tainted even for the dirt and squalor which they shelter; wooden chambers thrusting themselves out above the mud, and threatening to fall into it—as some have done; dirt-besmeared walls and decaying foundations; every repulsive lineament of poverty, every loathsome indication of filth, rot, and garbage; all these ornament the banks of Folly Ditch.

East of New Concordia Wharf, pristine developments give way to construction sites and local authority homes, a reminder of the established population for whom the river had, until the decline of its industry, been a place of work rather than a three-course lunch. Yet another twist in the power-play of disparate river interests is found beside Reeds Wharf with Downings Road moorings, where a cluster of barges are permanently occupied by a twenty-strong community: "people who have made a conscious choice to be part of the river," one told the *Guardian* in 2004. The barges have been decorated with trees and plants, while their occupants, here since the 1980s, have been praised for their recycling. Nonetheless, the greenery conceals deep-seated tensions between the occupants, supported by a broad church of politicians, and residents and developers who see the community as a blight on their cherished—and financially advantageous—river views.

Turner and the *Temeraire*; Sculpture and the Salters

From a vantage point hereabouts in 1838, the artist J. M. W. Turner watched the final voyage of a 98-gun warship and produced what would become one of his celebrated works, *The Fighting Temeraire*, showing the mighty naval vessel at the end of its distinguished life being pulled by a comparatively miniscule tug beneath a fiery-hued sky, seemingly as infinite as the river below. Debate continues as to whether the sun, shown in the east, is rising or (with artistic licence) setting. Just east of Cherry Garden Pier, the only reminder of Cherry Gardens (see p.177) and close to the Angel pub, is the curious sight of a sculptured gentleman on a public bench. Part of a series by Diane Gorvin, the figure depicts Doctor Alfred Salter (1873-1945), who did much to improve healthcare and local life in general, becoming Bermondsey's Member of Parliament in 1903; his wife became a local councillor and was elected mayor in 1922. The couple's daughter, Joyce, who died aged nine of scarlet fever, is also depicted beside the river, as is the family cat which sits on the river wall.

Rotherhithe and the Mayflowers

"The eternal river, ships, boats and barges, views over the water and landwards, many stairs leading down at low tide, piers, wharves docks, and a feeling of open airiness impart just the right atmosphere of present and past meaning," wrote Sydney R. Jones of Rotherhithe in 1943. Despite far fewer vessels, the river remains eternal and Rotherhithe's seafaring heritage remains apparent despite substantial redevelopment along a shoreline traversed by the two-mile-long Rotherhithe Street, one of London's longest thoroughfares.

Among countless seafarers who could claim intimate knowledge of Rotherhithe was Captain Christopher Jones (?-1622), whose voyages included that in command of the *Mayflower*, one of the two ships which sailed from Plymouth in 1620 carrying the Pilgrim Fathers across the Atlantic to settle what they also called Plymouth and what many white Americans call the start of their nation's history. Jones was buried in

Rotherhithe's St. Mary's Church; his burial site is unmarked but his part in the story of the Pilgrim Fathers is remembered with a much photographed marker. The ship itself was allowed to rot on a spot thought to be adjacent to the Shippe Tavern, rebuilt and re-named the Mayflower and coincidentally one of the few public taverns also serving as a post office, licensed to sell postage stamps; originally for the convenience of seamen, now for the convenience of tourists.

Surrey Docks and Deal Porters

Proximity to the Royal Dockyard at Deptford (see pp.183-4) encouraged ship fitting and repair yards to spread into Rotherhithe. With the 1697 Howland Great Wet Dock, the area gained London's largest, and then only, enclosed dock. Renamed Greenland Dock in 1763 when it served Arctic whalers, the ten-acre plot became part of Surrey Docks, which during the nineteenth century covered 460 acres of Rotherhithe and included nine separate docks, six timber ponds and a three-and-a-half mile canal.

At its height, Surrey Docks employed around a thousand deal porters ("deals" being a term for wooden planks) to unload timber and carry it to warehouses. Their heads protected by padded caps with long flaps covering their necks, the porters carried timber on their shoulders, stacking them in piles sometimes sixty-feet high. Their ability to reach the top of a timber pile by walking along single raised planks earned deal porters the nickname of the Flying Blondins, after a popular tightrope act, and the following comment from A.G. Linney who visited in the 1930s: "They wear leather 'backing' hats with a protecting flap which covers the neck, and the skill with which they balance a load of several lengthy planks on their lower neck and walk with their load often a considerable distance to the storage piles is astonishing. The more astonishing as they often have to travel along an avenue between piles, at a height of ten or twelve feet from the ground, where there is but a single plank-width for their feet to rest upon... Backward and forward for eight hours a day these men plod at their arduous task, and have rightly earned the reputation of being the steadiest of dock workers."

Deal portering was a trade often passed from father to son and one that evolved its own slang ("Surrey Docks" itself became rhyming slang for "pox"), but could do nothing to prevent the docks' post-war decline or their closure in 1969. Plans by the Greater London Council to build new housing estates across the former dockland lacked funds and enthusiasm, indicative of Rotherhithe's distance from the capital's concerns. Under the remit of the 1980s London Docklands Development Council (LDDC), Rotherhithe was reshaped with a conservation area around St. Mary's Church, given a new riverside path lined with imitation gas lamps as the former docks were filled-in and covered with low-rise homes ringed by cycle routes and parks, and dotted with public artworks that include Philip Bews' Deal Porters monument at Canada Water. With some justification, Sally Williamson dismissed the new Rotherhithe as "ticky-tacky housing and cheap industrial developments that many have come to associate with the LDDC's authority." Yet the sight of the Canary Wharf towers rising across the river might suggest Rotherhithe's good fortune at having being spared similar excesses.

The Brunel Engine House and Rotherhithe Tunnel

Unpretentiously sited amid a housing estate and announced by a slender chimney rising from a red-brick building, the Brunel Engine House held the steam pumps that kept the Thames Tunnel free of water during its long construction. Now holding a small museum documenting the first tunnel under the Thames, the engine house stands adjacent to the 42-foot-deep shaft used in the initial stage of tunneling. Brunel himself is remembered by Brunel Road, running parallel to a road named Tunnel Approach, not the route to the Thames Tunnel but the 1908 Rotherhithe Tunnel.

Costing £1.5 million, not including the £1,835 paid to 58 Thames watermen as compensation for lost trade, the Rotherhithe Tunnel opened in 1908, linking Rotherhithe with Stepney on the river's north side. At the opening ceremony, the Prince of Wales unlocked the gates with a golden key and then, as *The Times* reported, "the Royal Highnesses re-entered their carriage and proceeded through the tunnel to the pavilion at the northern approach, being again loudly cheered as their carriage disappeared from view."

To Deptford in the Footsteps of Pepys

To perform his duties as First Clerk, subsequently Secretary, to the Navy in the 1660s, diarist Samuel Pepys (1633-1703) was a frequent visitor to Deptford, formerly a fishing village on Deptford Creek, where the Royal Docks had been founded under Henry VIII in 1513. Taking the inland route across what were then fields and often pausing at a tavern called the Halfway House, Pepys frequently walked between Deptford and Rotherhithe (then known as Redriffe), and sometimes the Royal shipyard at Woolwich, recording such in numerous entries including:

1 June 1661: "From Deptford we walked to Redriffe, calling at the Half-way house, and there come into a room where there was infinite of new cakes placed that are made against Whitsuntide, and there we were very merry."

5 September 5 1662: "…walked all alone to Greenwich, and thence by water to Deptford, and there examined some stores, and did some of my own business in hastening my work there, and so walked to Redriffe, being by this time pretty weary and all in a sweat…"

19 September 1662: "I went alone to Deptford… At night, after I had eaten a cold pullet, I walked by brave moonshine, with three or four armed men to guard me, to Redriffe… I hear this walk is dangerous to walk alone by night, and much robbery committed here. So from thence by water home, and so to my lodgings to bed."

24 March 1664: "I walked very finely to Woolwich, and there did very much business at both yards, and thence walked back, Captain Grove with me talking, and so to Deptford and did the like-there, and then walked to Redriffe (calling and eating a bit of collops and eggs at Half-way house), and so home…"

The docks lasted three hundred years; Pepys' diary outlived them and continues to be read, and his name is immortalized at Deptford by a small park and a large 1960s housing estate on the site of the former Royal Victoria Victualling Yard. Of the estate, Norman Shrapnel wrote in 1977: "a massive exercise in modern rehousing which the local children… tend to call the Pepsie Estate."

John Evelyn's Deptford

Pepys was an occasional visitor to another diarist, John Evelyn (1620-1706), also an accomplished gardener and a founder of the Royal Society. From 1652, Evelyn lived at Deptford's Sayes Court and in 1698 rented the house for three months, at the request of the Crown, to Tsar Peter of Russia, who was visiting the Royal Docks to study shipbuilding techniques with a view to modernizing the Russian Navy. According to Hugh Phillips, each night the Tsar would "regale himself with a pint of brandy, a bottle of sherry, and eight bottles of sack, after which he went to the theatre." Peter and his entourage, whom Evelyn's housekeeper called "people right nasty", inflicted considerable damage on the house and the gardens, where the Tsar's biggest pleasure was being pushed through the hedge in a wheelbarrow. On his tenant's departure, Evelyn asked Sir Christopher Wren to assess the damages and submitted a bill to the Crown, which was duly paid. It was in Deptford that Evelyn chanced upon a woodcarver, Grinling Gibbons (1648-1721), introduced him to Wren and set in the motion the chain of events that led to Gibbons becoming acknowledged as a leading craftsmen of his time, working with Wren on St. Paul's Cathedral and other projects.

Deptford: the Royal Navy and the Gut Girls

Using Deptford and Woolwich as bases for building and servicing the fleet, the Royal Navy developed appreciably under Henry VIII, who also advanced maritime navigation by giving official recognition to the river pilots and seafarers based at the parish church on Deptford Strand, a group which eventually evolved into Trinity House, responsible for the maintenance of lighthouses, buoys and other maritime essentials. It was at Deptford in 1580 that Henry's daughter, Elizabeth I, knighted Francis Drake (1540-96) after his circumnavigation of the globe and declared that his ship would remain berthed here as "a memorial of national honour and imperial enterprise". The memorial received little care, however, and steadily fell to pieces, now better remembered by the replica at Southwark.

Deptford's docks became a centre of world shipbuilding, skilled shipwrights and the forced labour of convicts (held on rotting ships on the river) combining to produce such advanced vessels such as the three-decked *Sovereign of the Seas*, launched in 1637 as "the largest and most lavishly decorated and gilded warship afloat". Ships were also readied at Deptford for voyages of discovery, among them Captain Cook's *Endeavour* which departed in 1766 for the South Pacific, ostensibly to map the 1769 Transit of Venus but also making the first European navigation of Australia and the second of New Zealand.

Failure to embrace steam power, the silting of the riverbank and the period of peace that followed the Napoleonic wars all contributed to the Royal Docks' decline and subsequent closure. Between 1871 and 1913 the dock site became the Foreign Cattle Market, a scene of blood and guts to match any naval battle as imported cows, oxen and pigs were slaughtered and gutted by women nicknamed the "gut girls" and noted for their rough behaviour and coarse language. Of the cattle market, *The Royal River* insisted: "no person of nice tastes should think of visiting, beasts are being killed and dressed and quartered from morning to night, with an expedition which strikes the beholder as something unnatural and amazing."

In Deptford in the mid-1970s, a former bank clerk launched a Xeroxed music fanzine, *Sniffin' Glue*, which became the bible of the burgeoning punk rock scene. The former bank clerk was Mark Perry, who soon after took his own advice and formed a band, Alternative TV, and issued records on the Deptford Fun City label that helped bring the locality a certain renown. Much later, an influx of contemporary artists, pushed steadily eastwards by London's 1980s regeneration, opened the studios and galleries that helped Deptford acquire what *The Observer* in 2000 called, "a certain gritty chic" and the annual Deptford X Festival with two weeks of cutting-edge visual art exhibitions.

In circumstances that remain mysterious, poet and dramatist Christopher Marlowe (1564-93) was killed in a house on Deptford Strand in May 1593. The 1925 discovery of the coroner's report suggests that Marlowe died after being accidentally stabbed in the eye. Yet the discovery raised questions: what was the relevance of Marlowe's involvement in secret service work for the Privy Council? What were the links between three men who were with him in the room when he died? Was Marlowe's arrest ten days earlier for heresy merely a coincidence? Did Marlowe's sexual orientation play a part? More advanced conspiracists might wonder whether it really is Marlowe who lies in an unmarked pauper's grave in Deptford's St. Nicholas Church, remembered by a plaque on a wall.

Enter a Whale

John Evelyn's diary entry for 3 June 1658 reads: "A large whale taken betwixt my land butting on to the Thames and Greenwich, which drew an infinite concourse to see it, by water, horse, coach, and on foote, from London and all parts. It appear'd fast below Greenewich at low water, for at high water it would have destroyed all the boates, but lying low in shallow water incomps'd with boates, after a long conflict it was kill'd with a harping yron, struck in the head, out of which spouted blood and water by two tunnells, and after a horrid grone it ran quite on shore an died…"

Nearly 450 years later in 2006, another "infinite concourse" marked the appearance of a 19-foot northern bottle-nosed whale which travelled upriver as far as Chelsea and Battersea. Arriving on a Friday (thought to have taken wrong turns while seeking the North Atlantic, first into the North Sea and then into the Thames Estuary), the whale dominated the weekend news but the story brought an unhappy end. The stress of shallow waters, an attempted rescue and perhaps the constant presence of a TV news helicopter resulted in the creature's death as it was being carried by barge towards open water.

Greenwich

The most delightful spot of ground in Great Britain; pleasant by situation, those pleasures encreas'd by art, and all made completely agreeable by the accident of fine buildings, the continual passing of fleets of ships up and down the most beautiful river in Europe; the best air; the best prospect; and the best conversation in England.
Daniel Defoe, describing Greenwich *in A Tour Through the Whole Island of Great Britain*, 1724-7

Where Deptford might be acquiring a "gritty chic", Greenwich has been a social cut above the rest since 1433 when Humphrey, Duke of Gloucester, completed what he called Bella House, among the finest private homes in England and one which became a royal residence

following the duke's death, occupied first by Henry VI and his wife
Margaret (who named the house the Palace of Placentia) and by
successive monarchs over the next two hundred years. Reaching from
the river to the summit of what became Greenwich Hill, the palace was
the scene of banquets, jousts and royal hunts, and staged England's first
masquerade ball in 1516. It was here, too, that Henry VIII signed Anne
Boleyn's death warrant and where, four years later, he married Anne of
Cleves. The voyage of the newly-wed pair along the Thames to
Westminster was described by the Elizabethan Chronicler, Raphael
Holinshed: "…the King and she removed to Westminster by water, on
whom the Lord Mayor and his brethren, with twelve of the chief
companies of the City, all in barges gorgeously garnished with barters,
pennants and targets, richly covered and furnished with instruments
sweetly sounding, gave their attendance. And by their way, all the ships
shot off. And likewise, from the Tower, a great peal of ordnance went
off lustily."

Like her father, Elizabeth I held a special affection for Greenwich
and here received a cannon salute from Francis Drake aboard the *Golden
Hind* as it sailed towards Deptford in 1580 at the end of its world
voyage. Under Oliver Cromwell's Commonwealth, the palace was
stripped of its fittings, its paintings auctioned, and it was used as a
biscuit factory and as a holding place for Dutch prisoners of war.
Restored to the throne and a dilapidated Greenwich Palace in 1660,
Charles II tried to construct an entirely new royal dwelling composed of
three wings around a square facing the river, incorporating the striking
Italianate form of Inigo Jones' Queen's House, completed for James I in
1633. Pepys noted: "I observed the foundation of very Great House for
the King, which will cost a great deal of money." More money, in fact,
than the king could raise without upsetting parliament, and a partially
completed section became the King Charles Block of the Greenwich
Naval Hospital, designed by Sir Christopher Wren after William III
came to the throne in 1689 and decided Greenwich was no place for an
asthmatic king.

The Royal Naval Hospital

Moved by the sight of wounded sailors following the 1692 Battle of La
Hogue and inspired by the recently completed Chelsea Hospital for

soldiers, William's wife, Mary II, instigated the construction of a naval hospital at Greenwich. To accommodate the queen's insistence that the view of the Thames from the Queen's House be preserved, Wren used a symmetrical pattern of four main buildings with two domed towers, the Queen's House appearing as a delicate Palladian flower between them. Architects Hawksmoor and Vanbrugh completed the building after Wren's death and it welcomed its first ailing sailors in 1705.

The incongruity of the buildings' grandeur and the sickly naval veterans, who regularly complained of Spartan conditions and poor food, was elaborated on by Max Schlesinger in *Saunterings in and about London* (1853): "The architectural splendours of Greenwich Hospital are by no means destined to hide poverty and misery within. The gates are open. You may walk through the refectories, the kitchens, the sitting and sleeping rooms. Wait until the 'old gentlemen' sit down to their dinner, eat a slice of their meat, smoke a pipe of their tobacco, take a pinch from one of their snuff-boxes, admire the irreproachable white-ness of their cravats, take a seat at their side on the green benches which stand on the smooth lawn from whence they view the Thames, its sails, masts, and flags, the cherished scenes of their early career. Talk to them. They like to fight their battles over again in conversation, and will tell you whether they have to complain of the ingratitude of their country, and which is best (no matter how disgusted our German enthusiasts would be at the mere idea), to be paid so and so much per limb, or to starve on the general dietary of an Austrian Invalidenhaus, or rot in the streets of Berlin on an annual allowance which would hardly suffice to find a Greenwich pensioner in tobacco and snuff."

The Royal Naval College and Greenwich University
The hospital lost its pensioners, was acquired by the Admiralty and become the Royal Naval College in 1873, providing training to military officers. In the 1990s, it became part of the campus of Greenwich University, operating a maritime department but better-known for business, IT and music courses. To prospective students, the university's website promises "a stunning campus environment, rivalling the spires at Oxford." Jonathan Glancey concurred in the *Guardian*: "Other universities may have homes to rival the Royal Naval College, but none surpasses it."

The Royal Observatory

Recognizing the importance of astronomy to maritime navigation, Charles II appointed John Flamsteed (1646-1719) to the new post of Astronomer Royal in 1675 with instructions "to apply himself with the most exact care and diligence to the rectifying of the tables of the motions of the heavens, and the places of the fixed stars, so as to find out the so much desired longitude of places for the perfecting of the art of navigation." With wood, iron and lead from a Tower gatehouse, bricks from Tilbury Fort and £500 raised from the sale of spoiled gunpowder, a Wren-designed Observatory was constructed on the brow of Greenwich Hill. From here, Flamsteed invented conical projection, charted the eclipses of 1666 and 1668 and calculated 3,000 star positions in charts of hitherto unequalled accuracy published after his death as *Historia Coelestis Britannia*. Attempts to publish the charts ahead of their completion led to Flamsteed feuding with both Isaac Newton and his successor as Astronomer Royal, Edmund Halley, and to Flamsteed burning three hundred copies of the incomplete charts.

The Royal Observatory moved to less polluted skies in 1933, but the Old Royal Observatory serves as a museum of astronomy and timekeeping, and has the Greenwich Meridian running through its courtyard marking zero longitude and the baseline of world time. The meridian inspired Nathaniel Hawthorne to declare Greenwich "the very centre of space and time" in an 1863 essay, and many generations of schoolchildren to plant a leg in each hemisphere.

British Sea Power: the National Maritime Museum and the *Cutty Sark*

Any doubts as to whether Britain really once did rule the waves will be dispelled at the National Maritime Museum, adjacent to the Queen's House in the former Royal Naval College, where among two million artefacts are more paintings of ships, ships' captains and naval battles than anyone could ever wish to see. Temporary exhibitions often take more surprising turns: not least the 2004 Tintin At Sea, examining the nautical adventures of Hergé's cartoon creation.

With a hole bashed in its hull as an entrance, the *Cutty Sark* has been exhibited in Greenwich since 1954, the effect of visitors, rotting timbers and corroding ironwork being steady deterioration: a poor state of affairs for a ship that made its maiden voyage to Shanghai in 1870 in the age of the tea clippers, so-named for their clipping time off speed records carrying tea from the Far East. The *Cutty Sark* was most successful, however, carrying Australian wool and broke the London-Australia record in 1885, completing the voyage in 72 days. The preliminary stage of a planned £25-million restoration is currently underway, with the possible result of the ship being displayed as a life-sized ship-in-a-bottle, afloat on a glass sea.

The Greenwich Foot Tunnel
One of the two remaining pedestrian tunnels beneath the Thames, the Greenwich Foot Tunnel (see overleaf), its dome-topped entrance adjacent to the *Cutty Sark*, opened in August 1902 to link Greenwich with the Isle of Dogs, enabling West India Dock workers to end their dependency on ferries. Although the 1,214-foot tunnel now forms part of the National Cycle Network, riding a bike through it is illegal, and prospective users should also bear in mind the warning: "No person shall spit on or upon the tunnel or its approaches, stairs, lift, passages, or other means of ingress or egress…"

Greenwich Pier and the Trafalgar Tavern
Since it afforded a view of an unusually long stretch of the river, the public benches arranged along Greenwich Pier, point of call for London cruise boats, became a popular vantage-point in the great days of the docks and remain a berthing point for pleasure boats. For the better class of person, a trip to Greenwich Pier was also an excuse to take refreshment at the Trafalgar Tavern. Built in 1837 and frequented by politicians and writers—Dickens, Thackeray and Wilkie Collins among them—the tavern was noted for its whitebait dinners, typically consumed with iced champagne. The dish was served annually to Liberal Cabinet ministers at the end of the parliamentary session. At one such gathering, Lord Palmerston (1784-1865) allegedly looked down at his plate and suggested: "Let us all imitate this very wise little fish—and drink a lot and say nothing."

The pristine condition of the tavern today should not be a surprise: it was closed in the 1880s and used as a seaman's mission until re-opening in 1965 after a refurbishment in Victorian style with countless

paintings and prints of imbibing sailors added to its oak-panelled walls. Whitebait is still on the menu although one aspect of the past yet to be revived is the tossing of coins to urchins on the sands outside: a practice wrily recalled by A. R. Bennett in *London and Londoners in the Eighteen-Fifties and Sixties* (1924): "The dining-room… overlooked the river, and at low water an expanse of mud lay exactly under its windows. Cabinet ministers dined there only once a year at most; on other occasions humbler guests did and, at peace with all mankind after banqueting and speechifying, were wont to respond to musical invitations from ragged urchins assembled on the shore beneath by casting forth coppers, which, whether mouldy or not, speedily became muddy. The intellectual gratification of seeing youngsters roll over each other in the slimy filth must have been great, since the practice never seemed to stale."

Greenwich Peninsula

Writing of Greenwich in the 1930s, Arthur Mee added to his list of traditional attractions, "two huge gasholders, fifty years old, one the biggest in England, holding 12 million cubic feet." The gasholders, one of which remains as a skeletal frame, stood on Greenwich Peninsula, a marshy outpost that briefly held an Elizabethan watchtower and a gunpowder magazine before industry took root along its western shore. Victorian-era maps reveal businesses such as Edmunds Barge Builders, Gregg & Co. Seed Crushing Mills, Ashby & Sons Cement Works, and the Telegraph Construction and Maintenance Company. The latter were based at Enderbys Wharf and specialized in the production of telegraph cables, coiling them into vast cylindrical containers ready for deployment beneath the world's oceans. The peninsula's east side was occupied by the South Metropolitan Gas Company, supplying power to south London and, at its height, employing 3,500 people and the two gasometers which attracted Mee's attention.

Marking the Greenwich riverside's switch from royal history to industrial history is the extraordinary juxtaposition of Trinity Hospital's dainty seventeenth-century almshouses (rebuilt in 1812) against the industrial slab of Greenwich Power Station. Completed in 1910 for the energy needs of London's trams, the power station was fed by coal that arrived by barge and was unloaded along rails that still run above the riverbank. Now driven by gas and oil turbines, the power station provides back-up electricity for London's underground network.

The Millennium Dome

Appearing as an upturned flying saucer with antenna-like protrusions redolent of the Festival of Britain's Skylon, the Richard Rogers-designed Millennium Dome occupies the tip of the peninsula and became the VIP focus for London's millennium celebrations: a brief interlude of contrived happiness in the building's troubled history. As much a political controversy as architectural oddity, the Dome was conceived in 1994 by John Major's Conservative government with responsibility given to Deputy Prime Minister Michael Heseltine, also a leading figure within the London Docklands Development Corporation. High costs, slow progress and widespread derision of a plan for a large building of no specific purpose on a highly-polluted peninsula with limited public transport access did not deter the subsequent Labour administration from continuing the project.

Miraculously, the Dome was completed in June 1999, becoming the world's largest single-roofed structure and an instantly recognizable landmark. For many, however, the Dome was simply a series of farcical episodes that reached a climax, appropriately, on New Year's Eve 1999. On this invitation-only opening night, the Dome's VIP guests had to queue outdoors due to a transport hiccup, while the chimes of midnight saw a beaming Tony Blair coercing the Queen and Duke of Edinburgh into an embarrassingly self-conscious linking of arms and singing of *Auld Lang Syne*.

Open to the public throughout 2000, the Dome's Millennium Exhibition drew half its projected twelve million visitors and little positive response to the motley displays inside. Considerably more excitement was generated by the attempted theft of the Millennium Star diamond in November 2000 by thieves who battered their way through the perimeter fence, only to find police waiting for them inside. With no long-term use planned, the Dome controversy continued beyond 2000 when the empty building was reported to be costing £1,000,000 a month to maintain: the rare positive aspects being the removal of ground contamination and the Dome's provision of accommodation for the homeless over Christmas 2004.

In *London's Recent Architecture*, Ken Allinson called the Dome "a brilliant way of doing something inherently meaningless" and observed: "At the time of writing the dome appears to have no plausible future"— a comment that could have been made at anytime since its inception, despite advanced plans for it to become a "large indoor arena" from 2007.

The Millennium Village and Greenwich Ecology Park

Trumpeted by Labour's John Prescott in 1999 as "a tangible living example of sustainable development", the Millennium Village was planned to cover the east side of the peninsula with ecologically-friendly residential, retail and leisure developments for a mixed-income population. Much was the idea of British-Swedish architect Ralph Erskine (1914-2005), whose vision may have been to bring Scandinavian socio-economic integration to east London, but the project became almost as mired in controversy as the Dome; its ideals steadily abandoned, it became derisively dubbed the Yuppie Village.

Nonetheless, the scheme continues to take shape. Amid the gaily painted irregular apartment blocks ("the fearsome extrovert cheerfulness of it all... might overwhelm the less extrovert personality," suggested Allinson) is an innovatively designed primary school and a supermarket heralded as an "eco-superstore" ("fifty per cent more efficient in energy consumption than conventional supermarkets"). Another addition is the Greenwich Ecological Park where the tranquility of the pathways around a man-made lake is ruffled only by the legions of bird watchers sneeking peeks at bearded tits and chiffchaffs.

The Thames Barrier

Between the Greenwich Peninsula and the Thames Barrier lies New Charlton, a name optimistically suggestive of a community (the busy A206 divides Charlton itself from the river) but actually a stretch of the Thames still suggestive of the scene that greeted Norman Shrapnel in the 1970s, albeit with the old ladies replaced by CCTV: "The river path leading towards Woolwich and the new barrier is flanked by mountains of scrap metal and orchestrated with the rumblings and belchings of recycling processes. Small patient fires burn eternally, acrid smoke drifts over rusted pails and pools of black water, dead cars copulate in titanic pile-ups. Behind the riverfront the hellish air is more emphatic and achieves grandeur, especially at night when the gasworks blaze like a city of satanic palaces; and at the entrance to each, a little old lady sits in a small fireproof hut brewing tea."

When the Thames Barrier was declared open in 1984, few Londoners were familiar with post-glacial rebound or global warming, both regarded as contributing to rising river levels, though some may have been aware of the Thames' many attempts to drown the city, first documented in the *Anglo-Saxon Chronicle*: "(in 1099) the sea flood sprang up to such a height and did so much harm as no man can remember that it did before."

No respecter of power and privilege and unhindered by embankments, the river made frequent incursions into the centres of power at Westminster, Whitehall and Lambeth. Of a flood in 1238 Mathew Paris wrote: "Among other singular circumstances, the river Thames, transgressing its accustomed limits, flowed into the Great Palace of Westminster, and spreading itself, so covered the area that the middle of the hall might be passed in boats, and persons rode through it on horseback to their chambers. The water, bursting into cellars, could scarcely be drawn outside again." At Lambeth Palace in 1242, Stow's *Survey of London* records that "men took their horses because water ran over all." And Pepys' diary entry for 7 December 1663 runs: "There was last night the greatest tide that ever was remembered in England to have been in this River, all Whitehall having been drowned."

As London expanded through the nineteenth century and Lambeth became better known for its hovels than its palace, the river still showed no mercy. In *Street Life in London* (1877), J. Thomson and Adelphe Smith wrote: "The sufferings of the poor in Lambeth, and in other quarters of the Metropolis, caused by the annual tidal overflow of the Thames, have been so graphically described as thoroughly to arouse public sympathy... Feelings of apprehension and dread again and again rose with the tides, and subsided with the muddy waters as they found their way back into the old channel or sank through the soil. The public have settled down with a sense of relief; and the suffering People returned to rekindle their extinguished fires and clear away the mud and debris from their houses; to reconstruct their wrecked furniture, dry their clothes and bedding, and live on as best they may under this new

The Thames Barrier

phase of nineteenth-century civilization."

Even with improved embanking, the river still caused loss of life in the capital, not least in January 1928 when heavy snows swelled the upper river and violent storms caused a surge tide through the estuary that caused the Thames to burst a wall at Lambeth leading to fourteen fatalities. In 1944 J. H. O. Bunge's *Tideless Thames in a Future London* made a strong case for a barrier at Woolwich, while the 1953 floods that took three hundred lives around Britain and particularly affected Canvey Island created the momentum for better London river defences, culminating in the £534 million Thames Barrier.

Spread like a series of silver pagodas across the river, the barrier has ten gates arranged between nine concrete piers within which lifting gear is concealed beneath a steel canopy. The barrier can be raised within thirty minutes (though usually much slower to prevent dangerous waves), dividing the river from the sea and preventing high tides continuing upriver.

While it quickly become a minor tourist attraction and enabled Londoners to sleep more soundly, the Thames Barrier is expected to become ineffective well before its anticipated fifty-year lifespan ends. Changing weather patterns have made stronger surge tides more likely: by the end of 1989, the barrier had been closed in anger on four occasions; between 2000 and 2004 it closed 29 times. Protecting twenty-first century London from a raging Thames may come to depend on a new barrie; a ten-mile gateway across the river between Sheerness and Southend was proposed in 2005.

Part Four

The Widening River

East of the Thames Barrier, between the south shores of Essex and the north coast of Kent, lies an all but foreign land. A tract of marshes, mists, rip tides, rubbish tips, freighters, sinking buildings, the world's largest sugarcane refinery, reeking sewage and rotting hulks left over from the Napoleonic wars and D-Day, interspersed, like some hastily edited film, with sporadic tower blocks, remote pubs, and hippy encampments. Here, if anywhere on the map of England, be monsters.

Jonathan Glancey, The *Guardian*, October 2003

Anyone seduced into thinking that the Thames is all about *Three Men in a Boat* and views of Tower Bridge will have their illusions shattered by the sights, sounds and smells of the river between the Thames Barrier and the sea. On this stretch some 14,000 vessels annually carry fifty million tons of cargo between banks liberally studded with oil storage containers, grain silos, cement, paper chemical works, sewage plants and recycling facilities. Surprisingly, however, the Thames beyond the barrier is not without history nor expressions of natural drama. It was here that Elizabeth I rallied troops against the Spanish Armada, here that Defoe explored and found polygamy being practised, here that the real Pocahontas met an unfortunate end, and here that formerly malarial marshes now delight birdwatchers.

But an even bigger surprise is that, despite the chill winds, the smell of waste, the propensity to flooding and the lack of a transport infrastructure, these unsettling vistas have been labelled the Thames Gateway, Europe's biggest proposed redevelopment and earmarked as the solution to the housing problems of an expanding London. By 2016 these unlikely tracts are intended to hold 120,000 new houses in communities not yet conceived, let alone located or named. No less extraordinary, or controversial, are the £480 million bridge intended to

rise 150 feet above the Thames between Beckton in the north and Thamesmead in the south by 2012, and the £700 million London Gateway Port intended to invigorate two miles of the north bank as a deep-sea container terminal on the site of a former oil refinery.

Economic success or environmental and social disaster: no one is sure quite which, if either, the Thames Gateway will become. Beyond doubt however is that this section of the river is about to undergo twenty-first-century change every bit as drastic as that which re-shaped the Thames above and within London during the nineteenth century.

The Widening River: North

The Royal Docks are a defining feature of the riverside immediately east and west of the Thames Barrier, even though Silvertown and North Woolwich lie between them and the Thames itself. Like the docks, both communities are in advanced stages of regeneration, though the view from the river remains a strongly industrial one. A similar outlook continues to the former gasworks of Beckton and the car plant at Dagenham, beyond which lie the open spaces of Romney Marshes and the chalk cliffs that hold Purfleet. As the river widens, the shoreline reveals such contrasting sights as the enormous Tilbury docks, the wondrously sited St. Clement's Church, and Canvey Island—a reminder of the human story often concealed behind the river's commercial frontage.

The Royal Docks

Between 1855 and 1921 the three-mile-long swathes of water forming Royal Victoria, the Royal Albert and the King George V Docks were built parallel to the Thames at Silvertown and North Woolwich. Their magisterial titles symbolized the commercial importance of shipping to Britain, their technology—whether rail links from dockside sidings to the national network or hydraulic lifting gear—was cutting-edge, and their very existence a testimony to the endless expansion of global trade and the ever-growing girth of steam ships. Furthermore, the King George V Dock was the first to be built by the Port of London Authority (PLA), created in 1909 to smooth the booms and busts that had afflicted private dock companies. By 1939 the PLA had created eighty acres of new docks with six miles of quays and storage space for a million tons of cargo, employed 30,000 people and was indirectly responsible for the livelihoods of 100,000 more.

Marking the first fifty years of the PLA, a supplement in *The Times* praised the organization's success and suggested: "The second fifty years of the PLA may easily provide more startling surprises than the first." The reporter was remarkably prescient though not in the manner intended. Well before the next half century was up, the inefficiencies of traditional cargo handling were highlighted by the rise of containerization (quick loading and unloading; no need for warehouses) and ships served by larger, deeper docks at Tilbury and Northfleet. These factors, along with foreign competition, poor management and strained labour relations, led to the steady closure of London docks from the mid-1960s; the Royal Docks were all closed by the early 1980s.

The docks have since been the subject of countless regeneration ideas in varying stages of conceptualization, construction and completion: a process gaining a fresh impetus from London's successful bid to host the 2012 Olympic Games. The Royal Albert Dock has become an Olympic-standard rowing course and a regatta venue, overlooked on its south side by the silo-like apartments providing accommodation for students of the University of East London. Former dock workers who have never adjusted to the docks' decline are further tormented by the sight of planes landing on the quay of the King George V Dock, now the runway of London City Airport, which opened in the early 1990s and serves over a million passengers annually: most of them City workers jetting between European financial hubs.

Silvertown and North Woolwich

A product of the docks and the raw materials unloaded therein, Silvertown took its name from the rubber and telegraph factory of S. W. Silver & Co., soon joined among local employers by sugar refiners who included rivals-turned-partners, Henry Tate and Albert Lyle; their Tate & Lyle refinery is still a major local employer and an anachronistic addition to the shoreline. The rest of Silvertown is awash with new developments, including the green splash of Thames Barrier Park and loudly trumpeted spectaculars such as the still-evolving Silvertown Quays, an "exciting mixed-use development" set to include an enormously costly aquarium.

Adjacent to Silverton, North Woolwich spent years as a piece of Kent on the Essex side of the river: an anomaly stemming from an eleventh-century extension of manorial land across the river and ending with a re-organization of local government in 1965 but in the meantime enabling Woolwich to claim that more wealth passed through it than any other place in the British Empire. For late-nineteenth-century Londoners in pursuit of relaxation, however, North Woolwich was less a local government quirk than a place to enjoy the amusements at North Woolwich Gardens. Opening in 1851, the gardens boomed after the Bank Holidays Act of 1871 gave workers an extra day off, and was soon the only pleasure garden in the capital. As such, it provided a ready source of material for journalists in search of lightweight copy. One was Marcus Fall who appeared bemused by the sight of the beneficiaries of improved working-class education enjoying themselves: "…here cannot be less than three thousand to four thousand men, women and children in the grounds, there is not one whose name you can find in *Debretts*. The majority of the men are artisans, clerks, shops hands and small tradesman. There is no absolute rudeness but a good deal of horseplay. The humour is of the simplest order and takes the form of practical jokes." Despite a successful straw hat exhibition, the gardens' owner went bust in 1881. As the Royal Victoria Gardens, the site re-opened in 1890 having been bought by public subscription and continues to provide a pocket of greenery just east of North Woolwich pier.

The *Princess Alice* Disaster

In September 1878 a day-trip to Gravesend's Rosherville Pleasure Gardens (see p.224) ended in disaster when the *Princess Alice* collided with a collier just before docking at North Woolwich and split in two, sinking within minutes and causing at least 640 deaths. A reporter, W. T. Vincent, wrote of the scene at the *Alice's* Woolwich office: "The lifeless frames of men and women lay about, and out on the balcony, from which the directors had so often looked upon their fleet through the fragrant smoke of the evening cigar, there was a sight to wring out tears of blood from the eyes of any beholder. A row of little innocents, plump and pretty, well-dressed children, all dead and cold, some with life's ruddy tinge still in their cheeks and lips, the lips from which the merry prattle had gone for ever." The unusual and rapid decomposition

COLLISION OF THE *BYWELL CASTLE* AND THE *PRINCESS ALICE.*

of the bodies, which issued a smell so bad that police guarding them were issued with smelling salts, indicated that many were killed not by drowning but by poisoning, the sinking occurring shortly after the second of the day's releases from the new sewage pumping stations: many who initially survived the accident may have later succumbed to the swallowing of contaminated water.

An enquiry blamed the disaster on the *Princess Alice*'s captain, himself a victim of the sinking, but conflicting evidence suggests that the verdict was unjust, and that a true picture of the night's events may never emerge. One outcome, however, was the late 1880s introduction of sludge barges to carry solid waste, culled from the pumping stations' cesspools, out to sea.

The *Princess Alice* disaster occurred close to Beckton Gasworks, which covered 540 riverside acres with the men and machinery capable of providing gas for 4.5 million customers and a reassuring odour for Thames pilots uncertain of their bearings. The discovery of North Sea natural gas caused the gasworks' closure in the late 1960s; the site was reborn in 1989 as Beckton Alps when a large grass-covered hill formed from the gasworks' waste acquired a dry ski slope. The hill was demolished in 2001 and replaced with the promise of a snowdome offering skiing on real snow; a promise unfulfilled but possibly mutating into an indoor sports centre. As likely as a Thamesside Alps is the fact that the former gasworks stood in for Hanoi in Stanley Kubrick's 1987 film, *Full Metal Jacket*.

Towards Dagenham: Barking and the Roding

The Roding River, reaching the Thames at Barking Creek, and the invention of the welled smack, a vessel with a holed mid-section that allowed an inflow of water in which fish could remain fresh between being caught and taken to Billingsgate market, were instrumental in the rise of Barking's fishing industry. In the 1960s, Robert H. Goodsall noted of the creek: "Once this unpretentious stream may have been a haunt of anglers, but now the banks are industrialised and would seem to offer small encouragement for piscatorial endeavours." Oil depots, a sewage works and minor industrial sites continue to sit amid a pylon-dotted scrub and marshland landscape that continues east to the Ford works at Dagenham. A notable landmark, however, is the Barking Flood

Barrier at the Roding's mouth, part of the 1980s system of flood protection that produced the Thames Barrier and comprising two towering concrete pillars holding a barrier high enough to allow the passage of cargo ships but able to drop it like a gigantic portcullis when floods threaten.

In 1931 the Ford Motor Company opened a new manufacturing plant at Dagenham, a town evolved from the oldest Saxon settlement in the county of Essex to one described by the 1970 *Shell Guide to Britain* as having "much utilitarian urban housing of little distinction". The housing that so unimpressed the guide's authors was nonetheless highly desirable to its inhabitants, arriving from east London's slums during the 1920s and relishing inside toilets, electricity and gas, and gardens as offered by the new homes of the Becontree Estate. Built across four square miles, the estate become the largest council estate in the world with 27,000 homes and a population of 90,000, a big part of Dagenham's sharp growth in years to 1939, many attracted to jobs at Ford.

Spread across six hundred acres of former marshland, the Ford works included a power station, blast furnace, coke ovens, a foundry, railway sidings and a reinforced concrete jetty capable of berthing 10,000-ton ships. At its peak in the early 1970s, the Ford works employed 28,000 people, but the combination of a strongly unionized workforce and a management seeking to work within constraints of a multinational company made Dagenham a byword for industrial relations strife. Such problems coupled to wider economic changes led to the company's decision to relocate car manufacture and, in 2003, after producing almost eleven million vehicles, Ford at Dagenham was re-assigned to the production of diesel engines with a greatly reduced workforce.

Many occupants of the Becontree Estate, meanwhile, took up the opportunity to own, rather than rent, their homes under 1980s Right to Buy legislation. This turned the estate from the utilitarian drabness remarked upon by the *Shell Guide* into what Weinreb & Hibbert described in the 1990s as "a heterogeneous rash of neo-Palladianism, bankers' Georgian, mock Tudor, pebble-dash, and vertical crazy paving".

In his *Tour Thro' the Whole Island of Great Britain* (1724-27), Daniel Defoe recalled:

We saw passing from Barking to Dagenham, the famous breach, made by an inundation of the Thames, which was so great, as that it laid near 5000 acres of land under water, but which after near ten years lying under water, and being several times blown up has been at last effectually stopped by the application of Captain Perry; the gentleman, who for several years had been employed, in the Czar of Muscovy's works, at Veronitza, on the River Don.

The breach that Defoe observed was a notorious break in the river wall caused by a high spring tide and the flooding of Dagenham Creek in 1707, forcing enough mud into the Thames to create a major navigational difficulty. Numerous efforts to repair the breach failed. Samuel Smiles in his nineteenth-century *Lives of the Engineers* suggested "the engineering skill of England seemed... completely baffled by this hole in a river's bank." It took a 1714 Act of Parliament to approve rectification of the problem with public funds, followed by the digging of two sluices to relieve pressure and the driving of wooden stakes into the river bed to repair the breach; a process that took five years. Now a sizeable lake popular with anglers, the Dagenham Breach forms part of the Ford site immediately south of the A13.

Frog Island, Rainham Marshes and Purfleet

Though its name suggests a riverside refuge for amphibians, Frog Island is, according to the East London Waste Authority's website, "better known to locals as Ferry Lane Industrial Area" and is due to become the site of a state-of-the-art wood-built recycling facility. In keeping with the people-friendly ethos of the new-look estuary, the centre will include a visitor and education centre to enforce the concept of waste reuse. Between Frog Island and Purfleet, the 871 acres of Rainham marshes bring a rare glimpse of a riverside landscape unravaged by industry, a result of years of use by the Ministry of Defence as a rifle range. Now protected as an Area of Special Scientific Interest, the site was acquired in 2000 by the Royal Society for the Protection of Birds which is now providing the last undeveloped wetlands beside the Thames with an unobtrusive network of nature trails.

In the *Dictionary of the Thames*, Charles Dickens Jr. described Purfleet as "a pretty village with some picturesque chalk hills pleasantly wooded, and with a fine view down Long Reach towards Greenhithe and the Kentish hills." *The Royal River* concurred but added an intriguing caveat: "Purfleet is a pretty and interesting town, notwithstanding the uses to which it has been put, and the danger there must always be in living there." The danger came from five gunpowder magazines constructed at Purfleet from 1760 following an explosion at the Woolwich Arsenal. Each magazine could hold over 10,000 barrels of the combustible mixture, tended by men wearing soft flannel clothing and soft leather shoes to prevent risk of sparks. Minus its load, one magazine is preserved as an ancient monument while the 25-acre site on which the arsenal stood is largely filled by housing.

In the 1960s, long after the decommissioning of the magazines, Goodsall described Purfleet as "the old village nucleus submerged in a welter of industrial buildings dominated by the oil tanks of the Esso depot along the water-front." Cracknell was more succinct: "As you enter the town from the east you pass so many oil tanks that you begin to feel positively oily." Though declining, oiliness remains, much of the riverfront from Purfleet's chalk hill to the Tilbury Docks being a succession of cylindrical storage drums.

The outlook is a far cry from the celebrity high life enjoyed from the mid-nineteenth century when the whitebait dinners served at the Royal (then Purfleet) Hotel became a favourite of London socialites including, allegedly, an incognito Prince of Wales, the future Edward VII. The hotel remains, though its hard to imagine royals or even minor celebrities showing up for the Wednesday curry night or "a bowl of nacho corn-chips and 4 delicious dips".

Equally at odds with its present condition is Purfleet's appearance in Bram Stoker's *Dracula* as the site of the Carfax estate purchased by the Transylvanian count: "At Purfleet, on a byroad, I came across just such a place as seemed to be required, and where was displayed a dilapidated notice that the place was for sale. It was surrounded by a high wall, of ancient structure, built of heavy stones, and has not been repaired for a large number of years. The closed gates are of heavy old oak and iron, all eaten with rust."

Tilbury

Mammoths once grazed in the Thurrock area and archaeologists recently unearthed the remains of a jungle cat.
Thurrock: A Visionary Brief in the Thames Gateway,
www.visionarythurrock.org.uk (2005)

Mammoths and jungle cats might be long gone but the Queen Elizabeth II Bridge (see p.222) looms with a primeval intensity above the oil storage tanks, jetties and expanding mud banks of the riverside east of Purfleet. Wedged between West Thurrock marshes and the docks at Tilbury, Grays invites itself to be the butt of jokes regarding the aptness of its name to its lacklustre character. For Iain Sinclair in *London Orbital* (2002), the marshes between Grays and the Thames are an example of mutant ecology, an area where: "Lurid mosses lurk between the stone blocks of the embankment. Tyres, left in the mud, become rockpools. A lovely, lapping tidemark of oil, thick as elephant's skin. Abandoned shopping trolleys act as trellises for weeds and rubbery marine growths. Couch grass breaks through a tarpaulin topsoil." Another environmental curiosity is the Proctor & Gamble factory, which all but wraps itself around the Saxon-rooted, pilgrim-visited St. Clements Church. The oddness of the church's setting is matched by the oddness of its role as a blockbuster film location, staging the key funeral service scenes in *Four Weddings and a Funeral* (1994).

Twenty-six miles down river from Tower Bridge and with no road links until the 1930s, Tilbury Docks opened in 1886 as the too-far-sighted vision of the ailing East India and West India Dock Company. Built contemporaneously with the Royal Albert Dock at Silvertown, with which they were in competition, Tilbury Docks were strategically positioned to intercept London-bound cargo and deep enough to service all ships regardless of tides. The trade slump of the late-nineteenth century and rising competition from foreign ports did Tilbury no favours and propelled its owners towards bankruptcy.

In *The Mirror of the Sea* (1906), Joseph Conrad described the under-used docks: "These are very modern, but their remoteness and isolation upon the Essex marsh, the days of failure attending their creation, invested them with a romantic air. Nothing in those days could have been more striking than the vast, empty basins, surrounded by miles of bare quays and the ranges of cargo-sheds, where two or three ships seemed lost like bewitched children in a forest of gaunt, hydraulic cranes. One received a wonderful impression of utter abandonment, of wasted efficiency. From the first the Tilbury Docks were very efficient and ready for their task, but they had come, perhaps, too soon into the field. A great future lies before Tilbury Docks."

In the latter respect, Conrad was right. Under the Port of London Authority, Tilbury developed as a cargo dock and passenger terminal. A £30-million 1960s re-fit equipped Tilbury for container ships—in and out in 36 hours—and roll-on, roll-off carriers, while a 100,000-ton silo and a row of riverside mills confirmed its importance as a grain handler. Also in the 1960s, what Jerry White in *London in the Twentieth Century* labelled "a myopic trade union rooted in an obsolete past" saw strained industrial relations and persistent strikes that gave commercial advantage to rival docks with cheaper labour such as Southampton and Felixstowe. Despite its commercial fall as a general dock, Tilbury is (in partnership with Northfleet, directly across the river) a major container storage facility and offers its customers the tax advantages of freeport status.

From the 1930s, Tilbury became London's main berth for ocean-going liners, with fresh arrivals' first steps leading into Sir Edwin Cooper's voluminous terminal building. Incoming vessels included, in 1948, the SS *Empire Windrush*, bringing 492 arrivals from Jamaica, the first organized wave of Caribbean immigrants. The rise of air travel dimmed Tilbury's glamour, but with the overly-grand title of London's Cruise Terminal it remains a busy cruise ship berth, albeit one regularly threatened by plans for new facilities elsewhere. Most passengers in and out of Tilbury, however, are aboard the ferry to Gravesend.

Tilbury Fort

Its site directly downriver from the docks, Tilbury Fort was built under Charles II on a defensive position raised during the reign of Henry VIII. Initially intended to deter Dutch and French encroachment along the Thames, the fort was, ironically, designed in French style by a Dutchman, Sir Bernard de Gomme. High in cost due to its marshy setting and never firing a shot at any would-be invader, the well-preserved fort is unremarkable in all aspects save for its imposing cannon-decorated stone gateway.

On a hill overlooking the Thames at West Tilbury, about two miles from the fort, around twenty thousand soldiers gathered in July 1588 following the sighting of the Spanish Armada off Cornwall. As the country feared invasion, the reigning Elizabeth I moved from Richmond to Westminster and, on 8 August, advised that it was safe for her to do so, travelled by barge along the Thames to Tilbury, there disembarking and continuing to West Tilbury on horseback. At this time it was not known that the Armada had been effectively defeated, driven northward by Sir Francis Drake's use of fireships off Calais and later ravaged by freak winds. Fearing that the invasion force might re-group and attack, Elizabeth I addressed the troops with what would become perhaps the most famous speech of any English monarch:

> Let tyrants fear... I know I have the body but of a weak and feeble woman; but I have the heart and stomach of a king, and of a king of England too, and think foul scorn that Parma or Spain, or any prince of Europe, should dare to invade the borders of my realm; to which rather than any dishonour shall grow by me, I myself will take up arms, I myself will be your general, judge, and rewarder of every one of your virtues in the field.

While patriotic historians have long doted over the sentiment of Elizabeth's speech, it is less well recorded that events rendered it largely meaningless; it was apparent the following day that the invasion had failed and, far from being rewarded, Elizabeth's troops were, for many weeks, unpaid and close to starvation.

Canvey Island

"A wild and forbidding place is Canvey Island... there is a scant population of people who have their own ways methods of regarding strangers." So observed *The Royal River* in the 1880s of Canvey Island before going on to remark on the warmth and hospitality of the islanders, who then numbered less than two hundred. In those days Canvey, separated from the mainland by Holehaven Creeks and Hadleigh Ray, could only be accessed by ferry or at low-tide on foot across stepping stones. The acquisition of a bridge in 1931 helped cement the island's popularity as a do-it-yourself resort for east Londoners who responded to an offer of cheap plots of land on which they erected makeshift shacks as holiday homes. Donkey rides, a glass-walled "winter gardens", recreational clubs and the opportunity to collect mussels and whelks along the shore made Canvey Island a welcome break from the deprivations of the city. In 1933 the annually published *Official Guide to Canvey Island* insisted: "a week in Canvey will do you more good than a fortnight elsewhere."

Two hundred years earlier, Daniel Defoe had found another local curiosity, polygamy: "… all along this county it was very frequent to meet with men that had had from five to six, to fourteen or fifteen wives; nay, and some more; and I was informed that in the marshes on the other side the river over-against Candy [Canvey] Island, there was a farmer, who was then living with the five and twentieth wife, and that his son who was but about 35 years old, had already had about fourteen…" Defoe's discovery might be part exaggeration but carries a ring of truth due the detrimental effect of damp marshlands and outbreaks of a strain of malaria that proved less fatal to men than women, particularly those from the surrounding uplands where Canvey men typically found their wives. Many new arrivals survived less than a year.

Earlier still, Canvey reclaimed land and built sea defences under a London-based Dutch merchant, Joas Croppenburg, who was rewarded with a proportion of the new land. A small Dutch settlement that ensued in the early 1600s is chiefly remembered by two octagonal cottages, one of which, "the Dutch Cottage", now holds the island's museum. Despite antagonism between the Dutch settlers and islanders, the Dutch connection was played up during Canvey's resort phase with an annual "Dutch bazaar", locals parading in Dutch national dress and the Dutch names of thoroughfares such as Vaagen Road and Waarem Avenue.

Dating at least from the seventeenth century, the island's Lobster Smack Inn was recorded by Dickens Jr. as "very comfortable and unobtrusive… boating men are frequently accommodated with bed and board." He neglected to mention that some of the boating men were engaged in smuggling from boats moored just outside, despite the coastguard located next door. The inn is a rare survivor in a place where a unique past is rapidly disappearing despite the preservation efforts of the 37,000 islanders. Even a wartime concrete barge that became a local landmark and was demolished in 2003 has inspired a website (www.concretebarge.co.uk) and poetry in its honour.

The Flood of 1953

Canvey Island's sense of community was strengthened by the events of 1 February 1953. To keep rights over their land, the Dutch settlers had to maintain the island's sea defences but their departure caused the defences to deteriorate and by the late 1800s a levy was being charged on islanders for upkeep of the sea wall. An exceptional high tide in 1938 demonstrated the wall's inadequacy, but complacency was evident in the island's official guide of 1949: "The valuable and arduous work of the Canvey Island Sea Wall Commission, who keeps a vigilant eye on the present works, render (flooding) very, very unlikely now."

On the last day of January, 1953, a storm turned south off Iceland and, combined with an unusually high tide, travelled along Britain's east coast to bring death and destruction to Canvey Island (many coastal communities were also affected and 1,800 perished on the west coast of Holland) in the early hours of the following morning. Efforts were made to alert islanders to the dangers, and a few responded to the sounding of sirens and firing of maroons but most were asleep and only became aware of the danger when they woke to find floodwaters lapping around their beds. With no means of escape, whole families were forced to stand on furniture, climb into attics or onto roofs dressed, on a cold winter night, in only their sleeping clothes, hoping that the waters would recede. Of the 307 killed nationwide, 58 were Canvey Islanders. Miraculous tales of survival, such as the baby who lived after twelve hours afloat in a damp cot, were tempered by the sad tales of lost lives, not least the parents, and the young brothers and sisters, who spent the night holding dead children above water, believing them to be asleep. The names of the dead are recorded on the island's Flood Memorial (the fiftieth anniversary of the disaster brought plans for a memorial garden) although the practical legacy of their sacrifice are flood-resistant buildings, relief roads, annual flood drills and the ten-foot concrete sea wall that now girdles the island's shoreline.

Dr. Feelgood's Canvey Island

A more joyous reason for islanders' sense of solidarity and achievement began in the mid-1970s, when Canvey briefly became home to the most exciting rock music in Britain. The four islanders who comprised the band, Dr. Feelgood, played a raw and spiky r'n'b, relocating sounds more appropriate to the Mississippi Delta to the oil refineries, sewage works and marshlands of the Thames Estuary.

From modest beginnings, including using a pram to push their equipment, Dr. Feelgood began playing the small backroom venues of London's growing pub circuit and by the mid-1970s were established as one of the country's most popular live acts. Despite minor hits and a first album defiantly recorded in mono, Dr. Feelgood's recordings lacked the excitement of their shows until the release of the 1976 live album *Stupidity*: a rare instance of a number one album being recorded in Southend. Ironically, in taking rock music away from big stadiums and bringing it back to ordinary people in clubs, Dr. Feelgood helped pave the way for Britain's punk rock explosion—which would contribute to their own commercial downfall—although personnel changes and the yearly round of recording and touring inevitably took their toll on the band's energies and inspiration.

For Dr. Feelgood's small but global army of followers, Canvey Island has become a place of pilgrimage, not least to seek out the bench honouring the band's charismatic singer and harmonica player, Lee Brilleaux, who died in 1994, and attend the memorial concerts each May which celebrate the vocalist's life and music. With over twenty albums to its name, Dr. Feelgood continues to tour and record albeit with completely different personnel from the early days. Which, one feels, is precisely what the original members would want: far too much of Canvey has already been lost for ever.

The Widening River: South

Like nearby Deptford, Woolwich was dominated from Tudor times by its royal shipyards, and more uniquely gained the arsenal that supplied Britain's firepower as well as incidentally producing one of the country's leading football teams. To the east, Thamesmead became a much-discussed example of 1960s town planning in the shadow of Bazalgette's pioneering sewage works at Crossness. The new town was gouged from

the expansive salt marshes that line the river and which continue to warp themselves around Erith and Dartford, where the past spans Bronze Age tracks and the river's place in the treatment of smallpox. Gravesend, the south bank's final town of appreciable size, was once a first taste and last taste of England for international travellers—unlikely among them the native American heroine, Pocahontas—as well as a short-lived holiday destination for Londoners before the paddle steamer was eclipsed by the train. Further on, the strange estuary landscapes of the Isle of Grain and Hundreds of Hoo are perhaps a fitting conclusion to the river: the boundaries of land and water often blurred and once exciting the passions of writer Charles Dickens and artist J. M. W. Turner.

Woolwich

Woolwich today has little of its old nautical flavour. The people cannot get within sniffing distance of their river except in one or two places—out of several miles of waterfront there are only a few yards available to the public.

Basil Cracknell, *London River*, 1968

Complete with cantilevered foot bridge and views to the Thames Barrier and Canary Wharf, Woolwich's Resolution Walk has greatly improved local river access since Cracknell's observation. The missing nautical "flavour", however, has been less successfully replaced in a community where matchbox homes now fill the void left by the closure of once mighty docks and where naval and military associations reach back 500 years.

Created under Henry VIII for the building and repair of warships, Woolwich's Royal Dock's first project was the king's flagship, *The Great Harry*. Whether it weighed 1,000 or 1,500 tons (accounts differ), the *Harry* was, with a crew of 700, the largest ship not only of its day but for 250 years after it. Although innovative placement of heavy guns improved stability and increased the damage it could inflict on the enemy, the *Harry* saw action only during the 1545 French attack on Portsmouth and was destroyed at Woolwich by accidental fire in 1553. The docks stayed at the forefront of shipbuilding into the nineteenth century, their technology admired by Prussian architect Karl Friedrich

Schinkel (1781-1841), who visited in 1826, noting: "Huge sheds, usually two standing next to each other. Awesome anchoring equipment. Excellent smiths' workshop, big iron construction, steam engine, bellows, enormous great hammers."

Causing much local hardship, the docks closed in 1869. Fourteen years later, *The Royal River* optimistically saw in their stillness the prospect of a war-free future: "The once famous dockyard... is represented by great, empty, stone spaces, sloping to the river, and a pair of large, singular-looking sheds, stored full of gun-carriages and implements of war... No hammers resound there now, and the dockyard, silent and sleeping, might well be of the type of an age of national amity and absolute peace." Very soon, though, the author regained his senses: "...not so with the arsenal which is busy day and night with forging the bolts of war."

Woolwich Arsenal
The arsenal began in 1671 when the government bought 31 acres of Woolwich land for ordnance storage on a site beside the docks. By the end of the seventeenth century, it had developed into a munitions factory spread over a hundred acres and expanded further with buildings and testing sites collectively known as Woolwich Arsenal, developing bullets, rockets, fuses, percussion caps, shells, torpedoes and other battlefield implements. Employment at the arsenal surged during the Napoleonic campaigns and the Crimean War, and peaked during the First World War when its workforce rose from 10,000 to 72,000 (including 17,000 "canary girls", so called because exposure to high explosives turned their skin yellow). After the Second World War, despite a brief flirtation with atomic weapons research, the arsenal was scaled down and formally closed in 1994.

With ownership of the site passing to property developers and a painstaking clearing of unexploded ordnance from the grounds completed in 2001, the site was opened to the public, who, for the first time in 300 years, could stroll beside the Thames without being arrested on suspicion of spying. In the former guard house, a "marketing suite" offers houses and loft-style apartments in remodelled arsenal buildings. Within a few yards of their homes, residents can enjoy a waterside leisure centre and explore the three centuries worth of armaments manufacture documented inside a museum named, with schoolboy-pleasing drama, Firepower.

The promotional material provided by the developers, however, overlooks another facet of the arsenal's past: that it was partly built by convict labour and, from 1776, dead prisoners were commonly buried in mass graves on its land. Some re-surfaced as skeletons during a building programme in the mid-1800s; others presumably remain.

By another route, the arsenal's fame endures for sporting rather than militaristic connotations. In 1886 arsenal workers formed a football team, Dial Square, later re-named Woolwich Reds (following a gift of red shirts) and eventually becoming Woolwich Arsenal. In 1913 the team relocated to north London and evolved into one of the country's top teams under the briefer name of Arsenal, best known for many years to fans of rival clubs for defensive play that ensured games were won by a single goal.

The Woolwich Ferry and Foot Tunnel

We're so far off the map that nobody has found it worthwhile to close down the free ferry.
Iain Sinclair, writing of Woolwich in *Lights Out for the Territory*
(1997)

Since 1889 the Woolwich Ferry has been the only free crossing of the Thames east of Tower Bridge and, surviving even the rampant privatization of 1980s Britain, it continues today, though is currently threatened by a possible new £320-million bridge between Thamesmead and Beckton and plans for an expansion of commuter transport on the river. Equally far off the map and equally unlikely to feature in the average Londoner's knowledge of river crossings is the Woolwich foot tunnel. Opened in 1912, the tunnel (like those at Greenwich and Blackwall) was inspired by the former docker who became Chairman of the London County Council Bridges Committee, Will Crooks (1852-1921) partly as a response to the refusal by companies on the river's north bank to employ anyone from the south side, fearing absence or lateness if the ferry was unable to sail or was delayed by traffic.

Thamesmead

In the 1960s the London County Council explored a variety of schemes to create new housing for the capital: "the most spectacular decision was to use 1300 acres of the windswept Erith marshes on the southern bank of the Thames estuary, an apparently hostile environment of power stations and giant pylons and sewerage outfalls, for an aquatic New Town to house 60,000 people," wrote Lionel Esher in *Broken Wave: the Rebuilding of England 1940-1980*. The "aquatic New Town" became Thamesmead, squeezed between Woolwich, the river, the sewage works at Crossness and the A2016. With marsh waters pumped along a series of canals and into artificial lakes and a mixture of high- and low-rise housing, elevated at ground level to prevent flooding, Thamesmead on paper had a futuristic quality much admired by planners. Of the first phase Esher remarked: "The… housing of the early stages is indeed perhaps the most handsome industrialized project ever achieved in England. The linear blocks are highly sculptural but without brutality, and the towers, after the excesses of inner London, are human in scale. Above the first boating lake, a café hangs in mid air, and a smart shopping piazza overhangs children's islands."

Predictably, Thamesmead was embraced less warmly by those who had to live in it and, with time and changing administrations, inspiration and funding for the estate ebbed away until its ownership was assumed by a private trust. Whatever the merits of its architecture, Thamesmead never offered a fully improved quality of life for its occupants—only 12,000 by 1974 and around 33,000 today—and became blighted by low employment and high crime rates, worsened by the "dumping" by local councils of "problem tenants" in its towering blocks. System housing, geographical isolation and odours from the sewage works all help to make Thamesmead (its name was chosen by a newspaper competition; the winner received £20) a recipe for alienation where even the view from its raised riverbank, decorated with the ferro-concrete wind shelters resembling upturned boats and officially termed "heritage icons", does little to raise the spirits.

Its concrete barely dry, Thamesmead became a backdrop for Stanley Kubrick's 1971 film of Anthony Burgess' novel *A Clockwork Orange*. Having scanned architectural magazines in search of futuristic cityscapes, Kubrick clad the book's youthful gangs in white boiler suits and bowler hats and had them patrolling Thamesmead's walkways and underpasses in search of opportunities to inflict sexual assault and grievous bodily harm. While the movie's cult status ensures a steady trickle of visitors, its connections with a film initially criticized for glorifying violence did little to raise Thamesmead's self-esteem. By contrast, in the mid-1990s Thamesmead was the setting for Jonathan Harvey's play and subsequent film, *Beautiful Thing*, depicting the romance of young gay love.

Crossness Sewage Works: a Brief History of London's Excrement

To inhabitants of Thamesmead and surrounding communities, Crossness means one thing: the sewage treatment works that sit on the river's bank between Crossness itself and Jenningtree Point. But while locals might hold their noses, the rest of London should rejoice. The works are a descendant of the still-extant Crossness Pumping Station, one of four pumping stations that became the public face of a colossal Victorian engineering scheme, giving the capital its first proper system of drains and sewers and ending the epidemics that regularly afflicted the capital as well as the stench that pervaded it.

From early times, London's waste, be it animal carcasses, rotten food or human excrement, was thrown into gullies in the centre of streets, eventually being washed by rainfall into streams that forged a stinking route to the Thames. In 1290 the monks of Whitefriars, located on what became Fleet Street, petitioned parliament claiming that the odours from the Fleet River were overpowering their incense and causing death among the brethren. The 1594 invention of the water closet was a landmark in the disposing of human waste but was of no use in a city without proper drains and sewers or a reliable supply of clean water. By 1810 London was a city of a million people and 200,000 cesspits that frequently spilled their contents into living areas; together with contaminated standpipes, this caused regular outbreaks of typhoid and cholera. Exacerbated by Victorian London's sharp population increase and the rise of industry, the problem became acute during the hot dry summer of 1858 when what became known as "the Great Stink" forced the closure of parliament and statesman Disraeli to describe the Thames as a "Stygian pool reeking with ineffable and unbearable horror."

As government-created bodies gradually assumed control of London, the Board of Works was created and in 1855 Joseph Bazalgette was appointed its chief engineer. Twenty years later, Bazalgette and an army of workmen had given London 82 miles of new brick-walled super sewers to carry the outflow of 1,100 miles of older street sewers to pumping stations where it would be treated and released into the river following high tide, ensuring its passage out to sea. The pumping station at Crossness symbolized not just Victorian technical achievement with its fifty-ton steam-driven pumps, but a mating of engineering with what Pevsner called "a Victorian Cathedral of Ironwork". Within the pumping station's Romanesque exterior, complete with red brick arches and mullioned windows, was an interior of richly-decorative ironwork and polished brass handrails. The station was opened with due ceremony by the Prince of Wales who, after turning on the engines, sat down for a feast with 500 other dignitaries in a shed by the engine house. The celebrations, as it transpired following the *Princess Alice* sinking, were premature.

It took the Great Stink and the draping of parliament with sheets soaked in chloride of lime (intended to mask the stench) to galvanize Victorian politicians into resolving a health problem that had faced London for years. A similarly drastic event might be necessary to stimulate present-day governments into safeguarding the river and those who live along it. In August 2004 following heavy rains, 600,000 tons of raw sewage were released into the Thames to prevent flooding; around sixty such releases take place each year as the system, barely changed since Bazalgette's time, struggles to cope with rising rainfall and changing patterns of urban occupation. The sewage release caused thousands of dead fish, suffocated by bacteria that consumed the river's oxygen, to appear on the river's surface just as the government announced the shelving of plans for a £2 billion sewage tunnel to run 300 feet beneath the Thames from Teddington Weir to Crossness, apparently fearful of the effect on voters of increased bills. If no action is taken to relieve pressure on the capital's overloaded sewage works, however, politicians may end up not just with egg on their faces but something far worse lapping around their ankles.

Along the Bronze Age: Erith to Dartford's Salt Marshes
The industrial landscape that asserts itself west of Thamesside with the modern Crossness sewage works is continued by the Gehry-esque form

of the decommissioned Belvedere Power Station and a web of industrial plots that continue for several miles to Erith. An important dockyard under Henry VIII and thriving with the rise of river traffic, Erith sits between the waterway and the A2106: or, to give the road its proper name, Bronze Age Way, a title which seems an example of municipal sarcasm until one realizes that construction of this lorry-laden thoroughfare in a landscape of tower blocks revealed countless Bronze Age artefacts, reminders of the ancient tracks that once crossed this way to the river between 2000 and 500BC.

West of Erith across the mouth of the River Darwent, gritty symbols of commerce pockmark Dartford Salt Marshes, otherwise frequented by such visitors as the lesser black-backed gulls and Eurasian oystercatchers, just two of many bird species eagerly recorded by the binocular-wielding watchers who frequent these bracing wetlands. Save for noxious emissions from local factories and periodic governmental scheming to land a new airport somewhere along the estuary, the birds at least have the airspace to themselves. From 1911, however, the marshes were home to Joyce Green aerodrome, a test site for prototype planes of the fledgling Vickers company and a pilot training base during the First World War, despite the protestations of Air Vice Marshall Gould Lee: "To use this waterlogged field for testing every now and then was reasonable and to take advantage of it as an emergency landing ground for Home Defence forces was credible, but to employ it as a flying training station was folly and as a training station was lunacy." Historically, the marshes' isolation had facilitated other uses, not least smuggling and the staging of illegal bare-knuckle boxing and cockfights. According to Robert H. Goodsall: "Its advantages were obvious. Lookouts, posted in along the lane from Dartford, could give ample warning of 'the law's' approach, whereupon participants and spectators alike could take boats and cross to the Essex shore where the matches might be concluded in safety."

Opened in 2000, the pristine Darwent Valley Hospital stands between the marshes and Dartford itself. The new facility is a descendant of Joyce Green Hospital, one of the "River Hospitals" created by the Metropolitan Asylum Board to aid the treatment of smallpox. Set up in 1877 as London struggled to cope with repeated smallpox epidemics (300 cases a week during 1881), the Board also treated 20,000 people between 1884 and 1902 in "smallpox ships" moored on the river. A small

fleet of river ambulances operating from three riverside bases moved patients to and from the ships. Hostility in more populous stretches of the riverside, where residents and businesses feared contamination and lost income, caused the smallpox ships to spend their final years in the more sparsely inhabited stretch off Dartford. Smallpox's decline and the opening of the new hospitals enabled the ships to be sold for scrap in 1902.

Dartford Crossings

Over forty years in the planning and synonymous with rush hour traffic delays for almost as long, Dartford Tunnel has carried London commuters to and from Kent since 1963 (with a second tunnel added in 1980) and in 1991 became partnered by the Queen Elizabeth II Bridge. While entering the tunnel is a descent into a dark forbidding hole, crossing the bridge's 1,600-foot span brings scenic views of the Thames from 160 feet up, though the bridge itself is the most eye-catching item on the local landscape. The two crossings, the most easterly on the river, work in tandem: the bridge carries four lanes of southbound traffic; the tunnel moves four lanes north. Both charge tolls, the only free crossings are for conscientious objectors to private internal combustion: the pedestrians and cyclists who are carried across by shuttle buses.

Swanscombe and the Pit of History

Between Dartford and Gravesend, the Swanscombe peninsula juts a marshy elbow toward the Thames, at its tip a radar installation aiding river navigation and elsewhere the chalk quarries that once produced a valuable raw material. The disused quarries have since provided rich pickings for archaeologists; discoveries in the area suggest that nomadic hunters lived in makeshift shelters along the river around 250,000 years ago. At one such site in the 1930s two skull fragments were found. Their age was consistent with theories of early local human habitation, but their similarities to the later *homo sapiens* rather than *homo erectus* overturned established thinking on evolution and made the "Swanscombe skull" one of Britain's most significant palaeolithic finds. The skull is now well cared for in the Natural History Museum; its discovery site fares less well, just off a public footpath beside a drab housing estate and since 1986 indicated by a marker usually daubed with graffiti unrelated to archaeology though possibly of interest to students of recent human evolution.

Gravesend

Its name having no link with graves, Gravesend gained a creditable mention in the 1970 *Shell Guide to England*: "There is a great deal of Thames bustle; and the riverside has some fascination." Sadly, the author failed to explain what the fascination actually was. *The Royal River* did, however, pinpoint two key attractions of the town: "tea and shrimps, for which it has a reputation quite unique."

Occupying the first high ground reachable by ships approaching London, Gravesend became a disembarkation point for vessels too large to navigate further. With a royal licence granted in 1401, the town's bargemen enjoyed exclusive rights to ferry London-bound passengers the remaining 26 miles into the capital. They typically did so in a tilt boat, a craft resembling a Viking longboat with a capacity of 37 people and able to make the trip to Billingsgate in a mere four hours, charging a halfpenny per head. The river steamers introduced in the early 1800s ended the tilt boat route but transformed Gravesend into a destination in its own right, easily accessed as a daytrip from the metropolis. Within a decade, 20,000 people a week were visiting and the town responded by remodelling itself as Gravesend-on-Sea, developing spas, a cultural centre and in 1837 opening Rosherville Gardens: a former chalk pit transformed into a mix of botanical garden, zoo, scenic view points, funfair amusements and sideshows.

As Londoners voyaged downstream to sample Gravesend's recreational delights, foreigners travelling in the other direction found it a curious first taste of England. One such arrival was German socialist Eduard Bernstein (1850-1932) who, in his autobiographical *My Years in Exile,* describes a time-passing visit to Rosherville Gardens on his first day in England: "A vast garden, with fine pleasure-grounds and extensive fair-grounds, where there were arrangements for every possible amusement and pastime: swings, switch-back railways, roundabouts, shooting-galleries, Aunt Sallies, 'try-your-strength' machines, and many similar diversions... I wandered, somewhat restlessly, through the pleasure-grounds, rejoicing in the flowers of all sorts that grew there, and admired a steep and fairly lofty wall of rock-work, at the end of the garden adjoining the river, which was overgrown with climbing plants, while from the top of the wall one enjoyed a fine panorama."

As quickly as river steamers put Gravesend on the day-tripper's map, so railways took it off. By the mid-nineteenth century, the sands of Kent's channel towns were within easy reach of the capital and Gravesend's era as a resort town drew to a close. In an unlikely turn of events more than century later, the Walt Disney Company brought unexpected publicity to a footnote in Gravesend's past: the final resting place of Pocahontas.

Until misleadingly resurrected in a 1995 Disney film, Pocahontas was a largely forgotten Native American who died at Gravesend in 1617. The truth of her life was the stuff of myth and conjecture even before Disney became involved, and it probably began with seventeenth-century British incursions into North America and a meeting of English Captain John Smith with a Powhatan chief, the father of the woman who became known as Pocahontas (a nickname meaning "the naughty one" or "spoiled child").

In a disputed account, Smith described the young girl as having placed her hand over his head to prevent his execution by the Powhatan, thought to be a ritual intended to ensure friendship between Smith and the native people. Seemingly more certain is that the British tricked Pocahontas into visiting their colony at Jamestown in 1612, taking her hostage with the intention of using her as bargaining tool to secure the release of British prisoners. At Jamestown, however, John Rolfe, a widowed settler who would become known for creating a saleable strain of tobacco, took a liking to Pocahontas and the pair were married in 1614. Two years later in England, Pocahontas (now called "Rebecca") was presented to James I and became, along with her son Thomas, a public curiosity and an unwitting source of publicity for the Virginia Company, the commercial concern behind the Jamestown settlement.

In March 1617, at the start of a return journey to Jamestown, Pocahontas was taken ill with tuberculosis and was put ashore at Gravesend, dying soon after and buried in the medieval forerunner of the present St. George's Church. Here she is remembered by a statue of 1896 and set of stained glass windows presented by the Colonial Dames of America in 1914.

The Isle of Grain and the Hundred of Hoo

Ten miles from Gravesend, the busy towns of Rochester, Chatham and Gillingham cluster around the River Medway, each a contrast to the solitudinous banks of the Thames which wind east from Gravesend around the exposed peninsula forming the Isle of Grain and the Hundred of Hoo. Just as Gravesend has no connection with graves, the Isle of Grain is not an island and has no link with grain, its name derived from the Old English "groen", meaning "gravelley, sandy ground". Seen from the air, the peninsula is an intricate and softly undulating quilt in varied tones of green. Seen from the ground, it is a marshy and often foggy territory where roads either end abruptly as they reach reclaimed land or grow ever narrower as they weave through hamlets and around farmland before approaching the wall that lines the estuary.

The name Blythe Sands evokes thoughts of swimming costumes, ice-creams and donkey rides but the reality is an isolated and windswept carpet of beach where the indefinite fusing of land, sky and sea was painted by Turner as *Fishing Upon the Blythe-Sand, Tide Setting In*.

Similar thoughts, albeit with religious overtones, are evoked by All-Hallows-on-Sea. Not since the 1930s, however, has this tantalizingly-named caravan site offered seaside amusements worthy of the name; it only did so then because a railway made it easy for Londoners to visit. Standing in the way of a clear shot at invading Germans, the railway was dismantled with the outbreak of war; like day-tripping Londoners, it never returned.

As Iain Sinclair suggests in *Radon Daughters* (1994), a sad past is made sadder by the view across the river: "All-Hallows-on-Sea is a ghost, a resort that never was, a blemish. Bullied by marshland, it squatted the shingle of the North Kent shore, gawping enviously across the mouth of the Thames Estuary at the twinkle of Southend…"

Cliffe: a Village, not an Airport

In *London River*, Cracknell quotes an 1881 parish magazine article by the new rector of Cliffe, a port in its own right before land reclamation re-ordered its geography and marooned it inland: "We are out of the stream here and those who drift out of the stream float into a backwater, and the characteristic of a backwater is stagnation." Only 120 years later, Cliffe had its chance to become, if in obliterated form, something far grander than a backwater, selected as a possible site of a new London airport. By December 2003, the scale of local protest, legal challenges and financial uncertainties all helped to see off the scheme, though not the idea of a new London airport, which remains a spectre haunting the villages of south-east England.

Charles Dickens' Isle of Grain

Spending his childhood in Chatham and making his name in London, Charles Dickens left the capital in 1856 for a house at Gads Hill, between Chatham and Cliffe and with a good view of the Isle of Grain marshes from the top floor. In *Great Expectations* (1861), the marshes provide a suitably malevolent backdrop for the young Pip's first meeting with Magwitch, a convict freshly escaped from a ship about to transport him to penal servitude in Australia:

> Ours was the marsh country, down by the river, within, as the river
> wound, twenty miles of the sea. My first most vivid and broad

impression of the identity of things, seems to me to have been gained on a memorable raw afternoon towards evening. At such a time I found out for certain, that this bleak place overgrown with nettles was the churchyard; and that Philip Pirrip, late of this parish, and also Georgiana wife of the above, were dead and buried; and that Alexander, Bartholomew, Abraham, Tobias, and Roger, infant children of the aforesaid, were also dead and buried; and that the dark flat wilderness beyond the churchyard, intersected with dykes and mounds and gates, with scattered cattle feeding on it, was the marshes; and that the low leaden line beyond, was the river; and that the distant savage lair from which the wind was rushing, was the sea; and that the small bundle of shivers growing afraid of it all and beginning to cry, was Pip.

Dickens was fond of taking twelve-mile "strolls" to explore the marshes and surrounding villages, and allegedly once rowed across the river to enjoy a night out on Canvey Island. Much of the region is now called "Dickens Country", its protectors insisting with some justification that while Dickens' London settings have changed beyond measure or simply disappeared, the marshlands of the Isle of Grain are much as he left them on his death in 1870.

The London Stone: a Farewell to the Thames

The Port of London Authority's jurisdiction over the Thames that begins at Teddington ends close to All-Hallows-on-Sea, where a buoy at the head of Yantlet Creek and a stone (the "London Stone") record the fact and symbolize the surrender of the Thames to the waters of the North Sea. As W.G. Fernside put it in *Tombleson's Thames and Medway* (1834): "At this point the majestic Thames, having preserved that air of placid dignity and imposing grandeur which distinguish so eminently this monarch of British rivers, blends its immense volume of waters with those of the Medway, losing designation and destination, is engulfed in the mighty depth of the ocean."

Also at this point, where it is tempting to imagine the river in its death throes, we should perhaps remind ourselves that the majestic Thames is not a living thing at all but a mere body of water. That it appears to be much more, to be the true symbolic river of England as Sydney R. Jones suggested, is because the designation and destination it

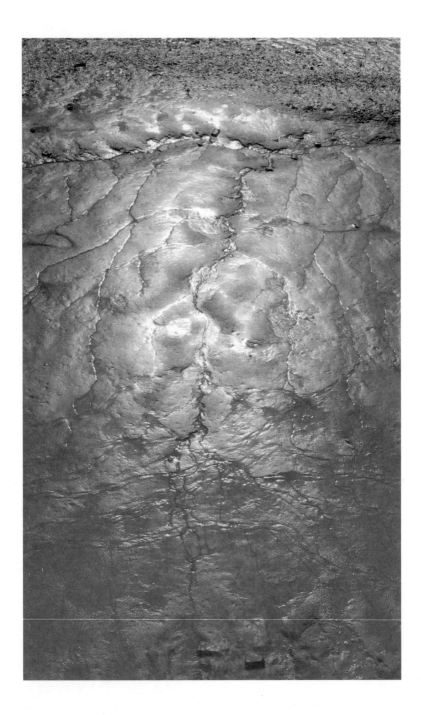

may now be losing is precisely what it has long given to those living within its sway. Whether as provider of sustenance, a means of transport and commerce, a subject for painters and writers, a target in wars or a gateway to the world, the river has determined the destinies of individuals and communities while shaping the course of English history. And just as history may have no end, neither has the river which continues to rise in a Gloucestershire meadow even as it merges with the North Sea—all the while and all the way along its course continuing to resonate with the symbolism and meaning which, over many centuries the people of England, and people beyond, have given it.

Further Reading

General

Andersen, J. R. L., *The Upper Thames*. London: Eyre & Spottiswoode, 1970.

Belloc, Hilaire, *The Historic Thames*. London: J. M. Dent & Sons, 1922.

Bolland, R. R., *Victorians on the Thames*. Tonbridge Wells: Midas Books, 1974.

Brown, Bryan (ed.), *The England of Henry Taunt*. London: Routledge & Kegan Paul, 1973.

Burstall, Patricia, *The Golden Age of the Thames*. Newton Abbot: David & Charles, 1981.

Conrad, Joseph, *The Mirror of the Sea and A Personal Record*. London: J. M. Dent and Sons, 1946.

Cornish, J. C., *The Naturalist on the Thames*. London: Seeley, 1902.

Cracknell, Basil, E., *London River*. London: Robert Hale, 1968.

Croad, Stephen, *Liquid History: The Thames through Time*. London: Batsford, 2003.

Currie, Ian, *Frosts, Freezes and Fairs*. Coulsdon: Frosted Earth, 1996.

Dickens, Charles, *Dickens's Dictionary of the Thames 1893*. Oxford: Taurus Press, 1972 (first published London: Charles Dickens & Evans, 1893, and in earlier editions).

Eade, Brian, *Along the Thames*. Stroud: Sutton Publishing, 1997.

Gibbings, Robert, *Sweet Thames Run Softly*. London: J. M Dent & Sons, 1940.

Goodsall, Robert, H., *The Widening Thames*. London: Constable & Co., 1965.

Hall, Mr. & Mrs. S. C., *The Book of the Thames*. Teddington: Charlotte James, 1980 (first published 1859).

Harrison, Ian, *The Thames from Source to Sea*. London: HarperCollins, 2004.

Hill, David, *Turner on the Thames*. London & New Haven: Yale University Press, 1993.

Jones, Sydney, R., *Thames Triumphant*. London & New York: The Studio Publications, 1943.

King, Tom, *Thames Estuary Trail*. Westcliff-on-Sea: Desert Island Books, 2001.

Mayo, Earl of, Adshead, S. D. & Abercrombie, Patrick, *The Thames Valley*. London: University of London Press, 1929.

Mindell, Ruth and Jonathan, *Bridges over the Thames*. Poole: Blandford, 1985.

Peel, J. H. B., *A Portrait of the Thames*. London: Robert Hale, 1967.

Phillips, Geoffrey, *Thames Crossings*. Newton Abbot: David & Charles, 1981.

Phillips, Hugh, *The Thames about 1750*. London: Collins, 1951.

Robbins, Michael, *Middlesex*. London: Collins, 1953.

Schneer, Jonathan, *The Thames: England's River*. London: Little, Brown, 2005.

Senior, W. *et al*, *The Royal River*. Henley-on-Thames: Gresham Books, 1983 (first published 1885).

Sharp, David, *The Thames Path*. London: Aurum Press, 2001.

Sharp, David, *The Thames Walk*. London: The Rambler's Association, 1990.

Shrapnel, Norman, *A View of the Thames*. London: William Collins & Co., 1977.

Thacker, F.S., *The Stripling Thames*. London: Fred S. Thacker, 1909.

Thacker, Fred, S., *The Thames Highway Vol. 1: General History*. David & Charles Newton Abbott, 1968 (first published London: Fred S. Thacker, 1914).

Thacker, Fred S. *The Thames Highway Vol. 2: Locks & Weirs*. David & Charles Newton Abbott, 1968 (first published London: Fred S. Thacker, 1920).

Wilson, D. G., *Thames: Diary of a Working Waterway*. London: Batsford, 1987.

Wilson, D. G., *The Victorian Thames*. Stroud: Alan Sutton Publishing, 1993.

Wilson, David Gordon, *The Making of the Middle Thames*. Bourne End: Spur Books, 1977.

Wright, Patrick, *The River in our Time*. London: BBC, 1999.

London and the River

Ackroyd, Peter, *London: The Biography*. London: Chatto & Windus, 2000.

Ackroyd, Peter, *Dickens' London*. London: Pilot Productions, 1987.

Allinson, Ken, *London's Contemporary Architecture*. Oxford: Architectural Press, 2003 (first published 1994).

Barker, Felix & Jackson, Peter, *London: 200 Years of a City and its People*. London: Cassell & Co., 1974.

Barker, T. C. & Robbins, Michael, *A History of London Transport, Vol. 1*. London: George Allen & Unwin, 1963.

Bates, L. M., *The Spirit of London's River*. Old Woking: Gresham, 1980.

Bell, Alan, *The Said Noble River*. London: Port of London Authority, 1937.

Bentley, James, *East of the City*. London: Pavilion, 1997.

Besant, Sir Walter, *London North of the Thames*. London: Adam & Charles Black, 1911.

Bignell, John, *Chelsea Seen from 1860 to 1980*. London: Studio B, 1978.

Bone, James, *The London Perambulator*. London: Jonathan Cape, 1950 (first published 1926).

Bunge, J. H. O., *Tideless Thames in a Future London*. London: The Thames Barrage Association, 1944.

Cameron, David Kerr, *London's Pleasures*. Stroud: Sutton Publishing, 2001.

Cherry, Bridget & Pevsner, Nikolaus, *Buildings of England: London 2: South*. London: Penguin, 1983

Chrimes, Mike, *Civil Engineering 1839-1889*. Stroud: Sutton Publishing, 1991.

Cobb, Gerald, *The Old Churches of London*. London: B.T. Batsford, 1942.

Coppock, J.T., & Prince, Hugh, C., *Greater London*. London: Faber & Faber, 1964.

Croad, Stephen, *London's Bridges*. London: Her Majesty's Stationary Office, 1983.

Cunningham, Ian, *A Reader's Guide to Writers' London*. London: Prion, 2001.

Dakers, Caroline, *The Blue Plaque Guide to London*. London: Macmillan, 1981.

Duncan, Andrew, *Secret London*. London: New Holland, 2000.

Eade, Brian, *Forgotten Thames*. Stroud: Sutton Publishing, 2002.

Ellmers, Charles & Werner, Alex, *Dockland Life*. Edinburgh & London: Mainstream, 1991.

Edwards, Brian, *London Docklands*. Oxford: Butterworth Architecture, 1992.

Fairfax, Bryan, *Walking London's Waterways*. London: David & Charles, 1985.

Fishman, William J., *East End 1888*. London: Duckworth, 1988.

Glinert, Ed, *East End Chronicles*. London: Allen Lane, 2005.

Glinert, Ed, *The London Compendium*. London: Allen Lane, 2003.

Godfrey, Honor, *Tower Bridge*. London: Murray, 1988.

Halliday, Stephen, *The Great Stink*. Stroud: Sutton Publishing, 1999.

Hardingham, Samantha, *London: A Guide to Recent Architecture*. London, Munich, Zurich: Artemis, 1993.

Hibbert, Christopher, *London: The Biography of a City*. London: Penguin, 1980 (first published Longmans, Green & Co., 1969).

Hunting, Penelope, *Royal Westminster*. London: Royal Institute of Chartered Surveyors, 1981.

Inwood, Stephen, *A History of London*. London & Basingstoke: Macmillan, 1998.

Jackson, Alan A., *London's Termini*. Newton Abbot: David & Charles, 1969.

Jenner, Michael, *London Heritage*. London: Michael Joseph, 1988.

Kent, William, *An Encyclopaedia of London*. London: J.M. Dent & Sons, 1970.

De Maré, Eric, *London's Riverside: Past Present and Future*. London: Max Reinhardt, 1958.

Linney, A. G., *Lure and Lore of London's River*. London: Sampson Low, Marston & Co., 1937.

Massingham, Hugh & Pauline, *The London Anthology*. London: Spring Books, 1951.

Mee, Arthur, *London*. London: Hodder & Stoughton, 1948 (first published 1936).

Milne, Gustav, *The Port of Roman London*. London: B.T. Batsford, 1985.

Morton, H. V., *H. V. Morton's London*. London: Methuen & Co., 1940.

al Naid, S.K. (ed.), *Dockland*. London: North East London Polytechnic, Greater London Council, 1986.

Nead, Lynda, *Victorian Babylon*. New Haven & London: Yale University Press, 2000.

Palmer, Alan, *The East End*. London: John Murray, 2000.

Panton, Kenneth, J., *London: A Historical Companion*. Stroud: Tempus Publishing, 2001.

Picard, Liza, *Dr. Johnson's London*. London: Phoenix, 2003 (first published London: Weidenfeld & Nicolson, 2000).

Picard, Liza, *Elizabeth's London*. London: Weidenfeld & Nicolson, 2003.

Pierce, Patricia, *Old London Bridge*. London: Headline, 2001.

Pudney, John, *Crossing London's River*. London: J.M. Dent & Sons, 1972.

Porter, Roy, *London: A Social History*. London: Hamish Hamilton, 1994.

Richardson, John, *The Annals of London*. London: Cassell & Co, 2000.

Saint, Andrew; Darley, Gillian, *The Chronicles of London*. London: Weidenfeld & Nicolson, 1994.

Sandhu, Sukhdev, *London Calling*. London: HarperCollins, 2003.

Saunders, Anne. *The Art and Architecture of London*. Oxford: Phaidon, 1984.

Schofield, John, *The Building of London*. Stroud: Sutton Publishing, 1993.

Sheppard, Francis, *London: A History*. Oxford: Oxford University Press, 1998.

Sheppard, Francis, *London 1808-1870: The Infernal Wen*. London: Secker & Warburg, 1971.

Sims, G.R. (ed.), *Living London (Vol. 3)*. London: Cassell & Company, 1903.

Sinclair, Iain, *Lights Out for the Territory*. London: Granta, 1997.

Stow, John, *Stow's Survey of London*. London: J.M. Dent & Sons, 1956 (first published 1598).

Sudic, Deyan, *Blade of Light: the Story of London's Millennium Bridge*. London: Penguin, 2001.

Sumeray, Derek, *Track the Plaque*. Derby: Breedon Books, 2003.

Walford, Edward, *Village London Vol. 1*. London: The Alderman Press, 1983 (first published 1883).

Walford, Edward, *Village London Vol. 2*. London: The Alderman Press, 1983 (first published 1883).

Waller, Maureen, *1700: Scenes from London Life*. London: Hodder & Stoughton, 2000.

Weightman, Gavin, *London River*. London: Collins & Brown, 1990.

Weightman, Gavin, *London's Thames*. London: John Murray, 2004.

Weinreb, Ben & Hibbert, Christopher (eds.), *The London Encyclopaedia*. London: Macmillan, 1983.

William, Norman Lloyd, *Tudor London Visited*. London: Cassell, 1991.

Williams, Stephanie, *Docklands*. London: Phaidon, 1993.

Williamson, Elizabeth & Pevsner Nikolaus, *London Docklands*. London: Penguin, 1998.

White, Jerry, *London in the Twentieth Century*. London: Viking, 2001.

Wright, Thomas (ed.), *A Traveller's Companion to London*. London: Robinson, 2004.

Fiction

Jerome, Jerome K., *Three Men in a Boat*. London: Penguin, 1999 (first published London: Arrowsmith, 1889).

Morris, William, *News from Nowhere*. London: Routledge & Kegan Paul, 1970 (first published London: Reeves & Turner, 1891).

Sinclair, Iain, *Downriver*. London: Penguin, 1991.

Websites

Rare it seems is the community, organization or devoted river watcher anywhere along the Thames without a website. Those listed below are the most generally informative, or simply the most curious, of a very large bunch.
www.bargemen.co.uk

Offers more than might be thought possible on the lightermen, watermen and bargemen of London's Thames.

www.derelictlondon.com.

Look under "waterways" for some seriously bleak depictions of the unregenerated, post-industrial Thames.

www.floodlondon.com

Examines the prospects of and the science behind a storm surge hitting the capital: not recommended for Londoners with a river view and a nervous disposition.

www.lbhf.gov.uk/external/thamesstrategy/default.htm

Find out what the London Borough of Hammersmith and Fulham are plotting for the future of the river between Kew and Chelsea; useful links to other local sites.

www.nationaltrail.co.uk

Operated by the Countryside Agency, includes a modest section on the Thames Path with general practical information and a diary of events taking place along its course.

www.portoflondon.co.uk

The Port of London Authority offers some intriguing historical pages and lots more on tidal timetables and where to berth your oil tanker or cruise ship.

www.portcities.org.uk/london

Comprehensive and accessible history of maritime London, from Roman times to the present day, enlivened by graphics and audio.

www.riverthamesociety.org.uk

Founded in 1962, the River Thames Society organizes events, offers annual membership and publishes a print magazine, *Thames Guardian*.

www.thamesweb.com

From the Thames Estuary Partnership, a conglomeration of local authorities, community groups and others, with an interest in the regeneration of the Thames Estuary.

www.thames21.org

Website of an environmental charity devoted to improving London's river in the twenty-first century. Lists forthcoming events for which visitors and volunteer rubbish collectors are always very welcome.

www.thames-path.com

General practical information on using the Thames Path.

www.victorianlondon.org

Excellent archive of the Victorian city, with much about the river and its users, and the diverse communities beside it.

www.visitthames.co.uk

The Environment Agency's invitation to mess about on and around the river, whether walking, boating or fishing; mainly of use for downloading or ordering their free print publications and maps.

Index of Literary & Historical Names

Index of Places & Landmarks